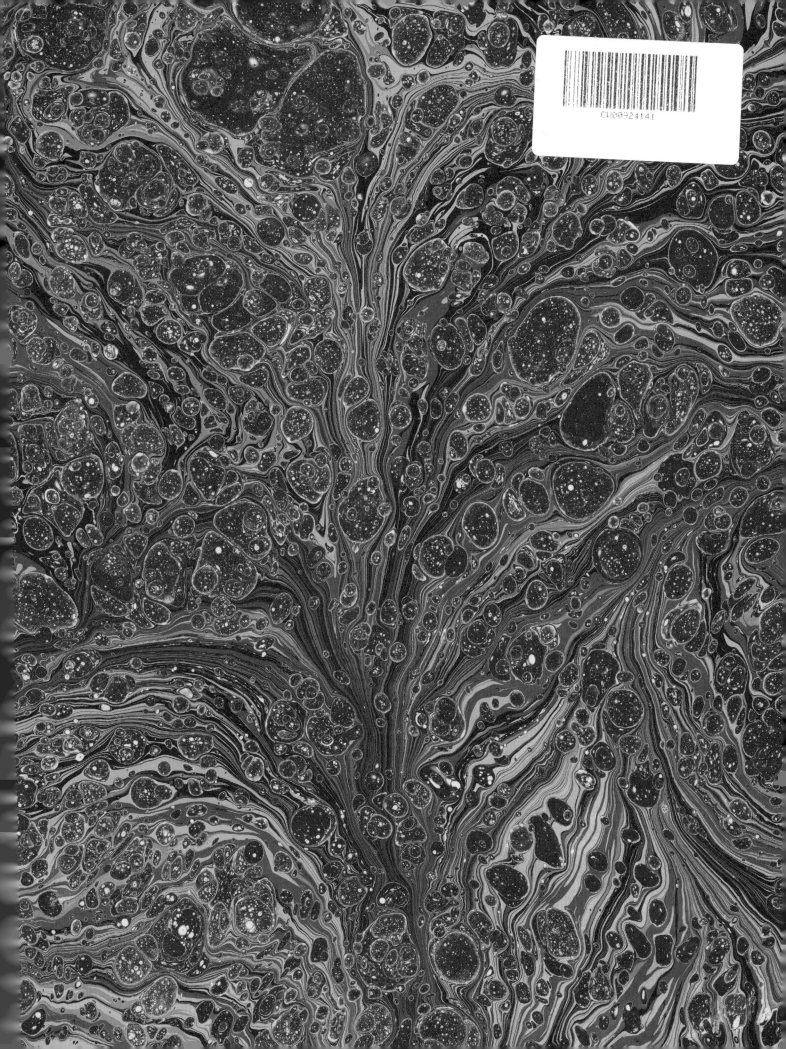

Volker A. Behr

Dornier Do X

DORNIER DO X

Volker A. Behr

4880 Lower Valley Road • Atglen, PA 19310

Book translation by Omicron Language Solutions, LLC.

Copyright © 2013 by Schiffer Publishing, Ltd.
Library of Congress Control Number: 2013953908

Printed in China.
ISBN: 978-0-7643-4476-3

This book was originally published in German under the title *Dornier Do X* by Volker A Behr by Motorbuch Verlag.

We are interested in hearing from authors with book ideas on related topics.

Published by Schiffer Publishing Ltd.
4880 Lower Valley Road
Atglen, PA 19310
Phone: (610) 593-1777
FAX: (610) 593-2002
E-mail: Info@schifferbooks.com.
Visit our web site at: www.schifferbooks.
com
Please write for a free catalog.
This book may be purchased
from the publisher.
Try your bookstore first.

Contents

Foreword
– Claude Dornier 1937

This book shows the Do X flying boat on land, in the water and in the sky, from the inside and out. Twelve years of continuous methodical development were necessary to establish the groundwork, which Swiss workers in Altenrhein then used to complete the aircraft in one and a half years. Another year passed before the thousandfold mechanics of the flying boat were coordinated with all of its components.

Perhaps one reader or another has noticed that I am speaking about a "flying boat" and that I don't describe the Do X using the common term "airplane." The word "flying boat" originated from the old Graf Zeppelin and today still sounds strange and a little unpleasant in the ears of some of the formal representatives of aviation interests. Some get wind of something new that doesn't suit them, others fear a competitor might rise against the Zeppelin airship. The old Graf Zeppelin already knew that the latter would not be the case. But clearly he also recognized that there are tasks that cannot be fulfilled by airships or airplanes; that something is still missing between airplane and airship, and must be invented. He chose me to fill in this gap. This is how he became a pioneer of the flying boat. There are few that know about this, and that is why it should be said here.

The first flying boat is now complete and will be tested on the ocean. It can't yet cross the ocean in one single,

uninterrupted flight, which has prompted many to ask: Why the enormous investment in time and money? Patience. Rome was not built in one day. Time and space don't move aside with one blow. Unless we can achieve the dream to move from the old world to the new world in twenty-four hours, many stages are still necessary.

In order to comprehend this, one only needs to look back at the history of steamship navigation. For one hundred years steamships have crossed over the furrowed ocean. In the 1860s, a letter from America needed fourteen days to arrive in Europe. By 1930, it arrived in seven to eight days. It took the steamship almost seventy years to reduce the travel time between the two continents by half. You just can't expect aviation, in its youth, to overcome the enormous space of the oceans. The first step has been made. The preconditions for lasting success have been met. The flying boat is here. For the first time, one can depart from protective harbors on a flight for long distances over the sea without having to risk life and limb.

Dr.ING. C. DORNIER BUILDER OF THE DO X 1929. Unique casting pattern from the estate of the Munich artist Karl Goetz (1875-1950). This 111mm diameter bronze medallion was also produced as a bronze and silver medallion in sizes of 59.5mm and 36mm. (Photo: Münzhandlung G. Hirsch Nachf., Munich)

The flying boat is equipped with all the tools of a modern ocean liner. In the hands of experienced seamen, we will soon gain enough knowledge to lead us to great things. Its economic rating, however, will establish the flying boat in its present form. The limit for commercial operation of the Do X, which rests on the current fuel consumption of the engines, is about 1,500 to 2,000km. You only need to look at a globe to see how extremely versatile the flying boat's application is today. Twelve metric tons of cargo can be transported between Buenos Aires and Montevideo, for example, which corresponds to 100 passengers and 2,000kg of mail or freight with a flight time of one and a half hours. Nine metric tons of cargo, or ninety passengers, can be transported between Hamburg and Southampton, or Marseille and Algiers, and nearly eight metric tons between Travemünde and Southampton. The Brindisi-Alexandria route can be covered in about six hours with forty-five passengers.

Especially interesting is the possibility of collaborating with fast seagoing ships, everywhere where the current flying range of the flying boat does not yet suffice. Thus, the flying boat could, for example, bring mail and passengers from Europe to the Cape Verde Islands or the Azores. Further transport from these islands could be temporarily carried out by ship to Natal or Bermuda. From there, the flying boat can again take over any further shipment.

These are only a few examples of the tasks that the flying boat can already cope with today. But what will it look like in the future? From 1918 to 1928, the largest transported load by an airplane increased from 3,700kg to 7,500kg. It took ten years to achieve a 100% increase. In 1929, the Do X flying boat increased the biggest load from 7,500kg to 22,000kg, thus tripling the heaviest load within a year. In light of these facts, can anyone doubt that we will witness loads of 100 metric tons or more in another ten years? This prospect, though, entitles us to hope, that in the fo-

reseeable future, the flying boat will have earned its place in air transportation history."

Claude Dornier's visions don't hide the fact that eighty years ago, long-distance international air transport was still in its infancy. The entire world hears the news of the Do X crossing the South Atlantic. With fourteen men on board, the Do X flies from the Cape Verde Islands to the Brazilian island Natal. This milestone in aviation, on the 4th and 5th of June, 1931, satisfy Claude Dornier's expectations. With the first "Jumbo" in aviation history, he not only succeeds in realizing a technically impressive design, but with the construction of three versions of the Do X flying boat, he also achieves a great feat for the aircraft industry. This book is documented with current research and it contains many unreleased reports about the progress and "life" of the three flying boats that were produced as well as new images from previously unknown archives. The pure hope that his Do X flying boat would take its place in aviation history ends in disappointment for Claude Dornier. By 1936, the German Do X 1 has already landed in a museum, and one year later the Italian Do X 2 and 3 are scrapped in La Spezia-Cadimare. In the end, he was on the wrong track with his flying boat and his vision for transoceanic transport. The 10th of August 1938 marks another milestone in aviation history. The Atlantic will be crossed and no longer used as a runway. A four-engine land plane with retractable wheel chassis, the Focke Wulf Fw 200 with the tail number D-ACON, flies nonstop from Berlin-Tempelhof to New York, and three days later, and flies back in a flight time of less than twenty-four hours. This spells the end of the flying boat dream. The future would belong to land planes.

Karl Goetz also dedicated a medallion to the 1938 nonstop flight of the Focke Wulf 200 Condor. (Photo: Münzhandlung G. Hirsch Nachf., Munich)

Introduction
– Portrait of a Legend

"First, we free these just delivered photo negatives from their old glassine envelopes and place them onto glass plates. Then, they are digitized using a special method and systematically documented. If our staff resources allow, this exceptional treasure will be put on the Web and be accessible through our homepage for all those interested."

During the conversation with Regula Zürcher in St. Gallen's State Archives in early-2011, some of the 88x119mm glass plate negatives wander from one cotton-gloved hand to another. "According to the information on the negative, that is Alfons Keppler, Business Director of Dornier-Flugzeuge AG in Altenrhein, photographed between May 23 and June 2, 1928. He looks quite skeptical in Ziegler's plate camera. His Do X world was actually still doing well in those days!" Shoptalk begins about the motifs of the almost 1,000 photos from Karl Alfred Ziegler, official photographer of DoFlug AG.

Beginning in mid-1927, Ziegler is employed by DoFlug, located in the eastern Swiss village of Altenrhein. He becomes the photographic chronicler of the most modern airplane factory in Europe at the time and the emergence of the three Do X flying boats. Many of his photos, some of which have been published for the first time in this book, remain unknown to this day and, after their rediscovery, are being prepared in the State Archives in St. Gallen for their grand entrance.

The same applies to the diverse collection of files from the Altenrhein factory archives. Claude Dornier's design and the thorough structural planning of his Do X are carried out in the mid-1920s in the Manzell plant near Friedrichshafen. All diagrams, reports, protocols, etc. are produced at Dornier Metallbauten GmbH. The history of the technical, financial and entrepreneurial problems fill up mountains of file folders until 1933.

At the end of the Second World War in 1945, the Dornier factory archives on the German side are stored in a bombproof underground shelter. It is unceremoniously flooded by French occupiers, which is the equivalent of a total loss by bombing. So where did all the original files for the development and testing of the flying boats come from? In Manzell, everything was planned out, and in Altenrhein things were built and tested. It was therefore necessary that all diagrams, calculations and further exchange of data were available in duplicate in Switzerland. What luck for Do X research and history! The DoFlug successor, FFA (the Flug and Fahrzeugwerk Altenrhein), in particular, preserves the archives, but only until the point of the ownership swap of the hangars and factory space in Altenrhein in the second half of the twentieth century. The new owners arrive with a large container to clean house. The DoFlug factory archives, which up until then have been slumbering away, goes off with all of the "old stuff" to the nearest local garbage dump. Because several heartbroken people observe the fatal cleanup, some of the files survive. The crowd hauls away whatever it can under two arms in a single run, and the randomly grabbed files later resurface in the hands of private owners in Switzerland. Therefore, we can now pore over Emil Rau's plans for the Do X 2's interior, read the thrilling report of the Do X 1's test flight on September 3, 1929, or envision the difficulties with the Do X 2's test flights over Lake Constance. All records of the fourteen flights are available in the original "for the purpose of producing the necessary copies." These files and much more have only been accessible again for a year.

Director face to face with the factory photographer. Alfons Keppeler has a skeptical look for Ziegler's plate camera. Altenrhein, end of May 1928. (Photo: Karl Alfred Ziegler, Staatsarchiv St. Gallen)

After decades of fading memories of the Do X flying boat, the first new book about the Do X, written by Peter Pletschacher, is released in 1979, also published by Motorbuch Verlag. The reason is the fifty-year anniversary of the Do X 1's first flight. The former publicity manager of Dornier GmbH presents the interested reader a number of rarely seen photos from the collection of the Dornier company archives, which was built after the war. Reproduced text documents make the book a fine reference source that lives to see three editions, which is remarkable for a specialized book. The 75th anniversary, the Do X's next obligatory date in 2004, awaits with a special homage to the flying boat. On stamp day, Deutsche Post dedicates a special postage stamp to the Do X – the first of its kind in Germany with Do X as the subject. The Post supports the publication of the fifty-five cent stamp in October 2004, with a new release in their series of anniversary editions. "A ship flies around the world, seventy-five years of the Do X" is journalist Jörg-M. Hormann's title. It is a thoroughly researched work with a philatelic emphasis that presents many new aspects regarding the history of the Do X. Most notably, the comprehensive biographies of the people surrounding the Do X, on board and on the ground, humanize the subject matter. Long stories and short stories can be read to understand the background of the Do X.

Two years later, a chronological sequence of events about the flying boat is published by Hormann. It covers Claude Dornier's first ideas up to the destruction of the Do X in the German Aviation Museum during a bomb attack on Berlin in 1944. All three works complement one another in their own way and bring more and more attention to the technical and historical life of the first large capacity aircraft in aviation history. Did you notice something? The gaps in time, in which the flying boat Do X is the subject, are getting shorter and shorter. This is a sign of the growing interest in the flying giants of the late-1920s. The best example, and confirmation of this, is a special exhibit in the new Dornier Museum in Friedrichshafen. It celebrates the eighty year anniversary of the first Atlantic crossing of an airplane, our Do X, with at least a fourteen man crew on board and the sensational splashdown, first in Rio de Janeiro, and then in New York Harbor on August 27, 1931. This book further complements a succession of descriptive books about the Do X flying boats, with up-to-date research.

May 2011
Volker A. Behr

"Dornier's flying boat is a thing of beauty." Contemporary metal model of the Do X 1. (Photo: Dornier GmbH, EADS)

Only a "Payload" Pays Off – Intentions of Claude Dornier

In early 1928, Claude Dornier speaks for the first time in front of the Royal Aeronautical Society in London about the history of his flying boat. The Do X 1 is under construction then and the contracts for the delivery of two Do X flying boats to Italy are signed in silence. One and a half years later and four months after the inaugural flight of the Do X 1 on July 12, 1929, Claude Dornier gives a much publicized speech during the annual meeting of the WGL (Wissenschaftlichen Gesellschaft für Luftfahrt, Eng: 'German Society for Aeronautics') in Berlin. At this point in time, the Do X 1 has just completed its famous 42nd test flight with 169 people on board, and the overloaded, heavily smoldering rear row of engines is surely weighing heavy on his mind as a huge technical problem. But that is nothing for the public to know about and certainly not for the critics who listen to his performance on November 6, 1929.

He describes in great detail the thought process that eventually led him to the design of the Do X: "… There were financial considerations to make before beginning construction on the first flying boat. To begin with, the decisive idea was that profitable transport of people in general will only be possible if a large number of passengers can be carried at the same time, along side all other modes of transportation. In order to achieve the necessary frequency, which is missing today, the public must be offered more safety, more space and more comfort than before. That inevitably leads to an enlargement of the dimensions. One then deems it extremely important to considerably increase the payload capacity. I have already pointed out that we aspired to make considerable progress with the construction of the flying boat, and today I can say that we achieved it. This is primarily based on the fact that, in a single blow, the payload of airplanes has been increased dramatically.

The decision to take on the construction of the Do X flying boat, was further influenced by thoughts of the industrial kind. Studying the development of aircraft construction has revealed to me again and again that the experience building smaller airplanes, also in metal construction, becomes, or rather has become, common knowledge, so that advances, which the German aircraft industry has favored for a long time, vanish more from year to year. In light of this fact, and especially with the development of the American aircraft industry, which will make its presence known in the world market within a short period, I am convinced that it is necessary for us to foster that area of aircraft construction, of which we have always been a leader, namely the construction of large airplane units. In this specialized area, it will require an even longer amount of time before other countries will have reached our present standing, and in the future, we will hopefully find the opportunity to far exceed what we have already achieved today.

From the outset, the prevailing thought with this design was, that to achieve the contrived goal, only technically proven ideas were allowed to be drafted. Every 'experimentation' was eliminated from the start. There is no doubt that the creative shape was shackled to some degree by these actions. But from the moment we began testing the flying boat until full-fledged flight, only about 100 working hours were dedicated to changes on the cabin, which proves, in association with the targeted flight performance, that these methods were correct."

Technical Steps to Build a Flying Boat

It all begins in the Summer of 1914 when Graf Zeppelin assigns his design engineer Claude Dornier to build a giant aircraft made of metal – a revolutionary construction technique he called "Metallbauten," literally "metal construction." An important element of this construction method is shell construction, which uses a rib frame connected by smooth plates to produce one interior space free of bracing. This technique will influence the development of airplane construction up until present day. Shell construction relies on the use of flat construction elements, or membranes, which are described here in this press release by Dornier Metallbauten GmbH from the 1930s: "… At this juncture, the sheet metal membrane applies a force of tensile and shear stresses that always act on the plane of surface, so it is not subjected to bending or rotation. If the thin sheet metal for the encasement of a space is now provided and brought to bear as much as possible, then we are talking about a shell. The resulting hollow body can withstand an incredible amount of stress. The well-known experiment with a chicken egg, which is squeezed in the hand and won't crack, even with all available strength, proves the resistance of a shell."

"After multiple tries," reports Claude Dornier in a 1921 speech held before the WGL, "a system of intersecting, U-formed profiles with double flanges proved to be the most suitable. The application happened in such a way that on the external side, made up of a stiff metal barrier, the profiles are arranged in the direction of the air current while inside they proceed under approximately a right angle. The reinforced profiles intersect so that no interruption on the cut surface is necessary, which results in particularly rigid walls. The interior profiles are very often simultaneously part of frames, spars, etc. By riveting the double flange U-profiles to the sheet metal, hollow bodies with great rigidity are created. The application possibilities of these profiles are immensely diverse and shape one of the main characteristics of the construction method I developed."

Behind these words hides one of the most basic inventions, which has become of vital importance for metal aircraft construction: namely, shell construction. It was applied to the fuselage, wings, tail units, buoyancy chambers, hull and sponsons. Without it, today's aerodynamic knowledge and corresponding plane designs as well as the everyday demands of airplanes would be utterly impossible. The first models with fuselages made in shell construction were the Dornier airplanes Do Cl 1 and Do Ca 1 produced in 1917. From a historical perspective, these hollow metal fuselages without actual framework emerged from the experiences building hulls and buoyancy chambers. The outer layer of these fuselages consists of smooth aluminum alloy sheets. Simple rib frames made up of double flange U-profiles are riveted in equal intervals. With larger fuselages, profiles are arranged lengthwise for bracing. Proper walers are usually not available and sway bracing is placed where heavy forces pass from the wing unit, motor mounting or the rudder, so that the fuselage remains completely hollow and the entire space can be fully utilized. Torsion and bending stresses of such fuselages result in extreme durability, and their production is quite simple with the technical methods and facilities at that time.

In 1918, shell construction, which had previously only been applied to the fuselage, is used for first time on wings, with the cantilever single-seat fighter Do D 1. It is the first plane developed with cantilever wings covered with smooth sheet metal and load-bearing skin panels. Claude Dornier recognizes the sweeping significance of the shell construction method for light metal construction. And all of the detailed questions in connection with shell construction – such as the design of fixed supports for the shell, force displacement, the design of openings and cut-outs, joint and rivet questions – are answered by Dornier. The principle of shell construction will prove to be one of the fundamental pioneering achievements for modern aircraft construction.

The groundwork for the construction of the first flying boat goes back to the year 1924. In the beginning, there was the "boat." From the first moment on, Claude Dornier is certain that the flying boat has to be more like a boat. Answering the question, "One or multiple decks?" is not as simple. But the decision for a single deck also happens relatively quickly. The first project drawing, labeled P 1106, bears the date September 27, 1924. Dornier then contemplates a so-called self-supporting boat, which, due to its great width, requires no further support.

It would go too far to discuss the many versions that are planned out before Claude Dornier and his staff arrived at project P 51223 on June 21, 1926. By then, several true to scale models are generated, which are used to verify the blueprint positions – something completely new in aircraft construction. The meticulousness of the Dornier workers goes to the point of an accessible 1:1 wood model of the fuselage with tail unit and engine layout. In the old flying boat

hangar in Friedrichshafen-Löwental, carpenters put together the model, which is finished in July 1927.

As of December 22, 1926, P51335 is the project number of the definitive form of the "giant flying boat," which is evaluated and then converted into a construction plan in the design office. During the course of this work, only minor deviations to project P51335 take place, with the exception of a design change to the sponsons. Both the design and the construction are kept secret for a long time until the German Navy loses interest in the Do X, which is originally intended to be a "torpedo carrier" and "gunship" to supply submarines at sea. The flying supply ship no longer fits into the minimized Navy's concept of sea-strategic gadgetry.

During the very first design from 1924, seven engines provide 4,200 horsepower. Dornier later makes it twelve engines with a total of 5,800 horsepower. After an engine conversion in 1930, the final output of the Do X 1a is 6,300 horsepower. In essence, setting the total at twelve engines can be attributed to the fact that 800 to 1,000hp engines, as essential as they had been in those days, were not considered as reliable as 500hp engines. One of the most difficult decisions is the choice and configuration of engines. The questions – water-cooled or air-cooled, open mounting of engines or housing engines in the wings or hull – kept Dornier and his men busy for over two years. In 1930, Dornier said: "When the decision was finally made for today's configuration, it seemed to be the best 'compromise' under the given circumstances. The determining factor for the choice of air-cooled engines for the first flying boat was the weight savings of over 3,000kg with these engines compared to water-cooled engines. This reduction of weight is so significant that even the somewhat lower fuel consumption of water-cooled engines doesn't balance out."

Dornier's deceptive technical argument, however, is only half of the truth regarding his decision. The reason for choosing air-cooled "Jupiter" radial engines from Siemens is the "German motor." The German authorities, financial backers of all activities surrounding the development of the flying boat, demand these engines be installed as part of the awarded contract. From the beginning on, Claude Dornier has a bad feeling about the air-cooled engine solution. He will be proved correct.

The tandem arrangement of the engines inevitably results from their quantity. With all their advantages and disadvantages, they are prevalent for more than a decade at DMB. When one is forced to use a larger amount of engines, it is by far the simplest, lightest and safest kind of engine assembly in the late-1920s and is therefore used just about everywhere. Claude Dornier adds: "By creating a double engine, the tandem arrangement reduces the number of units used by half. A tandem set of two engines, each with nine cylinders, for example, is barely more complicated than a single engine with eighteen cylinders. It is, however, considerably more reliable. First of all, the smaller engine is definitely safer than the larger engine, but then only half of the engine's power is figured when failures occur to the motor, gearbox or propeller. The drag of a nacelle equipped with a double engine, including its support structure, is not greater than that of a nacelle for a large engine."

From the beginning, there was no question that Claude Dornier's first flying boat had to be a boat, indeed a boat with a central hull, but not a twin-hull boat like the Italians favored at that time. After the quickly rejected consideration to use buoyancy props under the wings for stability on the water, Dornier inevitably comes back to the sponsons that were tested hundreds of times on the 'Wal' (English: 'whale') flying boat.

For the formation of the underwater shape of the flying boat, the Wal gives Dornier a treasure trove of experience. Claude Dornier remarks: "… The underwater shape, as far as the same shapes influenced by the take off process, were changed little compared to earlier built boats. The middle longitudinal ribs are kept the same. On its back end it is horizontal to the course of flight and turns into a slight V-shape toward the front. The parts of the bottom of the boat lying laterally to the longitudinal ribs form a slightly concave shape. The bow is sharply keeled, especially the parts that lie above the water line at rest in calm water. The sponsons penetrate the boat's sidewall, sharply rounded off diagonally to the direction of flight. This new kind of sponsons shape had not yet been slated for the project. It has static and hydrodynamic advantages. The height of the sponsons at the root becomes considerably larger, which makes significantly stiffer formation of the load-bearing organs possible."

An important characteristic of the Do X design is the flying boat's partitioning into three independent decks – a first for airplanes. The upper deck, the so-called "commando deck" contains the cockpit, captain's chambers, central control room of the engine unit and rooms for radiotelegraphy and auxiliary engines. The next deck is exclusively assigned for passengers – 23.5 meters long, about two meters high and 3.5 meters wide at its widest point. The lower deck contains the equipment, supplies, freight and baggage. Dornier does without a complete cantilever layout of the all-metal wings in order to maintain a surface that is as light as possible. Reasons of a technical-fabrication nature are also decisive in the choice for half-cantilever wings. The wing is designed as a three-sparred, threefold reinforced wing unit. This system, used for the first time with the Do X, yields a very distinct stiffness and torsional strength as a result of the special bond strength. There is also the guarantee that damage to a single upright or spar cannot influence the payload capacity of the entire system in a dangerous way.

Airmen and Pilots on board the Do X

In a speech from early-1930, Do X test engineer Heinrich Schulte-Frohlinde comments on the novelty of the flying boat from a pilot's perspective: "… The pleasing, aesthetic design of the Do X flying boat is distinct, like all aircraft creations by Claude Dornier. The flying boat is a thing of beauty, even without considering the size, novelty and audaciousness of this technical achievement. This beauty is accomplished by the clarity of static construction and the harmonious proportions of the building elements, whose form also gives the unbiased observer the impression of proper dimensions. For reasons of air safety, special attention was paid to the arrangement of the pilot seats during the Do X's design … You get the impression that the Do X's cockpit was the starting point when sketching its design – this is how convincing its great view and practical location is.

Upon viewing a new airplane, an airman always sits at the steering controls first in order to receive a first impression from this important spot. He walks over the sponsons of the boat through a convenient door on the inside and enters a cross corridor of the main deck. From this cross corridor, which connects the front and rear passenger chambers, the airman climbs up a ladder to the upper deck where the duty offices are located, like on ships. The Dutch pilot Scholte, known for his flights to the Dutch East Indies, writes about his first impressions of the Do X: 'When a pilot examines the upper deck of the Do X, the so-called service deck, he sees a dream of the future fulfilled, which was thought to be years away from realization.'

Probably every airman who steps aboard the captain's deck will instantly have a joyful and satisfying impression of the exquisite view from the cockpit, the practical roomaness of the navigation room and the perfection of the engine room. The spot with the best view, which is located near the center of gravity, was chosen for the pilots so that they have a view of the front of the boat before them and, with one look at the wings, they can also easily appraise the flying boat's condition in curves or in bad weather. The spot was also chosen for another reason: it offers a great advantage for estimating altitude when landing.

In front of them, the pilots only have the instruments needed for aeronautical command of the flying boat – no revolution speed gauge, thermometer, pressure gauges and the like. Only two collective rpm gauges for the motor groups on the starboard side and port side give information about the number of running engines and their average speed of rotation in conjunction with signal lamps. The pilots, of course, have the throttle in their power, but they can only operate the six starboardside and six portside engines jointly so that, in this regard, the flying boat is flown as a two-engine aircraft.

Directly behind the pilots, closed off by a wall with two large windows and a sliding door in the middle, is the navigation/captain's room. It is of quite ample size and furnished with a large map table and cabinet. Adjacent to it is the engine room with monitoring instruments and control levers for all twelve engines.

Powering-on, shutting down and warming up the engines takes place from the engine room, independent of the pilots. In special cases, the pilot can,

Clear panorama view from a high viewing position. Cockpit of the Do X, here the right seat of the second pilot or co-pilot. (Photo: Dornier GmbH, EADS)

however, activate a bypass switch to shut down the entire engine unit. The service alleyways, which lead to the individual engine nacelles, also empty into the engine room so that the head engineer can easily monitor the engine unit. The close proximity of the engine room to the captain's chambers assures that the ship's command can quickly be notified of all incidents. This still happens verbally or by hand signals since a more convenient way of mechanical transmission has not yet emerged.

Situated next to the engine room is a very large room for wireless telegraphy, and directly behind it the auxiliary engine room, where a two-cylinder, water-cooled DKW motor generates the power source. Using a gearbox, similar to an automobile's switching unit, the engine's output can be switched to a compressor, which uses pressurized air for starting the engines, while the generator of the light and power system is usually coupled with the motor. Providing the wireless telegraphy with electricity also takes place through this assembly, and other machines, such as the bilge pump, can be powered by the auxiliary engine.

Thus we have a complete and very successfully implemented separation of the crew from the passengers on the Do X, which is achieved by the centralization of the crew's offices in the upper deck. This outstanding idea was not as obvious as it appears to us now and was only possible with the division of the boat's hull into three entirely separate decks, which in turn was only feasible with a certain size of flying boat.

The middle deck, with space for the passengers, is divided in the front by a bulkhead. The capstan along with the necessary rope for sea maneuvers as well as the drift anchor and the like are located in the space that is formed up to the bow stem. This space is accessible from both the middle deck and the upper deck so that during maneuvers, such as tying or throwing out the towing line, the appointed man can reach the forward space from outside without entering the passenger space, or from the inside of the flying boat in case there are high seas and a danger of falling overboard. A hatchway leads from the previously mentioned corridor of the middle deck into the lower deck, where the operating supplies are stored and where space for heavier goods, like freight and baggage, is available.

The boat itself, at forty meters long, is remarkable in its novel construction. The under side, which reaches up to the floor of the middle deck, is the actual floating body. It is built with strong ribs and horizontal bracing – at two meters high, the keel beam, whose upper edge meets the floor of the middle deck, is the most important. Only the bulkheads reach up to this same height. With the slightest dip of barely 1 meter from a fully loaded flying boat, a deep, dangerous sinking, even with several flooded sections,

should not be feared. The middle deck of the flying boat could be kept completely free of troubling bulkheads to create an almost entirely free space for the passengers, which could then be freely developed. The bulkhead arrangement of the lower space was very carefully executed. The sponsons are also divided into several watertight areas that ensure stability on the water during breaches.

The forces of movement in water absorbed by the solid underside of the boat, upon whose roof the travelers are located, must be properly diverted to the wings. This is accomplished using three particularly hefty ribs, which hold and stabilize the three spars of the wings … Dornier's larger flying boats have a main step, or takeoff step, as well as a landing step. The takeoff step is divided by a stair-shaped, offset longitudinal step, which functions to reduce friction at higher speeds during the last part of takeoff. The bottom of the boat is strongly keeled. This eases rolling by splitting the waves and prevents strong blows to the boat during takeoff at sea. The keel narrows toward the steps and amounts to only a few degrees on the main step. The outside of the boat's bottom is arched slightly downward in the front. The purpose of this is to guide the water, which is split to the sides by the keel, downward to avoid larger amounts of spray. Without it, the water would go over the sponsons and shoot up to the motors. Curvature of the Do X was intentionally kept to a minimum since

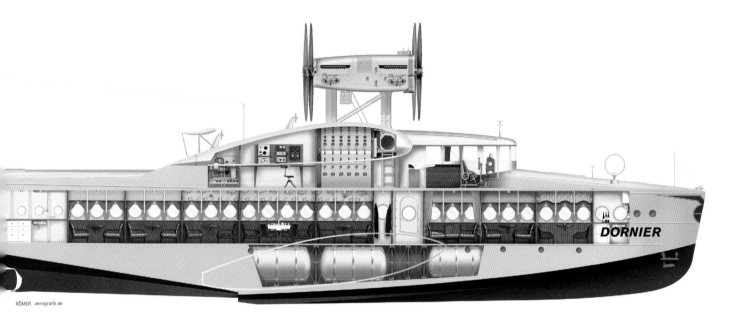

RÖMER aerografik.de

A cross section of the Do X reveals the partitioning into three decks. The command deck is located under the engine unit. In the center is the passenger deck, and below it the service deck with fuel tanks. (Illustration: Michael Römer)

excessive emphasis of this shape results in too much lift and would then involve unpleasant bouncing during takeoffs in rough water. This bouncing, during which the pilot has almost no control, can place a considerable amount of stress on the entire flying boat and must be countered with the appropriate weight disbursement. Another disadvantage is that high arching of the hull puts a very high tensile stress on the sheet metal, which causes riveted seams to loosen or even rip open. For this reason, DMB has always avoided ambitiously seeking out the necessary lift by making the boat as narrow as possible.

A wider boat has considerable advantages: it quickly lifts to the step (the Do X itself in only a few seconds), the contact pressure per unit of surface area decreases along with the overall stress on the boat, and finally, the downward curvature can be abandoned, which helps to prevent bouncing and makes landings smoother because the water can flow to the sides.

A wide boat results in a lower draught, another extremely valuable asset since there are numerous times when the water depth limits the ability to takeoff and land. Also, with lower draught the bulkheads used to connect watertight compartments can be arranged above the water level, which considerably re-

duces the risk of flooding into adjacent rooms when a compartment is leaking through open doors. Finally, the large reserve displacement of the hull gives wider boats a significant advantage. In swells, or if the boat is damaged, the available reserve displacement is crucial since it is mainly designated for the remaining buoyancy and stability. The impression of seaworthiness that the Do X makes to the unbiased observer is justified because the advantageous reserve displacement is preserved with the large hulls of a real ship.

The shape of the main step is very important for takeoff, but the landing step or tailskid also plays an important role. With its keeled shape, this structural component acts as a guiding blade when the boat rolls on the water. At higher speeds, the tailskid acts as an attenuator since it prevents too much angulation and lift of the boat's stem. The flying boat lands on this landing step, and since it is sharply keeled, it settles into the water smoothly. Due to their position on the back end of the boat, a guiding effect occurs immediately. The flying boat travels straight ahead and cannot swerve. This is essential for landings with crosswinds in narrow waterways, such as rivers, canals, harbors, etc.

When steered correctly in a crosswind, the flying boat moves in the direction of a river, for example, while the axis of an airplane, depending on the strength of the crosswind, forms a significant drift angle with its direction of motion, which coincides with the course of a river. As soon as the boat touches down with the tailskid, it is led immediately in the direction of movement by the path of tailskid and travels in the direction of flow. Landings of this kind have been made quite often by Wal flying boats in Marina di Pisa on the Arno, where over the course of the last eight years more than a hundred Wals were built and flown in. Due to the flatter formation of the main step, laterally sliding landings are accomplished without any risk.

The wings of the Do X, with an almost fifty meter span and 9.5 meter depth, has three spars. The spars are individually supported and fastened together so that failure of one spar still provides adequate flight safety. Instead of sliding 9.5 meter-long corrugates on to these spars, the sections created by the spars and crossbeams are covered by panels, so-called wing skin panels, about eight square meters in size, whose connections are located on the inside of the wings. This design makes it possible to cover the bare wing frame easily and quickly or to uncover them again for repairs and testing. The back end is installed separately in several pieces and can also be easily removed. The wings are tall enough on the inside, even though they don't involve a so-called thick profile, that they are even accessible in flight.

Achieving low frictional resistance was a priority when designing the steering mechanism. This worked out surprisingly well by using only ball bearings and tension wires; pulleys are completely avoided and are replaced instead by bell cranks. Freedom of movement was so great that the torsion of an idle flying boat is easier than with many small two-seated airplanes.

The rudders are balanced by special surfaces in typical Dornier fashion. It became apparent that the high steering forces of a Do X can be operated by hand, without help from rudder machines. The difference of forces between the rudder itself and the balance, which can have a strong effect on the aircraft but offset one another when steering, are kept low in all conditions so that they can be controlled. Refinements still seem to be possible, but can only be tackled after more flight experience.

It must have been something of a challenge to object to the twelve motors built on to the flying boat. This number inevitably resulted from the required power of about 6,000hp and the fact that reliable and tested motors with more than 500hp were not yet available.

The best spot for the motors proved to be the location above the wings. There the propellers were protected from spray water and the prop wash conveniently led to the tail unit and increased lift as a consequence, which is highly desired during takeoff. An installation inside the wings would only have been possible with water-cooled engines. This would have had to run in front of the wings with direct drive of the propellers and the propellers would have been positioned on the entire wingspan with the drawback of the leading edge of the wings reducing the effectiveness of the slipstream. Also, the outer motors would have been so far from the center of gravity that a failure would have caused torque. Restricting the number of propellers would again have to involve an extensive gear mechanism with propeller shafts and all of the disadvantages that come with it, such as heavy weight, lower reliability, difficult maintenance, etc., and the aerodynamic advantages would be completely lost as well.

The notion that installing the engines in the wings improves accessibility is only partly true. The spars, crossbeams and engine mounts that support the propeller bearings and shaft bearings, or the gear box if one is used, which are installed in this kind of confined space, do not make accessibility better by any means, similar to the housing in a special tandem nacelle. This guarantees completely acceptable accessibility in the current state of engine technology, especially to the tubing connections, carburetors, filters, etc. Large-scale works on modern airplane engines, whose movable parts are completely encapsulated, are just not possible with the relatively short flight times because the time, the crew and the available weight for replacement parts are not sufficient. The most important engine instruments are built into the engine nacelles of the Do X. Under special circumstances, a lever also makes it possible to move the throttle independently as well as the fire extinguisher.

As already mentioned, all engine instruments are joined in the engine room. Control over the flow of fuel also takes place here. It is pumped from tanks in the boat to two storage tanks located at the leading edge of the wings. Beforehand, the fuel goes through a double filter, which is carried out so that one-half shuts down and can be cleaned in flight.

A certain supply of oil is available for each engine. The oil, which flows from a large container stored in the boat, fills a small container in the nacelles. A signaling device indicates when the containers need to be refilled and also when the appropriate level is reached in the oil containers. The pumps, which send the operating fluids upward, are powered by electricity. For safety, mechanical power is also supplied by the airflow. In addition, special hand pumps are also provided for special cases, in harbors for example, when fuel needs to be pumped to the upper tanks.

The engines are furnished with Lamblin pumps, which draw gasoline out of both nose tanks. These pumps are designed as a double unit (one half is sufficient for each motor) so that one reserve is available. For extra security, a hand pump is built onto each side of six engines, which is put into service because the Lamblin pumps have no suction before the engines start.

Basically, the gasoline for the Do X is stored as deeply as possible, like with other large loads. The advantages of this positioning are: the heavy weights simply make the continuous heavy pounding during difficult takeoffs and landings in swells harmless since the inertia forces are now transferred to the water through the boat's bottom. Distribution of this weight to the wings would have resulted in tremendous strain for the entire wing assembly in swells. Furthermore, the gasoline supplies are safely stored by the larger distance from the motors."

This is the description of the functions on board the Do X from engineer and pilot Heinrich Schulte-Frohlinde's point of view.

Cash Flow in Difficult Times

In his autobiography 'Aus meiner Ingenieurlaufbahn' (English: 'My Career as an Engineer'), the eighty-two-year-old Claude Dornier concludes his recollections by writing about the financial history of the Do X and the hangar in Altenrhein: "I believe it was in 1925 (Note: July 1925). I had breakfast with the President of the German Aerospace Industry Association, Admiral Lahs (Note: at that time, Rudolf Lahs [1880-1954] was a frigate captain and leader of the air raid protection division, the camouflaged pilot division of the German Navy in Berlin. Admiral and Association President would come later). After eating we found a small, private office where we drank another cup of tea. Admiral Lahs was very well disposed to me. As an old Navy man he had a soft spot for seaplanes and was always happy to hear about my work on the subject. This time, though, the lively man was noticeably reluctant. He puffed on his cigar, as if to prepare himself for something he wanted to tell me, or ought to tell me. Finally, he broke the silence: 'Dornier, what would you say if a stranger gave you a pile of money to build a giant boat? Something that doesn't exist yet?' At first I was stunned in silence and in thought. Then, I simply said: 'I'd be happy to.'

Lahs hinted to me that substantial resources were available which someone wanted to provide for the continuation of my work in the field of large seaplanes. They trusted me and would offer me absolute freedom. I must say that my pulse quickened at this disclosure since the construction of a large seaplane was one of the greatest jobs, if not the greatest, I could have hoped for. I pulled my slide rule out of my pocket and planned. 'It will probably have to be fifty metric tons,' I thought. 'That costs a lot of money. We have to build a hangar and workshops, which means not only money, but a lot of time.'

Lahs had remained silent and was secretly pleased about my bewilderment. 'Dornier,' he said, 'we have the money, don't worry.' Just as he began to explain more, the door opened and a slim, tall man, who appeared to be a navy man at first sight, entered. He must have been a good friend of Lahs since the two spoke informally with one another. He spoke the

Building and Operating Costs for the Do X Flying Boat (RM = Reichsmark)	Do X 1	Do X 1a	Do X 2 and 3
Production costs			
Cost estimate from 1925	1,470,000 RM	-	-
Preliminary costs, order price, purchase price	2,370,900 RM	-	-
Model inspection	33,000 RM	-	-
Fixed price 1927	-	-	2,000,000 each
Final invoice from May 8, 1931 without engines	-	3,549,182.61RM	-
Engines and replacement parts (Curtiss) thirteen pieces ($7,500/piece) purchased by Dornier Metallbauten GmbH, Manzell 1931	-	417,411.88 RM	-
Acquisition by the German Reich according to current market value in July 1932	-	327,199.21 RM	-
Total production costs 1931	-	3,966,594.49 RM	2,000,000 RM each
Maintenance and repair costs (varies)			
Conversion from Siemens to Curtiss engines Summer 1930	-	509,578.89 RM	-
Ferry flight from Altenrhein to New York from November 1930 to August 1931 with repair stops in Lisbon (wings), Las Palmas (structure, upright ribs), Rio de Janeiro (hull) and Para (crankshaft) on November 14, 1931	-	1,464,864 RM	-
Engine overhaul in New York October to November 1931	-	102,691.88 RM	-
General overhaul in Altenrhein November 1932 to April 1933	-	119,207.39 RM	-

The figures shown come exclusively from contemporary sources from 1929 to 1933.
1. Budget records of the German Finance Ministry, here aviation entities, governmental interests in aircraft and aircraft engine industry, renovation of Dornier Metallbauten GmbH 1931-1932 (Federal archives Berlin, Sign. R2/5597).
2. Various source material from the author's archives

man's name so unclearly that I could not understand it. I call him the 'stranger.' He immediately joined in on our conversation. He said to me: 'So, Mr. Dornier, how many millions do you need then to build a great big ship for us?' Of course I could not answer this question on the spur of the moment and only said that it will require a lot of time and money to manage a job of this magnitude. 'The money is there,' he replied. 'But do you have the courage to attempt it?'

I answered that I couldn't imagine a better assignment and that I believed I could handle it. But money alone was not enough. I would need time and trust. 'You shall receive both,' the stranger said. I couldn't believe my luck. I felt a little anxiety before the upcoming task, but I didn't doubt for a moment that I would complete it. 'Let's have a drink to the success of the flying boat,' proposed Lahs and we had some glasses brought over."

This initial conversation between Claude Dornier, frigate captain Rudolf Lahs and the "secretive unknown navy man" was the moment that the Do X and the company for Dornier aircraft in Altenrhein were born. Presumably, the unknown navy man was naval captain Walter Lohmann (1878-1930). As the head of the sea transport division of the German Navy, he channeled millions in tax money through the Reichstag and made it available for military tech-

nology. The further development of speed boats, submarines, navy airplanes and probably the Do X as well were among the projects financed with "special funding" from budget items of the Reich's budget of Ruhr funds and bank credits since 1923. These were all armaments that were prohibited by the Versailles peace treaty. Disclosure of his activities culminated in the "Lohmann Affair" at the end of November 1927. As a consequence, Defense Minister Otto Geßler (1875-1955) had to step down and Admiral Hans Zenker (1870-1932), head of the Naval Command also resigned on September 30, 1928. Violation of budgetary law and channeling of public funds and tax money for private economic endeavors resulted in losses of twenty-six million Marks at the expense of the Reich Treasury.

In July 1925, Claude Dornier wondered who his investors would be. But Lahs ignored his question and answered: "You will sign a contract with the Ministry of Transportation and the money will come to you from this position. Don't ask again." Whether the Naval Command is considered the sole customer of the Do X, wanting to develop a "seaworthy experimental craft of the largest scale, which can be used as a remote reconnaissance aircraft, mine layer or torpedo carrier," has still not been clarified. In any case, the Ministry of Transportation allocates the promised funds from the budget. Claude Dornier finalizes the appropriate contracts for an initial 3.5 million Reichsmarks. Two million of it is designated for the construction of the new airplane factory and 1.5 million for the production of the first flying boat.

In September 1925, Claude Dornier assembles a planning group in Manzell for the giant flying boat project. It is the beginning of the later design department for the Do X flying boat. At the same time, the hunt for a suitable plot of land for a new aircraft hanger in neighboring countries is taking place. Due to the limitations of the Versailles Treaty, the new aircraft factory must be built in Italy or Switzerland. Dornier wants to implement his plans near the main Dornier factory in Manzell. After Swiss government circles show interest in the project and step in to help Dornier, a favorable site is discovered on the shores of Lake Constance. Altenrhein is the idyllic spot in undisturbed nature that will be dominated by construction machinery, steam-powered rams and water pumps in the following years. The nearly 100 hectare site for the new aircraft hangar, shipyard harbor and planned airfield lies about twelve kilometers from Rorschach in the delta of the old course of the Rhein. This choice of location is also necessary because the Navy later wants to carry out weapons tests for the flying boat at the place of production. In other words, Switzerland.

With the help of Swiss industrialist, Jacob Schmidheiny II (1875-1955), Claude Dornier initiates the creation of a public company for Dornier aircraft, the short-named Do-Flug AG. The German Reich owns 51% of the initial capital stock of over 3,150,000 Swiss Francs. Claude Dornier and Dornier Metallbauten GmbH split the remaining 49%. This 49% is an interest free, government loan irredeemable until 12/31/1935. The loan is to be paid off by the expected stock dividends. This is how Claude Dornier envisions it anyway.

But the problems begin already during the development of the land in Altenrhein. Due to rising water levels, the area is under water. It has to be dredged, drained and leveled before the construction can begin. Ground surveys reveal that for the foundation of the planned self-supporting hangars, over 12,000 meters of reinforced concrete piles must be installed. After all of the unpredictable problems, the expensive delay of the hangar's completion is set back by a year. Because of these "surprises," the German Reich a forced increase capital to 1,650,000 Swiss Francs in 1928. With a 76% majority stake, the German Reich is now the de facto owner of Do-Flug AG. A free-standing assembly hangar with a 40x60m floor space and 10m clearance height, a hangar with 75x60m floor space, and two production halls each with 60x60m floor space are built one after another for serial production. Together with the administrative buildings, this is the most modern aircraft factory in Europe. Founding Do-Flug AG in less industrialized eastern Switzerland is of considerable significance economically. Eventually, 700 to 800 skilled workers will work a single-shift operation in the assembly hangars, where the metal work, forging, propeller woodwork, painting, saddlery and anodizing, to name just a few, will be carried out. In 1927, an apprentice workshop is constructed to train aircraft builders for Do X assembly. The hangars are still standing today and belong to Park Altenrhein, an industrial park near the modern airport St. Gallen-Altenrhein and the aviation museum.

Fatal miscalculation. The money expected as income in relation to the concrete costs do not add up.

23

Anlage 4
Zu L.7. 9693/31.

Aufstellung

über die Gehälter der leitenden Angestellten der Dornier-
Metallbauten G.m.b.H. einschl. Berliner Büro.

		Monatsgehalt			
		Stand am 1.1.31 RM	Stand ab 1.2.31 RM	Stand ab 1.1.32 RM	Gratifika-tionen 1930 RM +)
Dr.Dornier	Geschäftsführer	2 000.--	1 840.--	1 500.--	6 997,50 4 000.-- ++)
Oesterle	kaufm.Direktor	1 700.--	1 564.--	1 330.--	3 600.--
Flittinger	Prokurist (techn.Leitung)	1 500.--	1 395.--	1 186.--	2 250.--
Mayr	Prokurist (Auslandsver-tretung)	1 300.--	1 209.--	1 029.--	1 875.--
Stahl	Prokurist (technisches Auftragsbüro)	1 100.--	1 023.--	600.--	937,50
	Büro Berlin				
Milatz	Leitung des Berl. Büros	1 665.--	1 665.--	1 500.--	3 000.--
Schulte-Frölinde	" "	2 000.--	1 840.--	1 200.--	1 125.--

+) Gratifikationen für 1931 sollen gegebenenfalls erst in der Gesell-
schafterversammlung im Juni 1932 beschlossen werden.

++) Dr. Dornier erhält 4 000 RM jährlich Aufwandsentschädigung.

Hard Times. The German Reich uses salary information
of the managing employees to decide whether to save
DMB GmbH.

In 1925, Claude Dornier's first calculation for the production costs of the Do X amounts to almost 1.5 million Reichsmarks. After being awarded the contract by the Ministry of Transportation, the purchase order price is set at 2,370,000 Reichsmarks in June 1928. The final invoice amount from May 8, 1931 (without engines) adds up to exactly 3,549,182.61 Reichsmarks. These cost trends generated little sympathy by government authorities. The conclusion of the developing friction with the German Reich: We will pay, but only once and never again.

With this decision, the scheduled serial production of the Do X becomes invalid and DoFlug AG's factory in Altenrhein is called into question. November 5,

1930 was a bitter day for Alfons Keppeler, the business director of Do-Flug. On the afternoon of this fateful day, the Do X 1a took off from Altenrhein with a 17 man crew for their flight around the world. The first leg follows the Rhein from Lake Constance to Amsterdam. The joy and expectations of all participants is great. The mood in Berlin, however, is completely different. Just minutes after take-off, the end of Dornier as an incorporated company has been decided. Alfons Keppeler (1895-1947) has to answer to the Ministry of Transportation in Berlin in a crisis meeting titled "Assessment of total costs of the Do X and closure of the factory in Altenrhein." The result: closure of the factory in Altenrhein and the voluntary liquidation of Do-Flug AG. It was a bitter day for those who played an important role in building the factory.

And for Claude Dornier things got worse. After a great deal of effort, the Do X 1a lands in Rio de Janeiro on June 20, 1931 and on July 6 the "Hoover Moratorium" comes into effect. In light of the developing global economic crisis, U.S. President Herbert Hoover enforces the one-year suspension of all war debt repayments despite opposition from the French. First and foremost, the German Reich is freed from reparation payments for one year – a fatal situation for Dornier Metallbauten GmbH. Two triple-engine bombers and a few Wal flying boats, which have been ordered by the Yugoslavian government as part of reparations business, are in the final stages of construction there. According to the invoice: Yugoslavia orders, DMB builds and the German Reich pays. The payments by the Reich are canceled abruptly due to the moratorium and now Dornier is on the verge of bankruptcy.

Frantic talks to save the business begin between the Reich ministries and DMB. Preserving Dornier, who along with Junkers is a leading airplane factory in Germany, is indeed wanted economically, but there is no consensus on how to achieve it. At any rate, DMB GmbH will be screened and prescribed the most frugal economic management.

Here is a good example of the dire situation. On November 24, 1931, Claude Dornier receives a very personal visit from Ernst Brandenburg (1883-1952) in Friedrichshafen. The department head at the Ministry of Transportation has traveled from Berlin to sort things out in a private discussion. In is his memo from December 1, 1931, he writes: "… After the departmental meeting concerning Dornier, I have spoken alone with Dr. Dornier about the earning capacity of his company. Secret information had been spread about Dr. Dornier obtaining an unreasonably high salary from the defaulted company due to his contract. Without reservation, Dr. Dornier gave me trustworthy information about his earning capacity. According to this information, he received a monthly salary of approximately 1,800RM in his capacity as executive director of Dornier Metallbauten GmbH and a monthly expense allowance of around 260RM. Dr. Dornier handed me a written statement on November 30, 1931, which is enclosed here, regarding the earning capacity of the other managers at the factory. For his role as executive director of the public company Do-Flug, Altenrhein, Dr. Dornier receives no income.

According to his statement, Dornier owns hundreds of patents. Many of them are of little value, but some are allegedly very valuable. In accordance with the contract that has now been signed between him and Dornier Metallbauten GmbH, 50% of the patents and copyrights belong to the company and the patent holder himself. As long as Dornier is a member of the company, the company has the exclusive rights to the patents in Germany and abroad. If Dornier parts with the company, he is also entitled to recreate his patents but not to hand over licenses. For the use and exploitation of the patents, the company pays Dr. Dornier nothing. If they sell building rights, they have to pay 40% of the gross proceeds to Dornier. Such license sales would have earned him variable yet continually dwindling annual amounts since 1924. The highest were the revenues from 1924, when he earned about 180,000RM from these license sales. In 1930 the falling proceeds from license sales amounted to around 60,000RM. The earnings came about exclusively through license sales abroad and were all related to the Wal model before 1924, which means they were generated without any financial support by the Reich.

Dr. Dornier believes that the exaggerated rumors regarding his income can be traced back to an earlier

established provision in his contract with the company, which assures him a progressive commission from sales if the net revenue comprises at least a 10% profit for the company. This commission was guaranteed to him up to 50,000RM, even when the company works without profit. But the entire provision was removed in 1929.

Beyond the exploitation of his intellectual property, Dr. Dornier considers the contract with the company to be his property. Under no circumstances is he inclined to relinquish this ownership. He wants to invest the assets acquired through his patents and his occupational activities, and the property belonging to him in Friedrichshafen, which he estimates to be worth considerably less than one million RM, so that he is still active in the German aviation industry, not just as an employee, but also as entrepreneur. Almost all of his liquid assets (ca. 380,000RM) in Dornier Metallbauten GmbH, which faced liquidity problems due to the loss of the Yugoslavia reparation installments, were lent without the security of a 1% interest rate under the Reich's bank discount. The trust that he put into the future of Dornier Metallbauten GmbH would also result from this. He would find himself in negotiations with the chairman of the company (Dr. Eckener) to discuss in what capacity he could participate, be it raising capital or purchasing shares in Dornier Metallbauten GmbH.

According to Dr. Dornier, Dr. Eckener is ready to explain to the Minister of Transportation that the contract between the company Dornier Metallbauten GmbH and Dr. Dornier is considered quite normal and fair."

An especially worrisome debt from November 14, 1931 summed up the state of affairs for Dornier's life's work. The involuntary, year old flight of the Do X 1a from Altenrhein to New York from November 5, 1930 to the date of invoice cost 1,464,864 Reichsmarks. A sum that had to be paid by DMB.

In the sunlight of success. The Do X 1 on the day of its maiden flight from Altenrhein. (Photo; Ziegler, DSLR)

Maiden Flight and Testing of the Do X 1

Heinrich Schulte Frohlinde (1887-1965) of Costruzioni Meccaniche Aeronautiche S.A. (CMASA) has already been employed for seven and a half years when Claude Dornier brings him back to Germany in 1929. Since 1921, the legendary Dornier "Wal" has been built and tested at the licensed enterprise of Dornier Metallbauten GmbH in Italy with substantial contributions by the engineer. Now Schulte-Frohlinde is to lead the testing of the Do X. He recounts the maiden flight and testing of the first flying boat in Altenrhein in his speech: "The Do X Flying Boat, Seen From the Standpoint of the Pilot" held in the "Ring of Pilots" in Berlin on March 11, 1930. The privately owned, typewritten draft from the Schulte-Frohlinde family is published here in excerpts for the first time.

"... Beginning work here at home, there could be no more honorable assignment bestowed upon me than the supervision of the Do X testing. I was all the more delighted to accept this assignment when Richard Wagner, a proven and talented pilot, was available to me to test fly the giant flying boat. I knew him already through longtime collaboration in Marina di Pisa and enjoyed our companionship on long Mediterranean flights with the Dornier Wal to Spain and Morocco. Test flights of Dornier aircrafts have always been directed by an engineer who generally takes part in the flights as a second pilot and is responsible for the entire process, the aeronautical as well as technical aspects. Of course the pilot is the real commander of the airplane in the sky. He has complete aeronautical responsibility and no one else dictates the operation of the controls.

Do X Director of Testing. Dornier engineer Schulte-Frohlinde (left) and his pilot Richard Wagner, head test pilot of DMB. (Photo: Ziegler, DSLR)

The accompanying engineer has to recognize the characteristics of the machine during flights and devise ways to correct defects, making suggestions and implementing them. This is best accomplished when the engineer assumes control over flight testing … As we prepared to test the Do X, it was soon clear to us that it was actually not a difficult task, as it can be with other new large-scale airplane models. On the contrary, throughout the entire process, which tries

to present consistent advancements to the previous airplanes of Dornier Metallbauten, there were no surprises at all. Only two dangers exist: first, that the balance of the rudder could be too large or too small, and second, that the balanced position of the flying boat would be disturbed by the stated trimming. An occurrence of both defects, however, could have serious consequences. To come right to the point, the flying boat proved to be completely balanced and quite easy to steer.

Personal preparation by the pilots for the maiden flight consists of frequent testing of the pilot chairs to get used to their position. Wagner takes sole control over the rudder. When he signals for help, the second man is ready to take hold of it. For the technical preparation, a dependable crew of sixteen men is assembled to be in position to immediately repair smaller problems. There are mechanics for every nacelle, skilled workers for the electrical system and instruments, etc. Furthermore, two larger motorboats are available: one is a service vessel with Claude Dornier as the commander, while the second is for passengers. Flag signals between the flying boat and service vessel are determined and messages delivered to those concerned.

Implementation of the program for the first test proceeds as follows: for the first rolling test, the flying boat is brought to the water with running engines. Before the Do X can swim freely, the service boat takes a towrope from the flying boat and tows in the direction of the channel in order to ease the departure and course bearing. In the meantime, the side supports are drawn into the sponsons. The towrope is thrown out upon instruction as soon as the Do X reaches the channel and is ready to begin the maneuver:

1. Determining steering ability on the water. After the towrope is cast off, the Do X begins the steering ability test, the results of which are important for properly reaching the buoy after the test is carried out. First, the steering ability is determined using the water rudder alone, then with the engines with the water rudder in a central position.

Maneuvering like a ship with the water rudder. The Do X travels with "caution" on Lake Constance. (Photo: Ziegler, Staatsarchiv St. Gallen)

2. Engine test. Engine tests are made on the water, each with two symmetrical nacelles. Should any faults occur during testing that require immediate correction, repairs are made either on board or back at the shipyard. If the repairs are made on board, the motors are shut off and the Do X is slowly towed by the service boat.

3. Taxiing tests on the step. As long as everything is good up to this point, the Do X will attempt to go up to the step to get a feel for the steering. This is repeated until the pilot on board the Do X has tested the balance and is satisfied with the steering and the proper functioning of the motor system and steering are assured.

4. Take-off test. Now the Do X flying boat will attempt to go airborne for the first time, but only a few meters above the water and without turning. The landing should take place by slowly decelerating.

5. Longer flight. After performing several take-offs, it will then be determined whether a longer flight or an appropriate discontinuation follows."

Program and Practice of the Maiden Flight

Of course, not everything goes according to plan, as is often the case in the aviation industry. As a result of slight vibrations on the flying boat's carriage, we prefer to go into the water with eight running engines. After completing steps 1 and 2, one engine stops and will not start again. We get up on the step at somewhat higher speeds to test the steering and to get the engine running again using the airstream. It starts up again just fine, but suddenly we find ourselves in the air, unintentionally. The take-off is barely noticeable and reveals, above all, that the rudders function well and the trimming is correct. We also immediately shed some light on another important point that had previously occupied us and whose solution could not be expected for certain – the estimated height above the water during landing. The pilots monocular lies about seven meters above the surface of the water when the flying boat touches the water ... During the World War, Dornier Metallbauten once set the pilot's chairs in the tip of a fuselage of a four-engined 1,000 horsepower flying boat with Maybach engines and 230 square meters of wing surface, while the boat's hull itself only contained equipment and weaponry. The view from this spot was ideal, but the landing was quite difficult. This flying boat, though, has different proportions since the fuselage floats freely about four meters above the hull. With the Do X, these difficulties do not occur at all. The length of the bow, which lies in front of the pilot, is about the same height that the monocular must have above the surface of the water. This eases the estimation so immensely that no difficulties exist and the landing can be made with the same security of smaller flying boats in which the pilot sits close to the water. The high water spray can never disturb the pilot during take-offs, another advantage of the Do X.

Crew of the maiden flight. Back on land the crewmembers assemble for a photograph in front of the Do X on the morning of June 12, 1929. In the middle in uniform is Richard Wagner.

Ready to slide off the boat trailer into Lake Constance. The Do X gets ready for a test flight. (Photo: Ziegler, Staatsarchiv St. Gallen)

Dynamic pressure measurements on the fly. Preparations on July 17, 1929. Both impact tubes on the hull can be lifted upward from the anchor room. (Photo: Ziegler, DSLR)

The Do X is towed out on Lake Constance by the company motorboat Altenrhein for take-off in the right wind. Spectators are almost always present. (Photo: Ziegler, Staatsarchiv St. Gallen)

After more take-offs on July 12, 1929, the first testing day, the Do X is moored to the buoy because the speedometer is not working and has to be repaired. Further test flights then follow without incident. During these flights we have already learned a great deal, although it must be said that we are still far away from being able to fly it properly and fully utilize it.

The model inspection with a flight weight of forty metric tons is carried out by Joachim von Köppen, head of the DVL flight department, and reveals that stability around all three axles passes. Particularly noteworthy is the result of flight ability test with engine failure. Here's the test report under point D: flight ability test of the flying boat during breakdown of: 1. an outer engine port side-nacelle III: the flying boat can (without relief by side rudder balancing) bank in both directions. 2. an outer nacelle port side-nacelle III (2 engines): the flying boat can (without relief by side rudder balancing) bank in both directions. 3. an inner nacelle port side-nacelle I: the flying boat can bank in both directions. 4. two inner nacelles port side-nacelle I and starboard side-nacelle I: the flying boat can bank in both directions. 5. two nacelles, starboard side-nacelle I and starboard side-nacelle II: the flying boat can (also without immediate relief by side rudder balancing) bank in both directions. 6. a nacelle starboard side-nacelle I and a nacelle starboard side-nacelle III: the flying boat can fly straight ahead with relief. The failed engines were throttled on idle; the other engines maintained cruising speed. No loss of altitude was detected during tests D 1 to 6.

Above Lake Constance during testing. One of many flights in the fall of 1929.

View of the back of the Do X from the top of a hangar. Clearly visible is the arrangement of the skylights in the engine room and radio room and the aft porthole. (Photo: Ziegler, Staatsarchiv St. Gallen)

Full throttle of all engines.
The Do X moving on the step
just before lifting off Lake
Constance. (Photo: Ziegler,
Staatsarchiv St. Gallen)

From these findings one can conclude to what degree the Do X flying boat is still able to fly and maneuver after failure of four engines, even if these are all on the same side. The accessibility of components, tubing, tanks and engines, makes monitoring and maintenance of the system considerably more important than with earlier airplane models. This has to have a great influence on the pilots and crew if the full potential of such a flying boat is to be exploited. It is no longer necessary for the commander himself to sit on the rudder and remain riveted to the spot for the entire duration of the flight. Of course he is free to take control of the steering himself, but his seat, especially in serious situations, is not on the wheel, but rather in the commander's room, where he has a complete view of the entire system. He will make difficult landings easier by estimating altitudes and announcing them to the pilot, just as we did in the beginning of test flights during hazy weather or with mirror-smooth waters. The commander will also prevent all non-critical messages being passed on to the pilots by the engine room. Instead of making a difficult situation worse, he can strive to relieve the already busy pilots during bad weather and judge for himself what measures should be taken when damages appear.

What Kind of Men and Professions Does the Do X Require?

Small airplanes guarantee control of movement in space, complete command by the pilot, great satisfaction and the exhilarating feeling of flying. In a flying boat like the Do X, the navigator's approach definitely has to be different. It immediately draws comparisons to nautical navigation, with the management of a large operation, like on a steamship for example. Claude Dornier deliberately separated aeronautical operations from mechanical operations when building the flying boat. Apart from the responsibility for the operation of the flying boat in its entirety, managing the navigation will have a greater significance than ever before thanks to the installation of wireless telegraphy and bearing systems, astronomical positioning, and the development of the weather service.

In the past, tracking the position of airplanes was primarily an intuitive art form practiced by experienced navigators, while today it is a science that uses all kinds of technical tools and requires study and theoretical knowledge. Of course, competence and experience will always remain important for navigation, which is why it cannot be referred to as a new profession. Pilots and navigators of the flying boat can only be a flier or an observer, who himself has extensive experience. Many pilots today still master everything that is required to operate a normal airplane in the sky. The majority will have sufficient knowledge and experience to assess the weather situation and to find their way using a map, compass and drift determination, and also have sufficient understanding of the engine system, often as much as a skilled technician. Servicing the wireless telegraphy, however, is impossible for most pilots; the separation of skills prevails here.

Where is the best reception? Detail of the loop antenna for the relay radio system that changed its position several times during the life of the Do X. From the radio room in 1930 to above the bar in the kitchen in 1933. (Photo: Ziegler, DSLR)

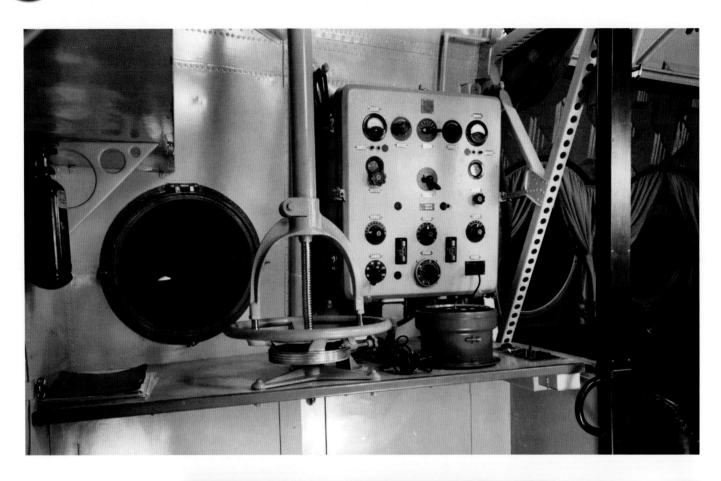

Relay radio system with a horizontal hand wheel for the rotating loop antenna. Here it is installed on the starboard side of the bar where it it remained from October 1930 to December 1932. (Photo: Ziegler, DSLR)

Experiments and testing. Stress measurements on the rods, spars and cross-beams in the wing unit of the Do X during assembly. (Photo: Ziegler, DSLR)

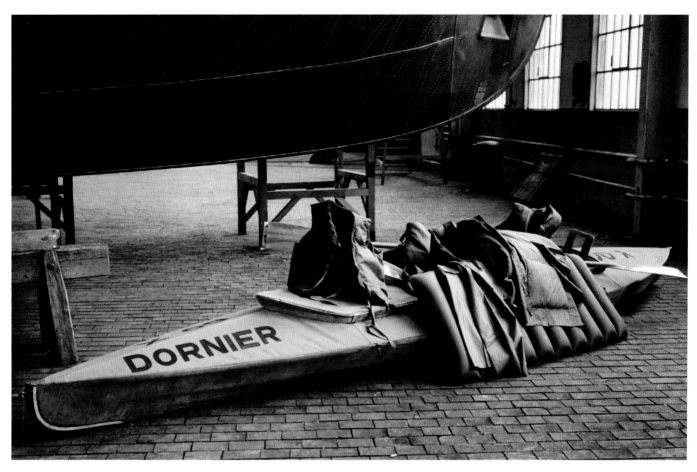

Spot-on for image promotion. From raincoat to life vest and air mattress to Klepper folding kayak. The company Klepper from Rosenheim equips the Do X in their favor. (Photo: Ziegler, DSLR)

Thus, it is not difficult to anticipate that commanding large flying boats will be technical and specialized. It will embrace similar functions like in sea navigation, where the machines are serviced by mechanics, the radio systems are serviced by telegraphists and the rudder is serviced by a helmsman, while the command and navigation lies with the skipper.

All comparisons are misleading though. Thus, a pilot on the hand wheel cannot be put in the same category with the helmsman of a ship. Due to the considerably higher speeds, the necessity to observe a balanced position and hovering capability as well as the transition of movement from a two-dimensional plane into three-dimensional space, steering an aircraft, in contrast to a ship, demands a lot more from the person steering. Aeronautical abilities, keen po-

wers of observation and quick decision making of the person steering are always essential for overcoming dangerous situations. Therefore, special talent is the most important prerequisite for the pilot profession and can never be replaced by thorough training and testing since training does not manage to create a fully adequate substitute for the qualities of character. To consider schooling a qualification to be a pilot is a mistake.

Some might wonder what has changed now versus then. For the pilot, quite a lot. Many advancements have been made in their profession. After creating flying boats like the Do X, we need able, experienced, aeronautically and technically trained operators who have mastered navigation. Only actual pilots with a lot of flight experience can be trained to become these commanders or flight captains. More accurately, it

The Do X 1a just before its water landing on Lake Constance. The hangars in Altenrhein can be seen in the background. (Photo: Ziegler, DSLR)

is up to the pilot himself to get advanced training for these major functions in order to concede the steering operations to younger pilots who will eventually take over the entire command of the flying boat, including the navigation. In this manner, it is clear that the age limit of pilots, up to the highest ranks of the profession, moves up considerably, than when the activity is limited to the control of the rudder.

We must also recognize the progress that technology has recently made with the automatic steering of airplanes. Experiments with mechanical devices that relieve people of the task of maintaining course while flying are so extraordinarily promising that we probably have to count on using such devices soon. This would be even more significant to the commander of the flying boat compared to the pure pilot. In light of these technical developments, the recruitment and development of pilots has to move in the direction of managing the flying boat as a whole, including navigation.

The commanders of large flying boats will also have take over additional rights and duties, which often results in a reduction of airfield management. The condition of the flying boat is monitored by them in the same way that the captain of a large steamer keeps the effectiveness of his ship up to date and verifies loading and the correct trim. The large crew must be impacted in a reasonable way, their working capacity and their weaknesses have to be made

known, and they have to understand how to enjoy their work. Of course, the commander is a good pilot who can fly with his head, or is able to assess the situation without feeling the pressure of the hand wheel in his fingers.

It is also extremely important that the commander is a capable seaman. The claim that the pilot of a flying boat has to have nautical training has been disputed a great deal. In this case too, training and testing alone are not sufficient – talent must be first and foremost. It goes without saying that a pilot of seaplanes has to be familiar with nautical rules and knot tying. If Odysseus used the same knots that a petty officer uses today (because their usefulness has been proven over the centuries) then there would be no point in inventing new ones. Seamanship must include the ability to be able to assess the effect of wind and water on flying boats. There are many examples where land pilots have become first-class seamen in surprisingly little time and are able to handle flying boats on the water masterfully.

However, with respect to the captain of a steam ship, the task of commanding a flying boat this way is much more difficult. His flying vehicle is frequently strained on the edge of stability when dealing with take-offs and landings on water, for example. So even a well-trained technical sense, which first develops after the appropriate experience, is a prerequisite to successfully lead a large flying boat.

Seldom photographed. The backside of the Altenrhein hangar with the flat administrative building. (Photo: Ziegler, DSLR)

In silver-gray for the first time. After the greenish protective coating of the duralumin fairings, the Do X gets its first finishing coat. (Photo: Ziegler, Staatsarchiv St. Gallen)

You can think twice about mankind's good fortune through technical advancements, but no one can doubt the progress of technology. Man feels the need to pursue a goal with his work and to distinguish himself in this pursuit. The pioneers of aviation made us believe that traveling quietly, safely and quickly through the air, over oceans and from one part of the world to another is possible. The Do X brings us one step closer to this.

During construction, Claude Dornier consciously tried not to endanger the success of the flying boat by testing for new solutions, as tempting as this would have been for the inventors and engineers. But the master revealed himself with this restriction. It is evident too that the cultural world feels this flying boat is more than just an interesting experiment by an inventor or scientist, but is there to help humanity. Some experts doubted the useful application of such a large flying boat in European commerce, as far as German aircraft owners were concerned. When Luft Hansa argues against it, saying that all traffic between Berlin and Oslo, for example, would not reach the capacity of the Do X, nothing is proven. The development of new, faster means of transportation also creates a new need and with it a larger number of passengers. If aviation were to become a difficult situation in Germany today and no immediate use

would emerge from the development of German aircraft technology then we want at least to recognize to what degree the Do X flying boat can contribute to strengthening German labor and Germany's reputation in the world. We at Dornier, anyway, believe that large flying boats will be the appointed aircraft for crossing oceans in the future. We think that the extensive flights over water this summer proves the usefulness of the Do X (Note: Schulte-Frohlinde's words in the summer of 1930).

Aviation is still quite young, even the development of aeronautical command has just barely begun and requires the constant cooperation of pilots to solve large problems such as flying in fog, locating position without ground visibility, etc. This evening I have tried to demonstrate to you that everything possible is being done in order to bring the highest degree of operational security to the Do X during flight by appropriately dividing the crew's obligations. It will surely not be difficult for proven German airmen to follow the train of thought expressed in lectures and to carry the added responsibility that is linked with the command of this kind of large aircraft unit."

With these words, Heinrich Schulte-Frohlinde ends his speech, "The Do X Flying Boat, Seen From the Standpoint of the Pilot" held in the "Ring of Pilots" in Berlin on March 11, 1930.

Weighing and weighing again. Nobody steps on the scale as often as the Do X. It was weighed with a boat transporter whose known weight is deducted for the final value. (Photo: Ziegler, DSLR)

For months the Do X is the focus of the press. Aviation, seafaring, commerce and even the tabloid press. Everyone is interested in the giant of Lake Constance.

Taken from the bow of the Do X. The slipway in Altenrhein awaiting the flying boat. (Photo: Ziegler, Staatsarchiv St. Gallen)

Back on land. Jacked up on the electrically operated boat transporter, the flying boat rolls from Lake Constance back to the hangar. (Photo: Ziegler, Staatsarchiv St. Gallen)

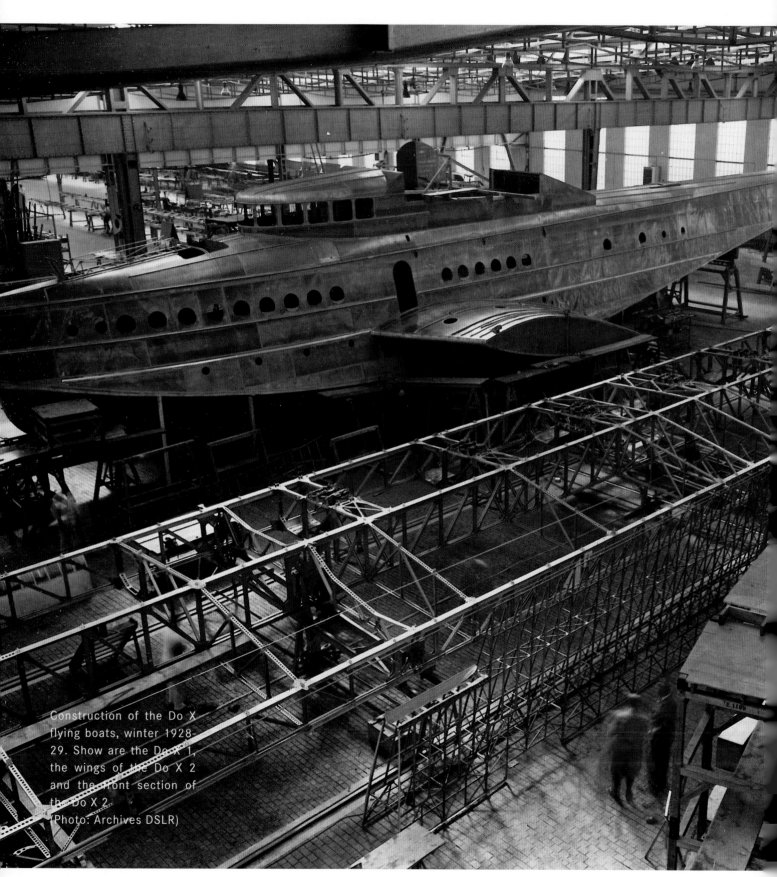

Construction of the Do X flying boats, winter 1928-29. Show are the Do X 1, the wings of the Do X 2 and the front section of the Do X 2.
(Photo: Archives DSLR)

Technical Details of the DO X 1 to the Do X 3

With the exception of the engine units, which are different on each Do X model and designed based on experience, the ship's frame, wings and tail unit are identical in their construction and design on all three flying boats. Because the flying boats are produced at almost the same time, only offset by a few months, requests for modifications resulting from testing and practical flight experience of the Do X 1 from the summer of 1929 are limited when implementing them into the Do X 2 and 3 models.

In the literature of the time and especially in Do X special editions of the Swiss magazine AERO-REVUE from 1931 and 1932, building specifications of the Do X 1 are reported in detail. Rediscovered and published here for the first time are the building specifications of the Do X 2 and 3. They come from a bundle of various original files from the inventory of DoFlug AG in Altenrhein that resurfaced in Switzerland in 2010. Twenty-one pages of typewritten text from July 9, 1931 are devoted to the "Building Specifications of the Dornier Do X Vas Flying Boat."

The Dornier model abbreviation "Vas" needs to be explained. In 1926 Dornier Metallbauten GmbH expanded their model abbreviation for newly built aircraft with a three-letter code. In this additional code, the first letter denotes the manufacturer of the motor installed. Obviously, consistency is not always possible here, as the model abbreviation of the Do X 1a with water-cooled Curtiss Conqueror engines shows. For Curtiss the letter "D" is used and the Fiat engines of the Italian Do X 2 and 3 are designated with a "V."

Almost complete Do X 1 in June 1929, a few days before its maiden flight. (Photo: Archive DSLR)

The first letter of the code is always capitalized and the other two letters are written in lower case. The second letter, always a vowel, offers a clue to the purpose of application: "a" for transport, "e" for testing, etc. The third letter denotes the design of the aircraft: "l" for land plane and "s" for seaplane. According to this code, the exact type designation for both Italian flying boats are Do X 2 Vas or Do X 3 Vas.

The building specifications, reproduced here in excerpts, apply to Do X model flying boats in the final technical state at that time. There was no update. Huge differences exist, as mentioned, with the engine units and the furnishings of the middle deck for the passengers. There are no differences among the three flying boats in regards to the their structural elements and use of materials.

Building Specifications of the Dornier Do X 2 Vas Flying Boat

Duralumin is predominantly used as building material, mostly in the form of smooth sheets and bands. The bands are fed into bending machines and each is molded according to the purpose of application. Cross sections, like those common in superstructures, are used for constructing the most heavily stressed parts on the flying boat. In these cases, pressed profiles are installed; steel is used predominantly used only for fittings and in places where increased risk of corrosion exists

View of both propellers on the front outboard III. and II. engine nacelles on the starboard side of the Do X 2 with Fiat A 22 R-engines.

screwing. Rivet heads are generally placed on both sides and are easily accessible for inspection purposes. Duralumin finished rivets are used with duralumin; to connect steel parts and steel with duralumin, steel rivets are used.

Construction is carried out in the familiar fashion for Dornier flying boats. The wings are positioned over the fuselage, which carries the load and the tail unit, and the engine unit is arranged over the wing unit. The rectangular outline of the wings passes over the largest part of the span with a fixed cross section. Each wing half is propped up by struts on the underside of the fuselage roughly in the center of its width. The engine unit consists of a total of twelve Fiat type A 22 R 430/600 CV engines, on which embedded propellers are powered by a gear unit that is built onto the engine housing. The engines are paired together in six nacelles, which sit on both front spars of the wings. For bracing, each nacelle blocks is joined together on its upper end by two profile braces.

Wings

The wings have a forty-eight meter span and 9.5 meter wing depth. The considerably rectangular outline only has a volume of 436m3 due to the rounding of the wing ends. The wings consist of a framework, from which the wing skin is easily detached. With the significant dimensions and the kind of engine unit construction, it was practical to use three spars instead of the usual two and to connect them together with crossbeams. Spaced 10.5 meters from the aircraft's center, three spars are intercepted by streamlined struts. The individual, nearly quadratic fields between spars and crossbeams are crosslinked and both sides covered by wing skin.

For the supporting the spars, pressed duralumin in the form of angled bars and plates is used; their dimensions are adjusted to the local stresses. The walers are connected to one another by filled rods made of pressed or rolled duralumin. Construction of the bars is carried out in a similar way. The skin fields are made of duralumin framework with stretched material and sealed from seeping water on the joints. The upper skin fields receive reinforced metal plating near the engine nacelles.

due to high stress. Where high compressive stresses require a precise central connection, seamless tubes are also occasionally built in, which are rolled to relieve connections on quadratic cross sections as long as they are advantageous. To reduce the weight of the wing skin, the fabric is stretched out as far as possible. Coating with paint, whose dependability is determined by a systematic series of tests, prevents decay of building materials affected by weather.

Connecting structural members is preferably carried out by riveting, which increases easy release by

Work on the three wing spars of the Do X 1 on December 4, 1928. With the long exposure of the plate camera used by Ziegler, diligent workers appear blurred. (Photo: Alfred Ziegler, Altenrhein)

Center spar of the Do X 1's wing unit after assembly in the factory building in Altenrhein. In the background is the Dornier Delphin II for practicing industrial arts. (Photo: Alfred Ziegler, Altenrhein)

Main crossbeam for two engine nacelles on their assembly stand. On the right, the contours of the crawl space for engine monitoring that will allow access to the engines later. A photo from December 30, 1928. (Photo: Alfred Ziegler, Altenrhein)

Wing skin panels being formed. To the left on their wooden construction frames and on the right in a finished condition before covering. (Photo: Alfred Ziegler, Altenrhein)

Behind the front spar, a crawlspace is located on the almost rectangular cross section, which is bordered on the underside by a smooth trough and on the sides by support tubes. It leads from the middle of the flying boat along both sides under the ladder shafts of the engine nacelles. The crossbeams between the spars lead forward up to the leading edge or trailing edge of the wings and thus allow for reasonable division of replacement pieces there. The connection of these pieces takes place on the protruding cross bars and the waler beams. The inserts formed on the wing's leading edges are plated with sheet metal, and their inwardly laid connections are serviced from the crawlspace. In front of the two inner engine nacelles, directly next to the switch room, fuel tanks, each with 300 liter capacity, lie in the nose of the main wing unit.

The cross bars protruding to the ailerons are connected on their back ends by brackets, which assume the load of the rudder and the fixed supports of the ailerons. The ailerons are twelve meters long and one meter deep. Considering deflection, the rudder shaft is split and cardanically coupled on the cut site. To ease the operation of the rudder, friction on the rudder shaft and on all control rod mounts is reduced by ball bearings. The bearing housings of the rudder shafts are attached with only a few bolts on the mentioned brackets to facilitate weight reduction of the rudder. During an aerodynamic moment on the rudders, compensation surfaces 4.5m long and 0.5m wide, which lie 0.7m above the wings, retain balance by means of their lifting forces. The length of the connecting rod between rudder and lever arm of the compensation wings can be changed to induce another state of balance.

Wing skin element for the underside of the wing unit on a wooden assembly frame. (Photo: Alfred Ziegler, Altenrhein)

Hull

The proportions of the fuselage are predominantly contingent upon the spacious accommodations of the payload capacity. The design of the hull is made with the aim of reducing drag as much as possible. Furthermore, the shape of the bow and hull is determined by the behavior of the flying boat during acceleration and deceleration. The bow is formed like a cruiser's, with stem posts sharply tapered, to prevent hard blows on the fuselage during swells. The sharp keel on the bow decreases steadily towards the aft and merges into a longitudinal step in the area of the main ribs. This longitudinal step continues just behind the cross step, which is located on the last main rib, to a displacement keel that enables smooth passage in the water and results in better control. In any case, the underside of the fuselage is lifted up strongly from the cross step (if it is compliant with the horizontal course of the aft deck) in an effort to bring the tail unit as high above the water level as possible. Due to the great width of the hull, the ribs steadily decrease in size toward the top and exhibit a slight arch on the upper side for the foredeck and quarterdeck. The main ribs receive attachments just above the surface of the water that serve as support for the sponsons, which provide lateral stability on the water in accordance with Dornier flying boats. The sponsons are divided into several bulkheads that are accessible through manholes and can be emptied of water leaks through drainage screws at their lowest point. The topside of the sponsons is accessible.

Assembly of Do X rib templates in a hangar in Altenrhein in early March 1928. Above the outer edges of the templates, the duralumin ribs are finished. (Photo: Alfred Ziegler, Altenrhein)

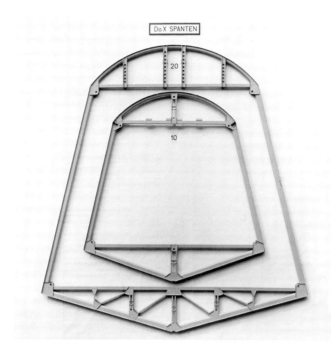

Rib #10 and rib #20 from the stern of the Do X flying boat. Photographed by Alfred Ziegler on October 26, 1928. On this day, the company photographer took photos of all of the Do X's ribs for documentation. (Photo: Alfred Ziegler, Altenrhein)

A look through the Do X rib templates from the front with a view of rib #43. Photographed by company photographer Karl Alfred Ziegler on March 5, 1928. (Photo: Alfred Ziegler, Altenrhein)

Upper left: ribs are aligned upside down on a mounting rack for mounting and assembly.

Upper right: stern ribs #1 to #21 on the mounting rack in Altenrhein. A Dornier Delphin II sits in the background. Two of these flying boats are being built by the newly formed Swiss aircraft manufacturer.

Left: ribs are positioned upside down. Braced with wires for stability with a view toward the stern on bulkhead rib #14 with a manhole for later inspections. (All photos on this page: Alfred Ziegler, Altenrhein)

Backbone of the Do X flying boat. Central longitudinal beam of the Do X 2 with paneled stern. A photo from October 10, 1928. (Photo: Alfred Ziegler, Altenrhein)

Detail of the central longitudinal beam of the Do X 2 between ribs #50 to #55 see from the port side. (Photo: Alfred Ziegler, Altenrhein)

The rib structure of Do X 2 before paneling, under construction on October 27, 1928. Clearly visible is the collision bulkhead rib #55 and the wooden shape of the sharply tapered bow stem. (Photo: Alfred Ziegler, Altenrhein)

The hold space is limited by the floor of the main deck. Above the main deck lies the command deck which almost protrudes over foredeck with its full ceiling height. The inside of the ship can be entered from both sponsons through doors on the side of the aircraft and one can go down to the hold or up to the commando deck through portholes here. The floor of the main deck is supported by crossbeams in the ribs and the three longitudinal beams. A lattice girder lies amidships with two meters of middle height. It begins three meters behind the bow and leads along under the whole main deck 23.5 meters up to the bulkhead rib before the empty rear fuselage. The other two longitudinal beams lie in the form of lattice framework directly on the side of the aircraft. Because the side longitudinal beams only reach up to the floor of the main deck, they proceed forward and backward with steadily decreasing height, so that the upper and lower flanges converge in the bow stem and on the bulkhead wall bordering the stern space. In order to keep the stern stiff enough, diagonals are used on the rear section of the longitudinal beams on the side of the aircraft and proceed through the entire height of the main deck. The main ribs are also reinforced by the diagonals lying on the side of the aircraft in the area of the main deck and are tightly fastened to the longitudinal beams so that they uniformly transfer forces of propulsion and lift from the three beams of the wings to the entire hull.

Paneling of the rib framework with riveted duralumin sheets. View of the ribs of the Do X 1's command deck from the stern on June 25, 1928. (Photo: Alfred Ziegler, Altenrhein)

Detail of the paneling of the Do X 1a during the stopover in the USA in the winter of 1931. Visible are the riveted panels at the 6th and 7th large portholes.

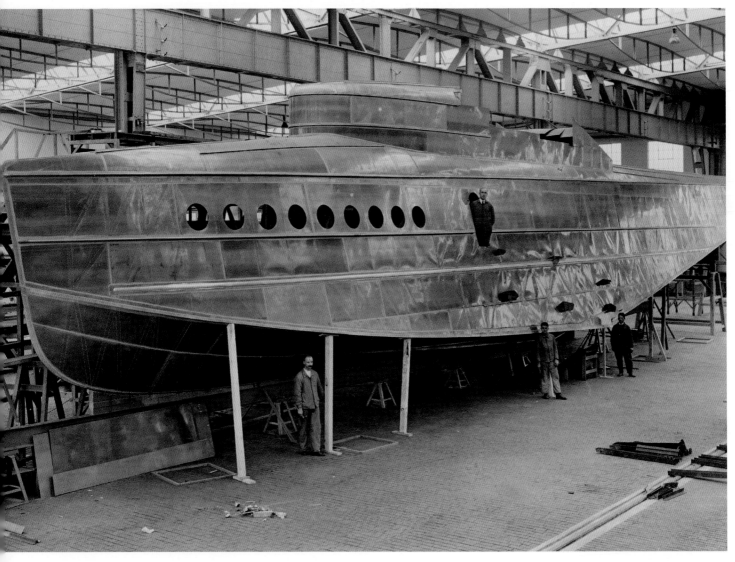

The Do X 1 in an advanced stage of planking, dated from December 4, 1928. Workers and an engineer are used as size comparisons for company photographer Ziegler. (Photo: Alfred Ziegler, Altenrhein)

The particularly high dynamic pressures in front of the cross step during acceleration and deceleration on water are transferred to the ribs between the longitudinal beams by two pairs of keelsons passing through. Ribs are taken out at the point of intersection with the keelsons and firmly connected to them. In total, the boat contains fifty-eight ribs spaced from 0.5 to 0.7 meters. These ribs form the partition walls as especially firm shear frames, which essentially only permit an opening to traffic in the boat's interior. The ribs that lie in between are the storage location for the fuel drums in the hold before the step.

Apart from that, the floor, side of the aircraft and deck are reinforced through further infills of panels on the inside, and the ship's outer skin remains completely smooth to prevent additional water and air resistance. Portholes (0.40m or 0.21m) are found in the aircraft's sides on the main deck; their centers lie 1.1 meters above the floor. Command and navigation rooms receive eleven large, rectangular windows 0.6x0.5 meters. The other rooms of the command deck receive natural skylights through portholes located on the topside of the fuselage.

Room Layout of the Three Decks

The foremost compartment of the command deck is the cockpit, which is separated from the captain's room by a wall with a sliding door. Behind the cockpit are the switch room for monitoring the engines, the soundproof lined radio room, and finally the tiny auxiliary engine room. The cockpit contains two pilot seats with double steering, adjustment devices for trim and rudder balancing, water rudder steering, and the necessary flight equipment for maintaining balance and course as well as throttle control and display units for engine performance. In the navigation room on the port side, a map table with an embedded compass and built-in cabin clock are provided for the captain. The layout is permanently installed so that no one lingers in the intersecting space on the front propeller level. In the switch room behind it, large indicator panels and switchboards are arranged on both sides behind the ladders leading to a crawlspace. This room contains devices required for monitoring individual engines and actuation mechanism necessary for their operation. The layout of the radio room is also permanently installed.

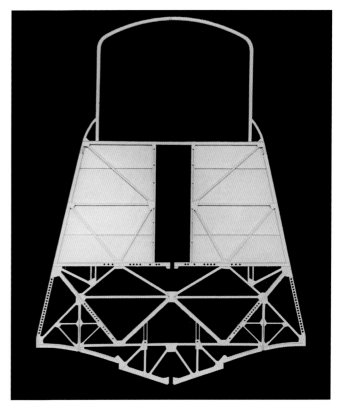

On rib #44 the three deck levels of the Do X are clearly visible. A 2001 replica of the rib can be viewed in the German Museum of Technology in Berlin.

A view of the production hall in Altenrhein, October 30, 1928. The Do X 1 under construction on the left and the Do X 2 on the right. (Photo: Alfred Ziegler, Altenrhein)

Front view of thc Do X 2's rib framework on October 27, 1928. (Photo: Alfred Ziegler, Altenrhein)

Do.X 2

The auxiliary engine room is accessible from here through the sternway and contains a 12/15 horsepower DKW two-cylinder, two-stroke engine with coupleable air compressor and generator, and all the small auxiliary engines that can be used anywhere.

On the main deck, behind the collision room – which is approximately 3m deep, sealed off by a bulkhead and is accessible through a porthole for bringing sea equipment from decks A and B – lies the passenger and crew quarters spread out over the entire length of the amidships main longitudinal beam of 23.5 meters and whose partitioning is essentially given by the already mentioned framework ribs. The rooms each receive different provisions according to their purpose on the flying boat. In the ship portrayed by the present description, a daytime lounge for twenty-four passengers is set up in the main rib section. A cloakroom is located behind the rooms equipped for accommodating the passengers. The kitchen lies before the stern bulkhead on the port side and two restrooms with washing facilities are on the starboard side. Again in front of that, between the kitchen and the restrooms on one side and the cloakroom on the other side, is the common room for the crew. This room on the main deck is 3 to 3.5 meters wide with 1.9 meters of headroom. The framework ribs allow for access ways between the individual rooms with an average width of 0.6 meters. The middle main rib even has a free opening of 1.2 meters width in order to preserve the assembly of the day room. The bulkhead ribs receive watertight, closeable manholes or bulkhead doors. The entrance to the main deck takes place, as mentioned, through doors found in the side of the aircraft directly before the foremost main rib, or the guest room. A 0.65x0.9m hatch in the quarterdeck directly before the stern bulkhead is provided as an emergency exit. A vertical, removable ladder on the bulkhead wall leads to the hatch. A 1.42x1.32m cargo hatch is available in the foredeck above the cargo hold.

The cargo hold lies in the lower hold directly behind the collision bulkhead. In the bulkheads behind it are the main oil tanks and two fuel tanks as well as another eight fuel tanks located between the three main ribs. For loading cargo there are ground flaps (0.58x0.71m); for loading tanks, clear openings are arranged (2.0x1.3m or 2.7x1.5m). Two panel sheets (1.5x1.3m) are arranged in the starboard wall for loading fuel tanks on to the main deck. Instead of being riveted, these sheet metal panels are bolted on and thus detachable.

Tail Unit

The tail unit is located at the tip of the stern and consists of the vertical stabilizer, which holds the tailplane at half its height. This tailplane is laterally supported by strut pairs that are securely fastened to a smaller tailplane on the rear fuselage with a 1° angle of attack. The tailplane (horizontal stabilizer) can therefore be considered a one-and-a-half-decker; of course only the wide, upper stabilizer has a rudder, while the lower stabilizer remains in one piece. The pitch elevator receives a triangular cut out in the center to enable the rudder to turn in the range 60° overall (30° to each side). Both spars of the vertical stabilizer are fixed to the corresponding ribs of the fuselage, but easily detachable by loosening the bolts. The rear spar of the tailplane pivots on the rear spar of the vertical stabilizer, and the front spar of the tailplane has an adjustable mount on the front spar of the vertical stabilizer so that the tailplane's angle of attack can be changed when idle. The strut pairs, which lead from the upper to the lower vertical stabilizer, are fastened to their spars and proceed underneath the lower stabilizer to the fuselage where they can be easily detached from the ribs. The rudder is connected with three ball bearings on the vertical stabilizer, and the pitch elevator is connected with a total of five ball bearings, whose housings are fastened to the rear spars of the stabilizers and can be easily detached so that the rudder can be easily removed. The ribs of the stabilizers and rudders are made with a light duralumin framework. The vertical stabilizer and tailplane are plated with sheet metal, while the rudders are covered with fabric.

The rudder is relieved by undivided auxiliary rudders, which pivot on the front spars of the tailplane. The rotation axis of the auxiliary rudders is located at around 4/10 of their depth so that aerodynamic moments in the opposite direction from the rudder and auxiliary rudders can be easily brought into balance by connecting rods, which engage in corresponding distances from the rotation axis.

Construction status on December 29, 1928. A view of the Do X 2 propped-up with its recently planked stern. (Photo: Alfred Ziegler, Altenrhein)

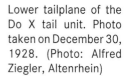

Lower tailplane of the Do X tail unit. Photo taken on December 30, 1928. (Photo: Alfred Ziegler, Altenrhein)

Internal half of the aileron on the port side. The twelve meter long, one meter wide aileron covered with airplane linen is divided in the rudder shaft and cardanically hung due to the risk of deflection. (Photo: Alfred Ziegler, Altenrhein)

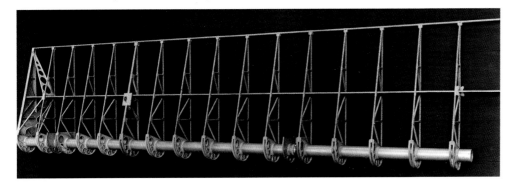

Rudder of the Do X before covering with airplane linen. Clearly visible is the mounting of the aft position lights in the center of the rudder. (Photo: Alfred Ziegler, Altenrhein)

Starboard pitch elevator of the Do X tail unit before covering with airplane linen on November 11, 1928. (Photo: Alfred Ziegler, Altenrhein)

This balance is not complete to warrant a noticeable resistance for the pilots. A rotation of the auxiliary rudders toward the main rudder (up to about ±8°) using the connecting rods during flight enables unidirectional course-deviating moments to balance out during potential engine disturbances, without forcing the pilot to continually kick out the rudder. The pitch elevator also has adjustable balancing. Before every rudder half, above the wings, the offset to the rudder can be adjusted by hand wheel up to about ±8° from the cockpit in order to also be able to balance changes in longitudinal balance without constant steering operation.

Fuselage, or hull, of the Italian made Do X 2 on the way from the production hall to the large hangar for the final assembly in Altenrhein on November 7, 1930. (Photo: Archive DSLR)

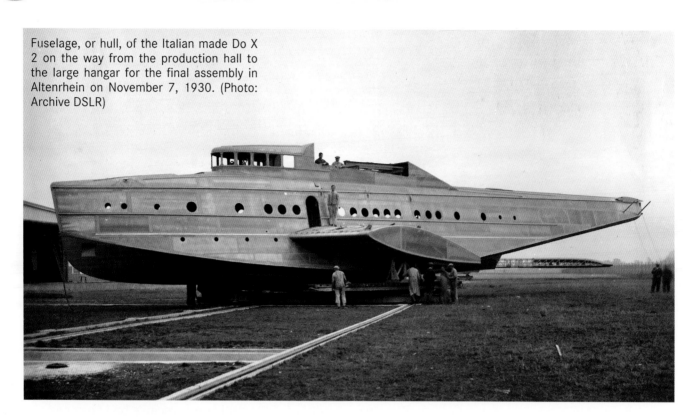

Wing unit of the Do X 2 in front of the production hall in Altenrhein on the way to the assembly hangar. (Photo: Archive DSLR)

Controls

As already mentioned, the flying boat is equipped with double steering. Steering is initiated by the pilot, as usual, through a steering column, which has a forward and backward wheel that influences the pitch elevator, and a hand wheel on its head that activates the ailerons. There is also a foot pedal for controlling the rudder. In order to require as little energy as possible for this, the pilots are provided with a large space. Because the reach of the rudder pedals is defined by the natural length of legs, attaining a large enough space for the pedals required arranging them on vertical levers that pivot around a horizontal axis positioned diagonally to the direction of flight. Transmittal of this rotation takes place on horizontal auxiliary shafts positioned in the very front of the cockpit, which are forced by toothed segments to equal deflection in opposite directions and directly carry the counter rotation lever for pull and back pull. The same auxiliary shafts thereby serve to ensure that on each base shaft a hollow shaft is put off and that the movement of the elevator levers are carried over. The hand wheels for operating the ailerons, which are connected by chains with stretchable rope, implement their movement in small turns of a vertical lever. Transmittal of steering controls from the vertical levers to the rudders takes place through tensile, seamless tubes. By using rods in place of cables, stretching of the pulling elements is prevented, which in its present form entails an unacceptably large backlash of the steering levers due to the significant lengths.

Through other horizontal auxiliary shafts it is also possible to bring the pull and counter pull rods of the rudder to the center of the boat protected by both sides of the central corridor and accessible toward the rear. On the rear rib, the aileron steering forces are now led vertically upward to the rear spar and along it to the ailerons. Rudder and aileron steering forces are made through other auxiliary shafts in the center of the boat and joined by the empty tail space up to its end where they are redirected by other rods on the rudder lever itself.

As mentioned above, auxiliary rudders and compensation wings of the tailplane are adjustable about the rudder itself in order to balance out constant rud-der disturbances. The hand wheels for activating the balancing equipment are located directly behind the port side pilot's chair. The degree of adjustment is shown by an indicator. The transmittal of adjustment movements is carried out by chains and stretchable intermediate rope.

On the back end of the displacement keel, which proceeds along the long step on the front of the boat, a water rudder is installed whose axis of rotation lies about a fourth of the way down the rudder's length, making it nearly torque-free. Operation of the water rudder is carried out by a hand wheel completely independent from the side steering since maneuvering in wind and swells occasionally necessitate opposing deflections for side steering and water rudder. It is, however, particularly practical to separate both rudders from one another in order to let disturbances of the water rudder affect side steering through ground contact. The cable pulls of the water rudder are led to the back together with the air rudder and run directly on to the segment on the rudder shaft. The guide pulleys of the cable pulls receive ball bearings.

Engine Unit

The engines are housed in six engine nacelles built onto the wings. Nacelles are spaced 3.6 meters apart and the front spar and center spar of the wings are connected by double bars spaced 0.56m apart. N-shaped nacelle supports, as seen from the starboard side, are positioned on the junctions of bar pairs and the front spar and a 1.85m connection piece inserted onto the double bar. The front and back supports of the engine nacelles are connected on their upper ends with profile-shaped, covered tubes diagonal to the direction of flight. Furthermore, a simple diagonal cross out is provided between nacelle I and nacelle II. The outer nacelle IIIs are supported against the nacelle IIs and against the wings.

The nacelles themselves consist of cross-sectional ribs which are connected to a horizontal, longitudinal beam on the upper ends at about half the nacelles height. The covering of the nacelle pieces are partly removable in order to ease inspection and maintenance of the engines. Two mounting boards, which can be stored on diagonal tubes on both sides

View of the two outer engine nacelles on the starboard side of the Do X 2 with Fiat A 22 R engines. (Photo: Archive DSLR)

of the nacelles, also help for this. On the front and back of the nacelle, the actual engine mounting for the water-cooled Fiat engines is found on the longitudinal beams.

In order to be able to set the propeller level of neighboring nacelles next to one another, attaching nacelle I SB, III SB and II BB takes place on the nacelle supports on ribs #3 and #9; those of nacelle II SB, I BB and III BB on nacelle ribs #4 and #10. This way, the propeller level is set at 290mm apart in accordance with the rib spacing, and a disadvantageous aerodynamic influence of the propeller blades is prevented.

Covering of the N-shaped nacelle supports and the nacelles themselves was specified according to aerodynamic aspects and carried out using duralumin sheets.

The front part of the nacelle is settled in here so that its form fits into the upper half of the propeller hood. In the lower half of the gondola's front part rests the honeycomb oil coolers.

Within the streamlined nacelle support covers are two bay radiators, the upper for cooling the front engine and the lower for cooling the back engine. Adjustable flaps are provided on the leading edge of the bay covers for regulating the cooling temperatures and also 0.92x0.45m square doors on the sides of the covers to ensure an exit from the nacelle shaft to the wings. The rear parts of the nacelle support covers, as well as the engine nacelles, are open (covered with wire grills) to achieve the best possible passage of air for cooling and ventilation of the radiators and engine housing. Exiting the nacelle from the crawlspace takes place by means on rungs through the nacelle shaft.

Twelve water-cooled Fiat engines each with twelve cylinders are provided for powering the propellers. Through a gearbox built directly onto the crankcase, the rotation speed transfers at ratio of 1,545:1 so that the highest rotation speed of the engine of 2,100rpm corresponds to 1,350 for the propeller rotation. Exhaust gases exit out of each cylinder directly into the open through short exhaust pipes.

Using the same engines for the pull and push propellers results in opposing sense of rotation so that the rear propeller acts as a kind of contra-propeller that cancels out the circumferential speed stream of the front propeller and can be transformed into usable axial speed. Despite an increase of stream velocity, considerably equal high-efficiency results, like with single propellers. Wood with brass fittings is provided as building material for the propellers to protect the edges.

With engine units of this size, operation and monitoring cannot be performed by the pilot alone. It is better to have a special switch room where the twelve engines can be monitored. From here the en-

The power for the Do X 2 and 3. Contemporary commercial from Italy for the Fiat A 22-R engine. The water-cooled straight V-engine included twelve cylinders.

gines can also be started in sequence by supplying compressed air and by using switchable starting magnets. Once running, they can then be monitored by reading engine speed, fuel pressure, oil pressure and temperature as well as water temperature.

The ignition timing control of the motors occurs independently from the gas regulation. The six throttle controls of a board side sit on a common axle with which they can be coupled. The axle is adjustable by rods from the cockpit so that the pilot can operate the engines all together or in groups separated by starboard side and port side. The pilot is informed by an engine display (light signals) about how many motors on each side are in operation as well as by an aggregate revolution counter about with what propulsion power the starboard or port side groups are working.

Fuel and Lubrication Systems

Fuel is housed in the ship's hold. Eight 1,500 liter tanks rest between the three main ribs and two 1,700 liter tanks lie in front of the front rib. Including the two aforementioned 300 liter tanks, the tank volume is 16,000 liters. For greater range the installation of another 1,300 liter tank in the front as well as two 1,700 liter tanks and two 1,300 liter tanks in the aft is possible so that a total of around 24m3 of tank volume is available.

The tanks are made with light alloy and stored under interleaving of shock absorbing materials on the inter-rib areas and over the entire diameter if possible. A disengageable line leads from the deepest point of every tank to a collection basin. From here, the fuel is forced out by a pump over a T-piece to both intermediate containers in the nose of the main wing.

Do X 2 during testing on Lake Constance. The factory building in Altenrhein in the background.

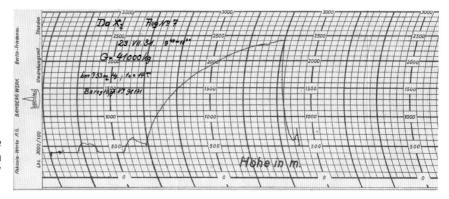

A document for altitude and flight time. Barograph of the Do X 2's flight #7 from July 23, 1931.

Blatt 5

Rotation speed and temperature protocol of the engine nacelles (A=aft, V=front) of the starboard side during the ninth flight of the Do X 2 on August 1 over Lake Constance.

Steuerbord				Gondel I (Motor A / Motor V)		Gondel II (Motor A / Motor V)		Gondel III (Motor A / Motor V)	
Event	Zeit			A: Umdr./temp./temp.	V: Umdr./temp./temp.	A: Umdr./temp./temp.	V: Umdr./temp./temp.	A: Umdr./temp./temp.	V: Umdr./temp./temp.
Rollen	16⁴⁰			800 67 62	600 52 45	600 78 50	700 72 58	700 58 40	700 70 52
				600 60 48	650 75 48	750 77 45	550 76 50	500 61 49	600 55 49
1. Start	16⁴⁸			1600 65 55	1700 62 58	1650 78 53	1660 75 63	1650 65 58	1660 70 60
				1600 60 50	1650 68 59	1650 76 46	1650 83 52	1800 70 55	1600 68 55
2. Start	16⁵²			1620 65 60	1740 65 70	1750 78 70	1660 75 70	1760 65 70	1780 70 70
				1800 72 68	1800 68 59	1800 74 45	1800 77 54	1800 78 70	1820 75 60
Steigen	16⁵⁵			2100 60 60	2420 68 70	2450 75 68	2000 75 68	2060 63 65	2000 70 65
				2100 72 71	2100 65 62	1900 73 45	2000 80 65	2000 68 70	2030 60 65
Steigen	17⁰⁰			2090 60 60	2100 73 70	2140 75 65	2000 73 63	2040 60 65	2000 70 65
				2100 73 72	2100 65 61	2000 73 67	2100 77 63	1990 70 70	2000 60 60
Steigen	17¹⁰			2090 58 65	2100 68 70	2150 72 65	2000 70 62	2040 70 65	2000 70 65
				2080 71 71	2080 64 68	2000 72 65	2110 76 66	1950 73 68	2050 68 65
Steigen	17²⁰			2040 58 65	2060 65 70	2120 70 63	2000 70 62	2040 72 63	2000 70 63
				2100 72 68	2100 70 66	2020 71 65	2120 74 64	1900 72 68	1900 72 63
Gleiten	17²¹/₂₂			1560 68 65	1500 60 68	1480 63 60	1500 63 60	1500 70 60	1550 60 62
				1400 72 67	1400 71 67	1380 70 62	1400 73 64	1430 68 60	1500 68 60
Vollgas	17²⁵/₂₇			2140 65 65	2120 68 70	2170 70 63	2020 72 62	2100 75 65	2020 70 65
				2130 73 70	2130 70 70	2050 73 65	2180 75 65	2050 73 68	2150 73 63
Reise	17³⁰			2000 68 65	2060 68 68 ³/₄	2060 72 62	1940 73 62	1980 78 65	1940 74 62
				2030 73 70	2030 70 89	2000 78 63	2000 76 65	1900 73 68	2000 73 68
Steigen	17³²/₃₃			2080 68 68	2090 69 68 ³/₄	2100 72 63	1980 65 62	2000 65 65	1980 68 65
				2070 73 70	2070 74 68	2000 73 65	2100 76 66	1900 73 70	2000 68 65
Reise	17⁴⁰			1980 65 65	1950 68 68 ³/₄	2080 70 62	1940 70 60	1980 63 63	1920 68 62
				2000 71 89	2000 69 68	1950 72 63	1950 63 63	1950 73 68	1950 60 60
Reise	17⁴⁵			2080 66 66	2080 68 70	2100 69 62	1980 72 62	2040 63 62	1980 69 62
				2050 71 70	2050 69 68	1980 72 65	2100 75 65	2000 78 60	2080 65 62
Landung abgestellt	17⁴⁷			1750	1755	17⁵⁰	18⁰⁰	1750	18⁰⁰

Altenrhein, den. 1. August 1931. Aussentemperatur: 25° Barometerstand: 725 9. Flug. Obere Zahlen = Centrale Untere Zahlen = Motorgondel

In order to be able to regulate the inflow to both tanks, a flow control valve is inserted on each branch line directly behind the T-piece. If too much fuel is delivered, it flows out of each tank through a return pipe back to the collection tank. Every engine receives the fuel from the intermediate tanks through a suction line driven by a pump with an overpressure of 0.2 to 0.25 bars on the carburetor. Both engines are given the possibility to be fed by a fuel pump through an interconnecting line in front of both carburetors of each nacelle. If necessary, all twelve motors can also be supplied with fuel by a wing tank through a connecting line. This offers more security for the fuel supply to the intermediate tanks. Instead of the stated pump, it actually has three pumps arranged on parallel uptakes – one powered electrically, one wind-powered gear pump and a hand pump.

Refueling all tanks takes place over large pipes, which lead from an outboard source through a filter to the collection tank. The openings for the tank hoses lie above the floor of the command deck on the outside of its wall in the rounded upper edge of the hull. Refueling the intermediate tanks takes place from the collection tank using the electrically powered gear pump or the hand pump. Thus, that a switchable outboard connection is built into their pressure line, the main tanks are also be emptied with one of these pumps. Every intermediate tank contains a drain line, which discharges into one of its return pipes. The fuel supply is determined by reading float gauges in the hold.

Vorläufiger Bericht über die Do-X,2- Flüge Nr.10, 11 u.12.
==

(Die Flugberichte der Flüge 1 - 8 liegen fertig vor; für Flug 9
siehe vorläufiger Bericht v.3.8.1931.)

Flugzeiten: Flug 1 - 8   = 380 min.
               Flug 9   =   59 min.

Flug Nr.10 vom 11.August 1931:
==============================

Flugzeit: 28 min.

Personenzahl: Deutsche Besatzung   14 Personen
               Jtalienische Besatzung 14 Personen
               Geladene Gäste   32 Personen
                            Total   60 Personen.

Zweck des Fluges: Prüfung der Flugeigenschaften und Vorführung.
               Wegen böigem Wetter und starkem Wind konnten keine Flug-
               messungen ausgeführt werden.

Startgewicht: 44,2 to.
Startzeit: 40½ sec. bei 10 - 12 m Wind.
Schränkung: 3¼°.
Schwerpunktslage: 34½ %.
               Bei 2⁵/4 schwanzlastiger Einstellung der Höhenausgleich -
               flächen war das Flugschiff bei 175 km/h und 1950 Touren
               in 250 m über dem See ausgeglichen.

               Die achteren Kühler stiegen beim Rollen nicht
               über 80° und konnten durch geringe Mengen hochgepumpten
               Kühler- Zusatzwasser leicht unter 80° gehalten werden.
               (Lufttemperatur 13°). Im Fluge hielten sich die Temperaturen
               der achteren Kühler in denselben Grenzen wie die der vor-
               deren Motoren. Alle Kühler konnten durch Regulieren mit
               den Kühler-Jalousien zwischen 65 und 75° gehalten werden;
               letztere waren dabei 1/4 - 1/2 geschlossen.

Blatt 2 zu " Vorläufiger Bericht über die Do,X,2 - Flüge Nr.10,11 u.12.
===

Flug Nr.11 v. 12.August 1931:
=============================

Flugzeit: 2 Std. 27 min.

Personenzahl: Deutsche Besatzung   = 13 Personen
               Jtalienische Besatzung = 14 Personen
                            Total   = 27 Personen

Zweck des Fluges: Siehe Flugprogramm v.10.August 1931 (40 to.)
Startgewicht: 41,7 to.
Startzeit: 35 sec. bei 3 - 4 m Wind.
Schränkung: 3¼°.
Schwerpunktslage: 35 %.
               Bei 2³/4 - 3½ achterlastig gestellten Höhenausgleichflächen
               ist das Flugschiff im Reiseflug ausgeglichen.
               Das Umtrimmen von 6 m/to. ist kaum merkbar.
               Prüfung der Flugeigenschaften ca. 35 min.(folgt besond.Bericht).

1.) Messung der Flug- Geschwindigkeiten:
       Bei 2150 Touren (Vollgas)   211 km.; ca.Flugewicht 41 to.
        " 1900   "   176 "   "   "   40³/4 to.
        " 1800   "   158 "   "   "   40½ to.
2.) Steigflug:
       3250 m über d.Meeresspiegel wurden in 47 min. erreicht.
       2700 m über Meeresspiegel wurden in 25 min. erreicht .
               Flugewicht beim Beginn des Steigens 40½ to.
               Gipfeltemperatur   - 4° Cels.
               Bodendruck   734
               Lufttemperatur a.Boden   + 17° Cels.
               Luftfeuchtigkeit   70 %.
       Die Barogramme wurden DMB - TY zwecks Auswertung übergeben.
3.) Die Vollgas-Drehzahlen der vorderen Schrauben lagen bei 2100-2150
       die der achteren Schrauben (davon 5 neue)   bei 2150-2200.
4.) Die Motoren wurden vor diesem Fluge durch das Fiat-Personal
       nachreguliert und die Düsen von den Turiner-Abnahmeläufen
       wieder eingesetzt.
5.) Ueber die Wasserkühler ergibt sich dasselbe Bild wie bei Flug 10,
       sowohl was das Rollen anbetrifft als auch die Temperaturen
       im Fluge.

Blatt 3 zu " Vorläufiger Bericht über die Do.X.2 - Flüge Nr.10,11 & 12
==

Flug Nr. 12 v. 13.August 1931 .
==============================

Flugzeit: 1 Std. 37 min.

Personenzahl: Deutsche Besatzung   = 14 Personen
               Jtalienische Besatzung = 14 Personen
                            Total   = 28 Personen .

Zweck des Fluges: Siehe besonderes Programm v.10.Aug. (45 to.).
Startgewicht: 45,4 to.
Startzeit: 60 sec. bei leichtem Seegang u. 4 - 6 m/sec. Wind
Schränkung: 3¼°.
Schwerpunktslage: 35 %.
               Die Prüfung der Flugeigenschaften ergab, dass die Bean-
               standungen betr. die Längsstabilität um das Höhenruder nahezu
               behoben sind. Besonderer Bericht über die Flugeigenschaften folgt.

1.) Messung der Fluggeschwindigkeiten:
       Bei 2000 Touren   187½ km.; ca.Flugewicht 44 to.
        " 1850 Touren   160 km; "   "   44 to.
2.) Steigflug:
       1800 m über d. Meeresspiegel wurden in 37 min.erreicht.
               Flugewicht beim Beginn des Steigens 45 to.
               Bodendruck   728
               Lufttemperatur a.Boden + 18° Cels.
               Luftfeuchtigkeit   74 %.
3.) Die Motoren, Kühler-Anlage usw. wurden in Ordnung befunden.
       Betr. Kühler-Temperaturen gilt dasselbe wie unter Flug 10
       angeführt.
4.) Betriebsstoff- Verbrauchsmessungen :
       Wegen böigem Wetter konnten die Betriebsstoff-Verbrauchs-
       messungen mit den Messtanks nicht vorgenommen werden,da
       die Benzinsäule zu stark schwankte. Die nachstehend
       angeführten Verbrauchsmessungen wurden mit der Siemens-
       Uhr vorgenommen.
       Brennstoff-Verbrauch:
       Im Reiseflug bei 2000 Touren mit 44 to. 7,2 kg/km.
       Im Reiseflug bei 1850 Touren mit 44 to. 7,58 kg/km.
       Es ist jedoch zu berücksichtigen, dass es etwas böig
       war und die gemessenen Geschwindigkeitswerte um ca.2-5 km/h
       zu niedrig liegen dürften, da auf der Messstrecke etwas
       Seitenwind herrschte. Im Uebrigen liegen die gemessenen
       Geschwindigkeitswerte sehr schön auf den Geschwindig-
       keitskurven mit dem zugehörigen Flugewicht. Durch die

Blatt 4 zu " Vorläufiger Bericht über die Do,X,2-Flüge Nr.10,11 u.12.
===

       Erhöhung der Fluggeschwindigkeit um 2 - 5 km/h. und durch
       die für den nächsten Flug (Dauerflug) vorgesehene etwas
       sparsamere Einstellung der Motoren dürfte der Betriebsstoff-
       Verbrauch innerhalb der garantierten Grenzen zu liegen kom-
       men. Ebenso ist zu berücksichtigen, dass die vorstehenden
       Werte bei 44 to. gemessen wurden, während dieselben im
       Vertrage nur bei 42,185 to. zu messen sind.

       Die Unterdruck-Messungen im Flügel ergaben beim Steigen
       52 - 60 mm Wassersäule; im Gleiten 76 mm Wassersäule bei
       teilweise geöffneten Schiebern.

       Zusammenstellung der Flugzeiten:

       Flug 1 - 8 .... 380 min.
       Flug 9 .... 59 min.
       Flug 10 .... 28 min.
       Flug 11 .... 147 min.
       Flug 12 .... 97 min.
       Total Flugzeit Flug 1-12   = 711 min. = 11 Std.51 min
       ===

Altenrhein, den 14.8.1931.
Fl - v.Mitterwallner

Verteiler: Doflug: KD, BD, FL, VD,
            DMB -   2 x
            Herr Gustosa 1 x.

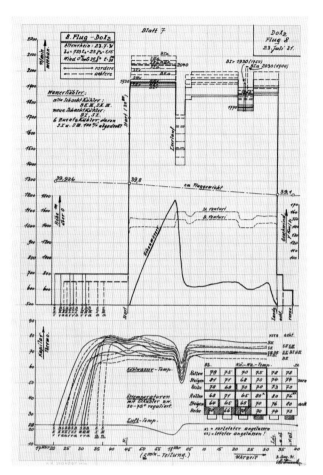

Coolant diagram from the eighth flight of the Do X 2 on July 23, 1931.

Front radiator of the Do X 2 in the nacelle shaft. Above, the air intake openings for the oil radiators. (Photo: Archive DSLR)

The lubrication system is comprised of six tanks, each with a tank volume of seventy-two liters that are hung in the center on the sidewalls of the six nacelles. There is also a main tank with a 1,300 liter capacity which is stored in the hold in front of the two 1,700 liter fuel tanks. The total volume of 1,730 liters is also enough for the maximum fuel tank volume of around 24m3. Filling the main tank takes place through tank lines from an outboard source, just like with fuel.

Through an electrically powered gear pump (in emergencies a parallel positioned hand pump in the hold), oil is forced over a distributor to the nacelle containers, where it is divided by a wall in both engine halves. The distributor allows the individual tanks to be filled up or in groups. The lubricant flows from the overhead tanks under a natural downgrade to the high-pressure pumps, which generate the re-

quired supplemental pressure for highly stressed parts. Through a low-pressure pump, surplus oil is forced back to the tanks and can be cooled by turning on the oil cooler, which is housed in the front of the nacelle, as already mentioned. Because oil becomes slightly viscous in cooler standing oil during longer immobilization of the radiator, a bypass line parallel to the radiator is switched on that carries the pressure oil through a crossover valve to the tanks. Lubrication temperature and pressure can be read on the nacelles and in the switch room by display units. Furthermore, warning lights that show the highest and lowest levels in the nacelle tanks are provided.

Cooling System

The main radiators are also arranged in the nacelle shaft and stored on the front spar of the wings. By covering the nacelle shaft, the lowest possible air resistance of the radiators is achieved. The radiator of the aft engine is aided by a small additional radiator on the nacelle roof. This additional radiator is switched in the main pipe of the cooling system and also contains the reserve water in the enlarged water tanks for the aft cooling system, while the reserve water of the front cooling system is housed in the bypass tank in the nacelle center piece. In order to ensure enough reserve water is on board during long flights, so that water loss can immediately be replaced during possible radiator leaks, and to be able to turn on increased water circulation amounts when starting the machine in hot regions, a fifty liter reserve water tank is found under each nacelle.

The water temperature is read on capillary thermometers in the nacelle shaft as well as on remote electrical thermometers in the switch room of the machine. Exceeding the maximum permitted water temperature is signaled by warning lights, which light up in the switch room if there is danger. Another control of the cooling system is the sinking of water levels in the nacelles' reserve water tanks, also signaled by electrical warning lights. Such signaling devices are unnecessary for the cooling system of the aft engines because the additional radiator lies in the main stream and above the main radiator.

Operational Equipment

As mentioned, display devices for monitoring the engine unit are installed for the pilot and show the number of available engines and the overall performance of each side. All other monitoring devices are found in the switch room. A special, small, current collector is provided for the very voltage-sensitive remote thermometer. Apart from the remote devices in the switch room, oil and fuel pressure gauges, oil and water thermometers as well as mechanical counters are arranged in the nacelle shaft of every engine to assure the reading. The devices for monitoring the flight are separate for each pilot, clearly arranged in front of the pilot's seat. The devices required for navigation should be situated in the command room or the navigation room.

The voltage of the entire electrical system, particularly the lighting, is twenty-four volts. A generator situated in the engine room serves as the power source and any unused electricity on board is absorbed by an accumulator battery. The entire network is operated from a board in the switch room, on which the fuses of the main circuit are also installed. The

exterior lighting is comprised of the usual five navigational lights on the bow, stern, starboard side, port side and, more importantly, white emergency lights on the wing ends and a toplight. A searchlight is also provided. The interior lighting is customized to room layout. Explosion-proof lights are installed in the tank compartments. Compartments, in which rods, cables and pipes are present, receive hand lamps. Important devices get their own lighting.

A two-cylinder two-stroke DKW internal combustion engine in the engine room can be coupled alone or together on the twenty-four volt generator, the generator for the radio installation or the compressor. Aside from the exterior and interior lighting described above, the electrical usage network comprises the electrical remote signaling devices, the signal installation and the driving motors of the fuel pumps. The compressor is used to compress pure air for filling the starter canisters. A cabin clock is installed in the cockpit, command room, navigation room and in the switch room.

The entire fire extinguishing system is supplied by the company Knock-Out S.A. from Torino. The fire extinguishers can be triggered automatically or randomly from various locations within the aircraft. To prevent the spread of fire, shut-off valves are built into the pressure pipes of the engine pumps and can be controlled from the crawlspace. The fuel rooms also have special fire extinguishers. To decrease the risk of combustion, fuel tanks and the entire compartment are vented outward. Leaking fuel can be drained through leakage points.

As already mentioned, a compressed air canister is used for starting the engines and from there the compressed air can be fed into each individual engine. Engine ignition takes place by toggle switch from the switch room using a starting magnet. A portable magnet in the nacelles can also be connected in case of failure of this starting magnet. Before starting, the compressed air that is forced into an air vessel from the compressor is used to inject fuel into each cylinder and to moisten the fuel pumps.

Two hand bilge pumps are used to bail penetrating water leaks that occur during damage to the hull; one of these pumps is firmly mounted to rib #44 and can be operated using rods from B-deck. The second pump is portable and can be fastened to provided mounts in the B-deck on ribs #21 and #44.

Pilot chair of the Do X 1a with trim wheels for rudder balance and a large steering wheel for the water rudder. (Photo: Archive DSLR)

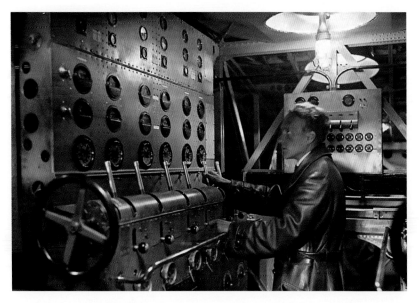

The engine room of the Do X 2 with engine monitoring for the port side nacelles, each with two engines. Behind the engineer is the switchboard of the Do X's electrical circuit.

Commercial for the "Knock-Out" fire protection system of the Italian Do X flying boat.

Longer suction hoses are provided for the bilge pumps in order to also pump water out of compartments where the pumps themselves cannot be brought.

The board bag contains the special tools and engine replacement parts that were delivered with the engines. The board sack has the most important tools and materials for smaller repairs on the flying boat. Propellers and nacelles are protected by covers when lying out in the open.

The radios for sending and receiving are installed in the soundproof radio room. This room also contains a table and chair for the radio operator. Signaling lamps are used for relaying orders and messages between the captain the crew. These devices transfer communications two-way between the command room and engine room, command room and FT room, engine room and tank compartment surveillance, and between the engine room and the individual nacelles. Sea equipment for propelling, anchoring, bringing in and docking in harbors belong the required gear.

Equipment of the Main Deck

Aside from being the collision bulkhead, the compartment between the bow and rib #55 is used to accommodate sea equipment, the essential gear for nautical maneuvers before take-off and after landing. Provided directly behind the collision bulkhead, between ribs #55 and #53 on the starboard side, is the radio direction finder.

On the main deck (B-deck), the space on the port side between ribs #55 and #44, and on the starboard side between ribs #53 and #44 initially remains without any detailed purpose. But the entire space is furnished with floors so that it is completely prepared for later installation of functional equipment. The space between ribs #44 and #42, into which access from the sponsons leads, is kept free from further furnishings since it is also the connection between the main deck and the hold, and also serves a purpose for the command deck.

The spaces between ribs #42 and #31 are furnished for day inhabitancy for the twenty-four passengers. Each compartment half of both other rooms consists of two banks, each with two seats and a folding table. The rooms are furnished according to the interior designs requested by the client. The center lounge between ribs #38 and #34 also has four seats in each compartment half, which are arranged around a table fastened to the wall. Both front passenger compartments receive full daylight through portholes on each side, four in the front and three in the back.

Behind the passenger cabin between ribs #31 and #28 is a cloakroom. Following this, between ribs #28 and #25, are the already mentioned crew quarters with eight seats. Behind it, between ribs #25 and #21, lies the kitchen with a table for electrical cooking equipment and kitchen cabinets for storing kitchen devices and supplies. On the starboard side at the same rib height are two washrooms with toilets. The space of the C-deck between ribs #55 and #50 are meant for the storage of post and baggage. Behind it, between ribs #50 and #28, the fuel and oil reservoirs are housed."

These were the building specifications of the Do X 2 from 1931.

Experiences From Two Years of Flight Operations

During a conference of the Technische Hochschule München (Technical University Munich) in the winter of 1931, Claude Dornier gave a little known speech: "About Flying Boats, Experiences, Comparisons, Conclusions and Outlook." The manuscript is published here in excerpts for the first time. It begins with a definition often scrutinized today:

"... I understand a 'flying boat' to be an aircraft that is also at home in the water and serves to transport large payloads across the sea. It is equipped with a central hull, similar to a ship's, which has several 'decks.' Apart from its size, the flying boat differs from the normal airplane in that the basis of its service on board largely depends on a division of work and conforms as nearly as possible to the operation of seafaring ships. The first flying boat, known by the name 'Do X 1,' was launched on July 12, 1929,

about two and a half years ago. In terms of the development of these vessels, we knew it was still a rather young technical structure.

It is not uninteresting to visualize the level of technology at the time of the launching of the first flying boat, the beginning of our observations. The largest payload capacity of an aircraft then was 7.5 metric tons. This was tripled overnight to 23.5 metric tons by the Do X 1.

Ideas about the possibilities of increasing the size of airplanes was strongly altered by these facts. Generally, the thinking at that time was that increasing size would be severely limited. Over the course of my speech, I will demonstrate that not only is it proven today that there are no insurmountable difficulties involved in increasing aircraft size, but also that the ratio of empty weight to vehicle payload of very large airplanes, even with the level of technology then, does not fall behind the values that are achieved by small airplanes under favorable conditions today. Great concerns also prevailed then regarding the possibility of handling very large aircraft. The opinion was that steering ability in the air could only be achieved with help from steering machines. The strength normally necessary by a single person would not be sufficient by far for handling the steering apparatus.

Significant doubts were also voiced regarding the take-off ratios and of the forthcoming behavior in swells. Generally speaking, the predominant view is that the stresses of the boat's hull would grow rapidly with the increase in size. Another absolute first in aircraft construction is the distribution of the driving power into twelve units; that means an increase of the engine quantity to about three times of what had been accomplished up to 1929.

The first practical attempt to carry out an extensive division of tasks on board was also met with an especially disparaging critique. The feasibility and usefulness of this work distribution, which inevitably must be proven as soon as aircraft sizes are increased above a certain degree, is one of the most important tasks of the young flying boat industry.

After brief references to the level of technology and the prevailing views when the first flying boat appeared, I will report about the experiences that have been collected since then, within a period of two and a half years.

An Engine Problem and Its Solution

These experiences refer to three different construction designs; the original model Do X 1, equipped with air-cooled engines, the modified with water-cooled engines Do X 1a, and the first of two flying boats commissioned by an Italian consortium, the designated Do X 2 (Umberto Maddalena) with water-cooled Fiat engines.

I reported in detail about the prototype aircraft in a speech before the WGL in November 1929. At that time, the experience gained by continuous operation was not yet available. The execution of tests in the winter of 1929/30 proved that the continuous output of the air-cooled engines was not sufficient. Indeed, the performances guaranteed by contract in terms of payload, speed and take-off power are already flawlessly achieved in one of the first flight tests on Sep-

tember 3, 1929 so that the final test flight of the Do X 1 takes place on February 20, 1930. But for it we were forced to fly partially with rotational speeds, which, as was soon proved, are considerably too high for the engine type used. Cooling the engine cylinder temperatures sufficiently and evenly also proved to be very difficult. On a large number of test flights, extensive measurements of the cylinder temperatures were taken and various ventilation layouts analyzed. We tried to achieve uniform distribution of temperatures by using ring-shaped air inlets, arrangement of canals and shafts of various designs, and finally by removing the forewing. These efforts are crowned with success to a certain degree, but nothing can change the discovery that the continuous output of the engine would fall short of the requirements that were the basis for the construction.

One of the forty-two test flights of the Do X 1, which were completed by October 21, 1929. (Photo: Archive DSLR)

Propellers of the Do X 1. A two-piece in the front, or two double-winged wood propellers with brass fittings and in the back, a one-piece wood propeller. The propellers came from Dornier's own propeller manufacture. (Photo: Archive DSLR)

Special airflow shafts for cooling the upper cylinders. View of the back row of the Do X 1's nine-cylinder Jupiter radial engine from Siemens. (Photo: Archive DSLR)

The solution to the engine problem comes from the USA. Two water-cooled Curtiss Wright "Conquerors" per engine nacelle. Clearly visible are the lamellas of the front cooling system on the front engines. (Photo: Archive DSLR)

A clear definition of an airplane engine's 'continuous output' did not yet exist in 1929. One had to rely on an intuitive estimate for it, which could always be expected from the engine due to its type tests in practical operation. This lack of knowledge made itself very noticeable when testing the Do X 1. Those bitter experiences do not contribute in the least to how one generally strives to make clear definitions of continuous output when acquiring or granting building contracts today. Without a doubt, it is also extremely important to make progress on this issue soon for international agreements. The choice of air-cooled engines took place then because the empty weight of the flying boat could be kept lower this way. This choice, however, was a false conclusion due to the lack of experience. The ratio of continuous output to normal output for the air-cooled engines was accepted as reasonable, whereby the comparison with water-cooled engines were strongly affected to their disadvantages. Applying the actual available continuous output during the first construction with air-cooled engines would have affected the overall performance of the flying boat so considerably that attaining the objective would have been impossible.

In spring of 1930, we were faced with a decision: using either a new engine with sufficient continuous output, about 420 horsepower, to produce practical proof for those who doubted the feasibility of the flying boat idea, or realizing that this new transportation tool possibly had to be buried for many years. In the meantime, the economic circumstances worsened so that it would be exceptionally difficult to find the means to procure new engines and make the necessary modifications upon installation. The demands of a continuous output of about 420 horsepower inevitably resulted in the decision for the water-cooled engine, and the fact that air-cooled engines of this continuous output did not exist then. In addition, the randomness of air-cooled engines in regards to uniform and sufficient cooling of individual cylinders is exposed.

Comparative calculations revealed that when using modern, fast running engines with water-cooling, and with an increase of engine unit weight by about one to three metric tons, that this excess weight will more than balance out through gains in continuous output. By this concession, the Curtiss Wright company succeeded in obtaining a suitable engine in favorable conditions. It concerns the new Curtiss Wright Conqueror engine, which represents advancements of the well-known Curtiss D 12.

Engine maintenance in October 1930. After insufficient oil cooling by each of two tubular radiators per engine, the newly installed oil radiators can be seen here on the starboard side of the engine nacelles. (Photo: Archive DSLR)

Well-deserved break. Only a few weeks after the reconstruction of the engine unit in 1930, the Do X 1a flies with double-bladed pressure propellers made of wood on the rear engines. (Photo: Archive DSLR)

This unusually light twelve cylinder engine is set to a 1:2 ratio. It has a dry weight of 396kg including the gearbox and the hub. Its peak output with n = 2,150 is 615 horsepower. The guaranteed continuous output with n = 2,150 is 415 horsepower. In order to reduce costs and building time as much as possible, compromises had to be made in more ways than one during the installation of the new engines. So it was necessary, for example, to retain the connection points of the old engine frame for the new engines. The impossibility of an enlargement of the propeller diameter resulted from this, which of course would have been very desirable considering the effectiveness of the propulsion system. To speed up the work as much as possible, the drop-shaped arrangement of the engine nacelle was ended and we made do with an ordinary profile construction.

The upper wings, which would have to be intentionally altered on the new nacelles, were also done away with. Cooling takes place through a front radiator with a 32m2 cooling surface and a belly radiator with a 28.2m2 cooling surface. The cooling system proved to be completely sufficient, even in equatorial conditions. Viewed from the standpoint of attaining the lowest resistance, however, the cooling system is imperfect and only evaluated as a compromise.

During testing it was soon revealed that the ending of the closed structure considerably limited accessibility to the engines in flight. For this reason, and also for the purpose of achieving a more organic and aerodynamic cooling system installation of the highest quality, the closed shaft of the new flying boats, the Do X 2 and 3, was implemented again and used for the installation of the radiators at the same time. Another improvement that was achieved with these new flying boats was that the oil coolers, which are attached to the outer sides of the nacelle walls on the Do X 1a, were built into the water coolers. The radiator covering takes place through two curved surfaces running along on double guides, and it forms the nose of the engine structure in a fully covered state.

Operation of the air-cooled Siemens engine of the Do X 1 occurs through compressed air, which is generated by an auxiliary motor with a built-in compressor. The mentioned procedure has proven to be very successful. Curiously though, starting engines with the aid of compressed air, which is common practice in Europe, is hardly known in America. For this reason, inertia starters (Eclipse) must be used for the American engines. These inertia starters can be integrated for electrical operation and for hand operation. We decided for the hand operation in order to save weight and costs. Testing revealed that the times for starting all twelve engines differed little with compressed air and with hand activation of the Eclipse. They normally fluctuate between four and eight minutes.

The weight for the complete starting apparatus with compressed air, including the compressor, but without its driving motor, amounts to 146kg. The total weight of the Eclipse system is 169kg. When comparing the weights of the engine systems of the three different constructions, with regard to the continuous output, the air-cooled design results in a weight of 1,885kg/hp, for the American engine a weight of 1,624kg/hp and for the Italian engine a weight of 1,620kg/hp. The propellers used up to now are all made of wood and manufactured in our own factory. The propellers of the Do X 1a, which had been exposed to the inclemency of all climate zones for more than a year without interruption, are still in perfect condition today.

The equipment facilities and supplies never gave rise to great difficulties. The large, 3,000 liter capacity gasoline tanks made of duralumin have held together excellently and have shown no deformations or noteworthy signs of corrosion. When designing the equipment facilities, we had the idea to store the gasoline in the bottom of the boat as far away from the engines and auxiliary machines as possible in order to decrease the risk of fire. This kind of equipment housing proved its worth brilliantly during a fire in a harbor in Lisbon and prevented an almost inevitable total loss of the first flying boat caused by any other fuel storage arrangement.

Port side wing panel of the Do X 1a right after the fire in Lisbon. The fabric covering of the wing is totally burnt off.

The Wings Remain Unchanged With All Versions

The wings remained almost unchanged with all three versions of the Do X. The rated load and structural safety, which underlie the calculation of the wing unit, enabled the approval of the flying boat for passenger transport group P3 up to fifty-two metric tons, according to the regulations at that time. The load transport group G2 with a weight of fifty-nine metric tons still corresponds to the security regulations valid in 1931. The tail unit has especially sturdy dimensions so that the stress of the flying boat through a gust of ten meter/second according to case G of the chartlet still lies far under the permissible limit of the rated load. The tail unit and wings are vibration-free. The wings are designed with three spars and bending braces and are covered with sheet metal or material covered plates, so-called wing skin panels, in 2.8x2.8 meter squares.

The first test flights show that significant negative pressure prevailed in the interior of the wings, which amounted to up to a maximum of 70mm column of water (centimeter of water). Because negative pressure within the wings was not considered when drawing up the static calculations, it had to be lowered, which worked in a satisfactory manner by installing openings in the proper places after various experiments. The novel construction of the wing covering proved their worth in the already mentioned fire in Lisbon, during which the skin of one wing half was completely destroyed. This fire did not begin due to a short circuit, as was reported in the press, but rather in the following way: the Do X 1a lay in the harbor in Lisbon tied to the buoy. It had been fueled up and cleared for take-off. On that day there was a strong wind and a gust blew a canvas tarp that had been laid out to dry on the boat deck onto the exhaust pipe of the DKW auxiliary motor, which, among other things, delivers electricity to the generator. This motor was in operation at the time since the daily weather reports were taken by wireless telegraphy. The tarp caught fire on the hot exhaust gas, smoldering pieces were driven by the wind onto the wing surface and before the mechanic, who noticed the event relatively quickly, could intervene, a large part of the wing had burned. Of course, this kind of accident would have been impossible during flight. Thanks solely to the ease of exchangeability of the wing covering the repair could be repaired in a relatively short time, out in the open and almost without any tools.

The Boat and the Accident in the Bay of Gando

Up until today, the necessity to reinforce or modify the hull, apart from trivial alterations on the stern step and the water rudder, only occurred once during the operation of the flying boat. During a take-off attempt with a heavily loaded machine in the Bay of Gando in Gran Canaria, the starboard sponson of the Do X 1a collided with a high ground swell at a speed of ca. 130km/h. A turning motion was initiated by the sudden deceleration and triggered unbalanced forces of inertia, which attempted to shear off the wings from the boat, so to speak, diagonally to the direction flight. Damages appear on the upper part of the three upright ribs, upon which the wings are mounted. After the all of the experience up this point, we couldn't anticipate these kinds of forces. This involved a new discovery, which might demand general interest. I would like to refer to the typically occurring damages, which were quite uniform and involved the upper parts of the upright ribs. The boat itself, as well as the sponson, remained completely watertight after the accident. The starboard sponson shows some local compressions and buckling, which normally appear during take-offs and landings of heavily loaded aircrafts. The thorough investigation of the damages to individual rods in the upright ribs enabled us, with help from some buckling and tensile tests, to draw interesting conclusions about the magnitude of the forces generated. We finally came to the conclusion, according to the presumptions of the DVL in 1931 for calculating the application of seaplanes that the same forces appear in swells above a Category 5.

The boat of the Do X 1a had not seen the inside of a hangar in over a year. For months it was exposed to the effects of seawater in all possible latitudes. Significant signs of corrosion did not appear during this time, so the boat can still be considered as good as new today. The hull has been carefully conserved,

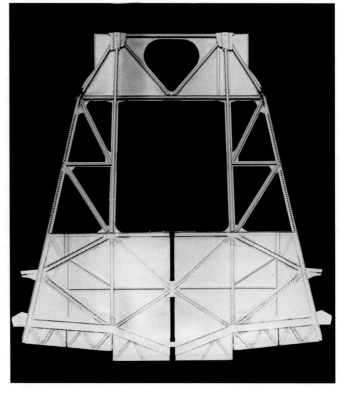

Upright rib #34. On the upper end, the attachment point of the rear spar of the wing unit. Horizontal and vertical forces meet one another on these points.

From the technical report of the Do X 1a from Lisbon to Las Palmas. Damages on the upright ribs after the impact with the groundswell in the Bay of Gando on Gran Canaria. Sketch created on March 21, 1932.

as much as possible, whereby quite primitive methods often had to be employed.

In order to perform these tasks, the crew had to repeatedly let the boat fall dry. By shoveling away the sand, all areas of the hull could be made accessible little by little. This kind of cleaning took place in Lisbon, Bubaque and in South America. The experiences up to now, with regards to preserving the flying boat, have been thoroughly gratifying. They reveal that preservation is substantially easier, more thorough and easier to perform than with smaller boats. The thicker sheet metal used when building flying boats combined with the significantly better accessibility of all inner parts, without a doubt increases the life of the hull considerably.

The retention of the flying boats' sponsons has really stood the test under the most varying of condi-

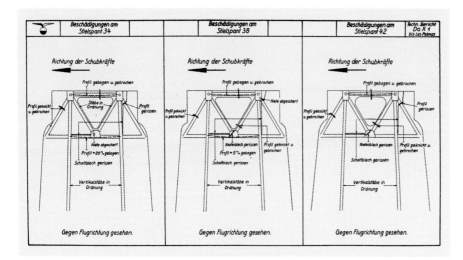

One of six connection points between the wing unit and the hull. Upright connector of the wing's center spar on the upright rib #38. (Photo: Alfred Ziegler, Altenrhein)

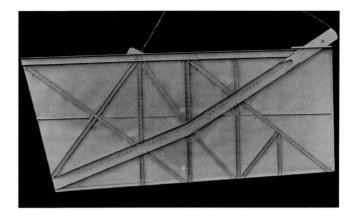

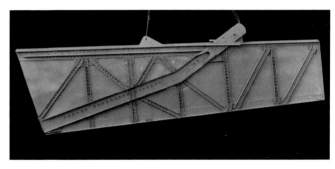

Bulkhead rib of the port side sponson. Here is the center bulkhead rib #38 (above) and the rear bulkhead rib #34 (below). Photographed on January 2, 1929. (Photo: Alfred Ziegler, Altenrhein)

Assembly of the starboard sponson of the Do X 2 in winter 1928. (Photo: Archive DSLR)

tions. The sponsons are exceptionally convenient for exiting and boarding as well as for carrying out all possible nautical maneuvers and other tasks, such as fueling, for example. When placing an Allweiler pump, which are always carried along on board, on the sponsons, it is possible to fill up to 6,000 liters of gasoline per hour. Furthermore, the sponsons make exiting and boarding very easy. They also enable simple and risk-free docking of boats in heavy swells, and they protect the hull from collisions with other vessels. No one really thinks about what kind of attractive force a flying boat has on all smaller and larger vehicles situated in its proximity. It is always a big worry for the ship's command, to keep all boats from ramming the flying boat or from boring it into the ground after a successful landing.

Trim sacks in action. For stability at anchor or moored on a buoy, cylindrical sailcloth containers are attached under the wings on each side, which dampen the heeling of the flying boat.

The stability properties of the flying boat were tested under very difficult conditions and always found to be adequate. Its behavior when being towed and on the buoy is excellent. The flying boat has repeatedly had to withstand winds of 80 to 100km/h for many hours on the buoy. The verdict is still out on its seaworthiness in regards to takeoff and landing. But one thing is certain: it surpasses the seaworthiness of today's smaller boats by far. In order to make mooring on a buoy as safe as possible in strongly variable gusty winds, so-called "trim sacks" are used with very good success. They are cylindrical sailcloth containers, which are fastened to the wings with ropes a certain distance from the center and left in the water where they fill up with water and are immersed up to their upper ends. As soon as a strong gust tries to tilt the wings, the trim sack on the opposite side is raised and increases its weight with every centimeter it surfaces, resulting in a backing moment. The damping is excellent. Thanks to previous experiences, this kind of stabilization will become a valuable aid in the operation of flying boats.

Flying Far and Wide With The Flying Boat

All there is to say about the flight characteristics is that everything that is demanded of many smaller airplanes is met by the flying boat in every way. All rudders are smooth and so well balanced that the pilot doesn't need to overexert himself even during hours-long flights in bad weather. Especially remarkable is the quietness of the flying boat even in strong gusty weather. Cases of seasickness are rare."

Claude Dornier elaborates more in his speech and approaches the topic of flight performances of the various versions.

"In a take-off curve diagram, the take-off curves of the three different flying boats are recorded (the take-off time of each according to flight weight). The curves for summer and winter are recorded to some extent, which show the impact of temperature on starting ability. The values recorded in the diagram, as long as nothing else is noted, relate to take-offs in calm water and without wind in European waters. To

Fairly decent waves. The Do X 2 on the buoy near Altenrhein during a storm on Lake Constance. It wouldn't have been so dramatic with trim sacks. (Photo: Archive DSLR)

this day (Note: winter 1931), the largest weight lifted off the water was achieved by the Do X flying boat in Lisbon: it amounted to 54.5 metric tons. The influence of the tropical climate on take-off conditions is considerable. For example, with a take-off weight of forty-six metric tons on the flying boat Do X 1a, the take-off time in European waters was about forty seconds, a take-off from Bolama in Guinea-Bissau during tropical summer required 123 seconds. The average temperature during the take-off attempts in Bolama was 27° C and the humidity ranged from 87% to nearly 100%.

The flying boat comes up to the step relatively quickly with weights up to fifty-four metric tons, but then can't be lifted, so that a take-off with fifty metric tons in Bolama is impossible. For the take-off curves of the Do X flying boat it should be noted that the propellers used at take-off made fifty revolutions too few. Time and means for new propellers were not available. The take-off times can be improved considerably with the appropriate propellers. At Porto Praia a take-off was executed with 51.7 metric tons in 26° C and 64% humidity. There was a slight wind, a groundswell of around two to three meters high and moderate sea conditions ... On various occasions the take-offs were also strongly affected by mussel formation on the hull.

When judging the climbing rates of the flying boats, one must be sure that all three models are equipped with normal engines of lower compression. By using highly compressed engines or blowers, the climbing rates can be greatly improved. When designing flying boats intended only for civilian purposes and for flights across the ocean, a large ceiling is not the goal. Considering the enhancement of seaworthiness by reducing the wing span results in a very low wing aspect ratio of only 1:5.

On the diagram of Do X flight speeds, speeds are applied as a function of revolution speed … With air-cooled engines these rotation speeds are: n = 1,700, corresponding to a continuous output of 300 to 320hp; with Fiat A 22 R n = 1,950, corresponding to a continuous output of 520hp and with the Curtiss Conqueror 2,150 from 415hp. One can see from the diagram that the version with air-cooled engines can only be flown with a nearly empty machine with the permissible continuous output. The speed values recorded in the diagram refer to a height of about 700 meters above normal zero. When flying just above the water, speeds increase at the same revolution speed by 10 to 12km. This would have been especially useful for the Atlantic flight.

The average traveling speed of the Do X 1a on the route from Friedrichshafen over Rio de Janeiro to New York, which was 24,800 km and required a total of 146 flight hours, was 170km per hour. The average rotation speed during this flight was n = 2,170 … For the assessment of the flight performance, the resource consumption per kilometer, gasoline and oil, is particularly important. For the Do X 1, this was determined to be 8.2kg/km. While the consumption for the air-cooled engine version was only determined over relatively short routes or times, the consumption rate for the Do X 1a is a firm medium value over more than 30,000km and amounts to 7.45kg per kilometer. The oil consumption of this model is particularly low and amounts to no more than 30kg per hour for all engines. During inspection by the authorities, the resource consumption of the Umberto Maddalena was determined to be 6.95kg/km.

Resource consumption data always refers to flights using all engines. With long-distance flights the average fuel consumption rate can sink considerably through a gradual stabilization of engines corresponding to the decrease of flight weight.

Comparisons and Conclusions

In order to form a clear picture of the level of flying boat construction at that time, the achieved performance, as previously compiled, should be compared to the performance of normal multi-engined airplane models.

To be able to do this it is still necessary to specify the empty weight of the three different versions according to the most recent state. For our other observations, the Do X 1 will be left out because a flight with continuous output was not possible. Between the empty weight of the Do X 1a with 31,198 metric tons and the Umberto Maddalena with 33,185 metric tons there is a difference of around two metric tons, which is ascribed almost entirely to the weight of the engine units. The engine weight of the Umberto Maddalena is high because special requirements were set by the client with regard to the cooling systems.

In the comparison table of various modern sea and land planes with the Do X 1a flying boat and the Umberto Maddalena, the following values were recorded: number and type of engine, nominal and continuous output, empty weight, normal and maximum payload capacity, normal and maximum take-off weight. payload capacity percentage of flight weight and payload capacity per 1hp of continuous output, resource consumption in kg/km as well as for the payload capacity metric tons per km, the maximum speed, the traveling speed. In cases where the continuous output is unknown due to experiences, it will be assumed at 0.70 of the homologated performance. In the table, literature references are included. Unfortunately, properly determining the empty weight from technical publications can only be done in rare cases. Therefore, it is not possible to reduce the compared aircraft, to which I specifically refer, to a common denominator. It should be assumed that components are included in the empty weight of some aircraft comparisons, and are probably missing in the empty weights of the flying boats, or vice versa. Special consideration should be given to the fact that, for a large number of the aircraft being compared, only 'calculated' performances are available. For this reason, the actual empty weights are often significantly above those contained in the table. Also, a large part of the models to be compared have air-cooled engines. One can assume that for normal aircraft planned with multiple engines and built within the last two years, the average payload capacity percentage of total weight with a normal load amounts to 36%, with a maximum load up to 45%. The Do X 1a flying boat has a ratio of 35.7% and 42.8% respectively, which falls in line very well with the development of other aircraft. The highest speed for seaplanes is indicated in the table with 220km. It was achieved by a twin-engine model, which is the last member of a more than ten years development. It is only slightly above the maximum speed of the Do X 2. The payload apportioned by one horsepower of continuous output is between 2.89 and 3.39kg according to the table. The corresponding value of the Do X 1 is 3.38kg. In this regard, the flying boat is marching to the top along with normal multiple-engined machines that currently exist.

Unfortunately, accurate data about the resource consumption of foreign machines is unavailable, with the exception of the Junkers G 38. A 1930 edition of Luftwacht (Eng: Air Guard), reported on the flight performances of the Junkers G 38 on page 287 due to model testing by the DVL. The recorded values in the table were taken from this report. The consumption of operating resources is listed with 2.1kg/km in cruise flight. The resource consumption for tonne-kilometer related to the payload capacity results from the table data calculated for the G 38 with 444 grams, for the Do X 1a with 431 grams and for the Umberto Maddalena with 454 grams. For one of the newest triple engine land planes Savoia Marchetti S 71, the resource consumption per tonne-kilometer is specified with 459g. The payload capacity percentage of the G 38's flight weight amounts to 26.4 % for normal take-off weight, 33.8 % for maximum take-off weight, while the corresponding values for the Do X 1a are 35.7% and 42.8 % respectively. It is assumed that the G 38 can still take off with more than twenty metric tons, so that the payload capacity percentage of the flight weight possibly improves with the maximum weight. But it is not known whether the structural safety allows an increase of take-off weight above twenty metric tons. The maximum speed for the G 38 is specified with 194km/h, while it amounts to 196km/h and 206km/h for both flying boats (according to findings by the DVL and Registro Italiano). The comparisons with the G 38 are especially in-

teresting because these machines, as land planes, had an actual advantage weight-wise over the flying boat. The ceiling of the G 38 with twenty metric tons is quoted with 3,150m and the ceiling of the Do X 1a with forty-eight metric tons is 2,120 meters.

The landing speed of the G 38 is only 92km/h. For the flying boat this is about 130km/h. The G 38 is an aerodynamic, especially well built airplane, whose design met a series of performance enhancing measures that came for the flying boat in due time. In particular, I refer to the following characteristics of the G 38 which had not yet been used with the flying boat at that time: high F/b2, engine system in the wings, low cycle stresses for the propeller, shaft extension, retractable radiators, metal propellers, very strong trapezoid shape of the wings, operating resources in the wings for load balance. The impact of these measures is reflected in the considerably better climbing capability and the low landing speed of the G 38 compared with the flying boat. Nevertheless, the flying boat outperforms in speed, resource consumption per tonne-kilometer, and payload capacity percentage of empty weight. This can only be explained in that the absolute size increase of the aircraft in itself holds new possibilities, even for improving and increasing its performance. The construction data of the flying boat was defined five years ago. Significant modifications since then are not possible. In the meantime, technology has not stood still and if new flying boats are designed today, they will surely have a number of performance enhancing measures, like the ones that have been applied to the G 38 in such exemplary fashion.

Even the almost primitive aerodynamic construction of the flying boats at that time, from today's standpoint, resulted in the same possibilities for performance enhancement, which are already more or less exhausted with most modern airplanes. Because the performance of past flying boats can compete with that of most modern multiple-engined airplanes, the further development of the flying boat shows great promise.

I have lingered on these things for a relatively long time because false ideas have been spread in public and also in professional circles about the performance of the flying boat. I would be pleased if my remarks would lead to a more factual assessment of these questions."

Technical Data of the Dornier Do X

Dimensions			
	Do X 1 (Nov. 1929)	**Do X 1a** (Oct. 1930)	**Do X 2 and 3** (1931)
Serial number (AG for Dornier-Flugzeuge, Altenrhein)	01	01	02, 03
Dornier type designation	Do X 1 Sas	Do X 1a Das	Do X 2 Vas, Do X 3 Vas
Wings and tail unit			
Wing span	48.00 m	48.00 m	48.00 m
Aerodynamic surface area (Wing unit and ailerons)	450.00 m2	450.00 m2	450.00 m2
Aerodynamic surface area with upper wings	486.20 m2	-	-
Wing depth	9.50 m	9.50 m	9.50 m
Wing aspect ratio	5.12	5.12	5.12
Maximum sash height	1.28 m	1.28 m	1.28 m
Wing skin panels	3.60 x 2.80 m	3.60 x 2.80 m	3.60 x 2.80 m
Ailerons (length x width)	12.00 x 1.00 m	12.00 x 1.00 m	12.00 x 1.00 m
Compensation surfaces (L x W) 0.7 m above the wings with repair stops in Lisbon (wings), Las Palmas (structure, upright ribs), Rio de Janeiro (hull) and Para (crankshaft) on November 14, 1931	4.60 x 0.5 m	4.60 x 0.5 m	4.60 x 0.5 m
Spacing between engine nacelles	3.60 m	3.60 m	3.60 m
Tailplane (L x W)	15.00 x 3.30 m	15.00 x 3.30 m	15.00 x 3.30 m
Surface area of vertical stabilizer	19.0 m2	19.0 m2	19.0 m2
Surface area of tailplane	33.4 m2	33.4 m2	33.4 m2
Distance from the elevator to water line	6.00 m	6.00 m	6.00 m
Airframe			
Total length	40.05 m	40.05 m	40.05 m
Ribs (numbered from the back to the front)	58 pieces	58 pieces*	58 pieces
Rib spacing	0.50 to 0.70 m	0.50 to 0.70 m	0.50 to 0.70
Maximum fuselage width (without sponsons)	4.80 m	4.80 m	4.80 m
Maximum fuselage width (with sponsons)	10.60 m	10.60 m	10.60 m
Maximum fuselage height	6.40 m	6.40 m	6.40 m
Total length of passenger cabin	-	23.50 m	10.00 m
Average width of passenger cabin	-	3.20 to 3.50 m	3.20 to 3.50 m
Headroom of passenger cabin	1.90 m	1.90 m	1.90 m
Number of large portholes on passenger deck (diameter: 40 cm without frame, 42 with frame)	34	58	34
Height of porthole center from the floor	1.10 m	1.10 m	1.10 m
Number of small portholes on passenger deck (diameter: 21 cm without frame, 23 cm with frame	8	14	11
Number of porthole on the service deck (diameter: 14 without frame, 17 with frame)	8	8	8
Number of skylights on the command deck (diameter without frame: 2 x 40cm, 1.25 cm, 2 x 21cm)	5	5	5
Number of skylights in wing crawlspace (Cellon, diameter: 15 cm)	8	8	8
Number of windows in the command and navigation room (measurements: about 0.60 x 0.50 m)	10	10	10
Fuselage volume with sponsons	400.0 m3	400.0 m3	400.0 m3
Total height (with running propellers)	10.25 m	10.25 m	10.10 m
Draught empty (with 50 metric tons displacement)	0.80 m (1.05 m)	0.80 m (1.05 m)	0.80 m (1.05 m)
Metacentric height with 50 metric tons	4.58 m	4.58 m	4.58 m

* Sixty-three pieces after repairs in August 1933.

Engine Unit

	Do X 1 (Nov. 1929)	Do X 1a (Oct. 1930)	Do X 2 and 3 (1931)
Engines			
Number and type	12 x Siemens "Jupiter" VI U	12 x Curtiss "Conqueror" GV 1570	12 x Fiat A 22 R 430/600 CV
Engine cooling	Air-cooled	Water-cooled	Water-cooled
Number of cylinders per engine	9	12	12
Cylinder arrangement	Radial	V-alignment	V-alignment
Cylinder bore	146 mm	130.2 mm	135 mm
Cylinder stroke	190 mm	161.1 mm	160 mm
Stroke volume per cylinder	28.6 liter	25.73 liter	27.4 liter
Compression ratio	5.3 : 1	5.8 : 1	5.6 : 1
Ignition	2 spark plugs/cylinder	-	-
Starting method	Compressed air	Eclipse inertia starter and hand starter magnet	-
Lubrication cycle	280 liter / hour	-	-
Oil consumption	16 - 20 g / hp-hr	-	-
Fuel (gasoline/benzine)	(70/30)	-	-
Propellers			
Material (wood with brass fittings)	Laminated wood	Laminated wood	Laminated wood
Front row, 6 puller propellers, clockwise rotation	2 x double-bladed	1 x four-bladed	1 x four-bladed
Back row, 6 pusher propellers, counter-clockwise rotation	1 x four-bladed	1 x four-bladed	1 x four-bladed
(August 4 to mid-October 1930)	-	1 x double-bladed	-
Propeller diameter	3.60 m	3.55 m	3.55 m
Displacement in propeller plane	0.29 m	0.29 m	0.29 m
Revolution reduction engine : propeller	2 : 1	2 : 1	1,545 : 1
Revolutions / hp at take-off	875 / 465	1,000 / 535	1,100 / 485
Engine performance			
Continuous rotational speed limit per engine	1700 n/min	2150 n/min	1850 n/min
Continuous output per engine	310 hp	410 hp	500 hp
Maximum rotational speed limit per engine	2100 n/min	2450 n/min	2100 n/min
Maximum output per engine	500 hp	610 hp	630 hp
Engine output (total maximum output)	6,000 hp	7,320 hp	7,560 hp
Engine weight			
Single engine	330 kg	396 kg	487 kg
12 engines (operational)	5,461 kg	5,219 kg	6,237 kg
Cooling system	74 kg	1,691 kg	2,394 kg
Starting system	146 kg	169 kg	148 kg
Engine operation	224 kg	208 kg	249 kg
Propellers with hubs	1,102 kg	796 kg	1,075 kg
Engine unit total	7,007 kg	8,083 kg	10,103 kg
Engine structural weight / hp (continuous output)	1,885 kg/hp	1,624 kg/hp	1,620 kg/hp

Structural Weights

	Do X 1 (Nov. 1929)	Do X 1a (Oct. 1930)	Do X 2 and 3 (1931)
Wings (including supports and upper wings)	7,559 kg	-	-
Tail unit	878 kg	-	-
Control system (rods, etc.)	363 kg	-	-
Fuselage	8,314 kg	-	-
Engine nacelles (including control boxes)	1,147 kg	-	-
Coating	350 kg	-	200 kg
Airframe overall	18,611 kg	19,094 kg	19,063 kg
Engine unit	6,668 kg	8,063 kg	10,103 kg
Fuel system	1,236 kg	1,200 kg	1,200 kg
Lubrication system	359 kg	485 kg	474 kg
Engine monitoring system (display instruments)	229 kg	254 kg	263 kg
Flight monitoring (measuring instruments)	20 kg	36 kg	36 kg
Navigation (compasses, etc.)	15 kg	36 kg	36 kg
Lighting	196 kg	250 kg	250 kg
General equipment (instrument panel, etc.)	85 kg	90 kg	90 kg
Auxiliary operational equipment (fire extinguishers, DKW motor, tools, protective engine covers, etc.)	428 kg	700 kg	700 kg
Communication medium (soundproof FT cabin, etc.)	8 kg	370 kg	370 kg
Nautical equipment (anchor equipment, bilge pumping system)	268 kg	400 kg	400 kg
Furnishings (including passenger deck)	200 kg	695 kg	634 kg
Empty weight	28,323 kg	31,673 kg	33,619 kg
Empty weight / hp (continuous output)	7.52 kg/hp	6.26 kg/hp	5.32 kg/hp
Payload (normal)	-	17,300 kg	15,300 kg
Payload (maximum)	23,300 kg	23,300 kg	17,630 kg
Payload / hp (continuous output)	-	3.38 kg/hp	2.89 kg/hp
Payload percentage of take-off weight (normal)	-	35.7 %	31.6 %
Take-off weight (normal)	45,164 kg	48,500 kg	48,500 kg
Take-off weight (maximum)	-	51,300 kg	54,500 kg
Fuel supply (normal, for a 10-hour flight)	-	16,700 liters	16,000 liters
Fuel supply (maximum)	-	22,700 liters	22,000 liters
Oil supply	-	1,900 liters	1,730 liters
Resource consumption (gasoline, oil)	270 g /hp /h	7.45 kg/km	6.95 kg/km

Flight Performance

	Do X 1 (Nov. 1929)	Do X 1a (Oct. 1930)	Do X 2 and 3 (1931)
Highest speed with maximum payload	-	196 km/h	206 km/h
Highest speed without engine covering	211 km/h	-	-
Traveling speed at an altitude of 420 m	175 km/h	170 km/h	180 km/h
Landing speed	115 km/h	115 km/h	112 km/h
Climbing time with a 45 metric ton take-off weight 0-1000m (1000-2000 m)	19.0 min (–)	9.0 min (14.0 min)	11.0 min (24.0 min)
Ceiling with a 45 metric ton take-off weight	1,550 m	3,000 m	2,200 m
Crew (record flight on October 21, 1929)	18 men	-	-
Crew	16 men	16 men	16 men
Passenger seats (record flight on October 21, 1929)	151 people	-	-
Passenger seats	-	66 seats	24 seats
Crew seats	-	-	8 seats
Maiden flight	July 12, 1929	August 4, 1930	May 16, 1931 (Do X 2)

The figures and values given here originate exclusively from contemporary sources of the years 1929 to 1933.

1. "Das Flugschiff DO-X" (Eng: The Do X Flying Boat) speech by Claude Dornier on November 6, 1929, given at the annual assembly of the German Society for Aerospace in Berlin (print, author's archives).
2. Unpublished "Building Specifications of the Dornier Do X Vas Flying Boat." The building specifications for both the Do X 2 and 3 flying boats, produced for Italy, originate from July 9, 1931 and has the company's internal number 1079/4, with the author's initials F/Schä. ("Swiss Collection of 2010," archival finds property of the Dornier family, Munich).
3. "Über Flugschiffe, Erfahrungen, Vergleiche, Folgerungen und Ausblick" (Eng: About Flying Boats, Experiences, Comparisons, Conclusions and Outlook), a speech by Claude Dornier, given at the 1931 conference of the Technical University Munich (print, author's archives).
4. Various source material from the author's archives.

Claude Dornier's Perspective On the Big Mistake

Claude Dornier then begins to talk about the role that the flying boat will have in the future of seaplane passenger transport.

"For many it is clear: airplanes that will cross the ocean have to be seaplanes. This means they have to be vehicles that include a boat or floats so that they can take off from the water and land on it again.

However, this view, which I myself fully support, is not yet accepted by all of those with an interest in the development of overseas air transport. There are still a lot of people who believe that the future 'ocean airplane' should be one with wheels, a so-called land plane. Some are still guided by the notion that a land plane always has a somewhat larger flying range than the seaplane due to its relatively lower weight. But today, the required flying range for an ocean crossing with sufficient payload and security is far from being achieved, even for land planes.

From a transportation standpoint, land plane ocean crossings, which were performed with great bravura, are insignificant. With all of those attempts, the machines had been so over-strained that they didn't meet the demands of construction and opera-

In 1936 at the International Aviation Exhibition in Stockholm, Dornier presents the model of the "ideal Do X" and explains it to Gustav V, King of Sweden (with top hat).

tional safety, which must be met in the interest of a regulated implementation of air transport. A one-sided increase in the flying range of land planes over the seaplane is not expected. The top speed of the seaplane today is even higher than any land plane. Each new aerodynamic or static improvement and every advance in engine construction benefits seaplanes just as much as land planes.

The proponents of the land plane as the definitive ocean aircraft further assert that there is no high seas-capable airplane so it would be better to just give up on the idea of a sea landing. To that, one must reply that a series of seaplanes have proven that landing and floating at sea for many days is possible. Unfortunately, it is also easy to prove that unforeseen landings will never be completely avoided. But what about the land plane? It has probably occurred that damaged airplanes were floating around at sea, carried for days by their empty fuel tanks or air pockets, and eventually saved; the crew on board this kind of airplane, however, cannot compare with the crew of a well built sea plane. In my opinion, any attempt to cross oceans with land planes will prove erroneous in the long run.

What will the seaplane for long journeys look like? Here too there is still a huge disparity of opinions. The boat idea, which I have always supported, has made considerable progress in recent years. Nevertheless, there are still a large number of supporters of floatplanes and the so-called double boat, which in the end is nothing more than an airplane with two floats. Proponents of the two float system, or the double boat, base their preference for this arrangement on the great lateral stability that can be achieved with it on the water. Experience has shown, however, that a flying boat can be built with a central hull that has sufficient stability characteristics in all circumstances with the normal operation of seaplanes. Increasing the stability above a certain value, though, is not necessary, and actually, undesired.

Side view of the "Ideal Do X." Model with aerodynamically
perfected engine unit. (Photo: Archive DSLR)

The model of the "Ideal Do X" corresponds to the Do X
2 and 3. It was produced by the apprentice workshop of
Dornier and is currently on display in the Dornier Museum
in Friedrichshafen. (Photo: Archive DSLR)

A front view of the model "Ideal Do X." (Photo: Archive DSLR)

Two floats and a fuselage, or two boats, will always be heavier than one boat and will always have more resistance. Also, their manufacture is more expensive.

The structural advantage of load distribution with a larger width of wingspan, which at first glance is expected for the double boat, does not actually occur because the increased stresses that appear during landings and take-offs more than balance it out. 'The long-distance seaplane will be an airplane with a central boat, a so-called flying boat!' Economic feasibility and safety will be decisive in the choice for the aircraft being considered.

The crew of a vessel that will venture thousands of kilometers out to sea and remain in the air twenty or more hours will always be made up of at least six people: two pilots, two men for radio duty and navigation, and two mechanics. This is the absolute minimum. It's obvious that this expenditure on personnel cannot be made when transporting only two or three passengers. If the number of passengers is increased tenfold, then crew will barely double. The cost of crew per passenger will amount to about one-fifth.

The same observations line up in regards to resource consumption and amortization of the flying equipment. The outcome: cost effectiveness is only possible when the costs can be passed on to a larger number of passengers. As soon as the flight duration exceeds ten or more hours, the required minimum number of passengers, namely about twenty to thirty, almost inevitably results in the dimensions of today's flying boat, if the necessary comfort for passengers and required safety installations are made available.

The availability of these comforts and the necessary safety measures is a prerequisite for attaining a reasonable frequency. A good frequency, however, is in turn the prerequisite of any economical transport. We conclude that air transport of people over wide sea routes will only be achieved by using flying boats. And then there is safety. Safety at sea requires reserve displacement, freeboard, protection for the propellers, protection of the tail unit, efficient message service, space for comfortable execution of navigation, sufficient accommodations for the part of the crew not on watch duty, the possibility to carry luggage, and the convenient deployment of life boats. Safety in the air demands a

high degree of serviceability of all parts; that means accessibility to the wings and boat in all important areas and storage of operational resources far away from the engines. These requirements again inevitably result in the proper dimensions, as they are epitomized in the Do X. You can't just venture out on the ocean in a nutshell.

What does it mean when the Umberto Maddalena or the Wal D-2069 taxis slowly in the same swell? Let's place ourselves in spirit on board both vessels. As a passenger on the Wal, we hear the waves thunder against the side of the aircraft, slight breakers come over the deck now and then and splash against the portholes. The crew is already soaked after just a short time. The swaying of the boat has made some passengers go pale.

On the flying boat you are 'dissociated,' so to speak, from the swells. You will probably see a cute little wave that will occasionally lap the sponsons, but that is it. I am not exaggerating when I say that, psychologically, for those situated on board the flying boat, the swell shrinks by half. This feeling of security, which only enlargement can give, is important. Much more important, of course, is the effective increase in safety achieved in the wake of enlargement.

As already mentioned, the present flying range of all airplanes, even land planes, is still too low to guarantee cost effectiveness on large overseas routes. We must ask ourselves which possibilities there are to increase the flying range, or performance, of large flying boats. The principle measures for this are: reduction of the structural weight, aerodynamic refinements, reduction of resource consumption, and improving take-off performance or take-off weight. A significant reduction of the empty weight without diminishing the structural safety seems very difficult, as long as one has to work with the present building materials. By using trapezoidal or triangular shaped wing contours, placing loads in the wings, as well as further refining the static formation of the wings, it is possible to increase the aspect ratio and the carrying surface with approximately the same weight.

Further weight savings for the wings and tail unit are achieved by using profiles with a very low center of pressure variation. Weight savings for the hull seem possible, if it works out to store operational resources in a kind of double floor since this achieves a significant reduction of stress on the boat's connections during take-off and landing, also by reducing the landing speed using flaps, divided wings and the like.

The resource consumption available today lies between 230 and 250g/hp-hr. Consumption figures of 160 to 180g/hp-hr have recently been achieved by diesel engines. It appears possible, in the not too distant future, to improve flight performance by using heavy fuel engines. But for the time being, one will have to trade lower resource consumption for higher engine weight so that gains will first be achieved on routes that exceed at least six to ten hours flight time.

Aerodynamic refinement is possible by choosing better profiles with a fixed center of pressure, improving aspect ratio, remote operation, reducing radiator drag, reducing propeller cycle stresses, installing a 'free wheel' between the propeller and the hub in order to be able to shut off engines as weight decreases (without increased performance loss by idle or rotating propellers) and improving the boat coefficient.

Ideally, we assume that a 20% reduction of the empty weight would be possible. Furthermore, we assume that the resource consumption per hp/h, which amounts to about 250g today, would sink to 175g. If we were to also implement the aerodynamic refinements so that we acquire a 20% increase in speed, one would get, under the assumption of a non-stop route of 4,000km, the following comparative values for the 'Wal' and 'Do X' models: The payload of the Wal would be 175kg compared to 3,656kg for the flying boat. The consumption of operating resources with 100kg payload would be 1,600kg for the Wal and only 490kg for the flying boat.

These comparative values show quite clearly that the desired economic conditions on long-distance oversea flights can only be achieved with an enlargement of the dimensions. While the crew's share of the 100kg payload on the Wal equals 230kg, it sinks to 33kg on the flying boat. On the Wal, transport of a 100kg payload would require 630hp, and only 180hp on the flying boat. The acquisition costs of airframes

The Do X 2 on Lake Constance before the ferry flight to Italy with a fresh coat of paint. (Photo: Archive DSLR)

plus engines for the flying boat amounts to half of that necessary for the Wal. These numerical values are not absolute values, but their relation to one another is essentially fixed. In recent years, people have often questioned whether all of the money and work that went into the development of the flying boat is justified. People particularly like to point out again and again that the flying boat was ahead of its time and ahead of market needs. The skies over land have been conquered by airplanes in the last decade. The much larger airspace over the seas today is still unconquered by aircraft heavier than air. As long as vessels lighter than air don't come into question, it can only be opened up commercially by the flying boat. This fact also underlines the justification for previous and future efforts to design and develop flying boats."

This concludes the remarks by Claude Dornier in his speech, "About Flying Boats, Experiences, Comparisons, Conclusions and Outlook," during a conference at the Technical University Munich in the winter of 1931.

And What Kind Of Paint Do The Do X 1 and Do X 2 Have?

One of the most frequently asked questions is: What kind of paint do the Do X flying boats have? Only meager clues are found on the black and white photos of the flying boat, which have had to satisfy model makers and airplane historians. In the St. Gallen's state archives there is a document that answers the question for the Do X 1a by and large. On March 13, 1934, Do X flight engineer Otto Eitel from DoFlug in Altenrhein wrote a list titled "Conservation of the Do X 1 Flying Boat." Apparently a new coat of paint is due. At that time, the Do X lay moored in Friedrichshafen and awaiting its fate. In his two-paged typewritten text, Otto Eitel mentions the topic:

"1. Boat above the water line – 1929, in the shipyard in Altenrhein: nitro-silver: base gray, finishing coat silver. Supplier: Süring Berlin. Paint is flaking off in places; also was not seawater resistant because it was observed that the color film became porous and very raw after a certain time, especially on the sponson deck and on the boat's sidewalls."

It must be mentioned here that the protective lacquer of the flying boat's duralumin plating in 1929 had light to dark green tones. That also applied to the first base coat and the finishing coat for the Do X 2 and 3. In black and white photos, the protective coat appears very dark and blotchy because the fly-ing boats were also coated with military camouflage in their testing phase before the first paint. The greenish protective coating of the aluminum component parts is part of the scope of delivery of the aluminum factory. It shimmers because a uniform color tone was not requested, only a surface protectant against corrosion.

The text from Otto Eitel continues:

"July 1931. Without previous leaching off, the entire boat was sprayed with nitro-aluminum (supplier: Syndicato Condor in Rio de Janeiro). This paint, as anticipated, did not hold well due to the insufficient pretreatment. October 1931. One coat with colorless boat lacquer and aluminum in New York. August 1932. One coat of gray oil paint (supplier unknown) in Travemünde. Spring 1933. One coat of DKH lacquer light green/green (supplier Lackfabrik Dr. Kurt Herberts, Wuppertal) in the shipyard at Altenrhein. The DKH lacquer lost its color tone and gloss very quickly.

2. Boat under the water line. Fall 1929 in Altenrhein. Base: one coat of diamond gray oil paint and one coat of KZ silver spray. Spring 1931 in Las Palmas. One coat of KZ silver spray. KZ silver proved a failure. July 1931 in Rio de Janeiro. The floor was mostly scraped and leached off. The corrosion present today, especially on the lamellas, mainly formed as long as the KZ lacquer was on. Since then, it has not changed much. In Rio, subsequent preservation was useful and proved to be the best. Base: one coat of Inertol (supplier: Syndicato Condor). Finishing coat: two coats of Antieorosivo International I and one coat of Antieorosivo International II, one red poison color (supplier: Krause & Köpke, Rio de Janeiro). Spring 1932 in New York. One coat of paint with tar color (supplier unknown).

August 1932 in Travemünde. One coat of paint with Interol. Spring 1933 in Altenrhein. One coat of paint with Interol."

Interol is still used today as a clear coating material on a bitumen base. Developed in the beginning of the twentieth century, Interol was used as a protective coating on concrete and steel, on foundations, small iron parts, gutters, mast steps, etc. Ideal corrosion protection for the subfloor of the Do X.

Paint sample of an extensive series of tests with various paints and weather tests for the Do X. (Photo: Archive DSLR)

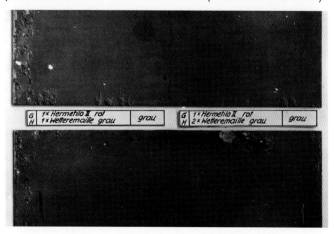

Point 3 of the text from Otto Eitel is short and describes the paint for the tail unit, the engine nacelles and the metal plated wing skin panels under the nacelles. They are identical to the above-water paint.

Point 4 deals with the paint of the wings. With the first covering, three coats of titanine red and two finishing coats with titanine aluminum are used. Titanine, a lacquer for airplane fabrics, was supplied by the English manufacturer Titanine-Emaillite Ltd. In Hendon, when airplanes were covered with linen. The English magazine "The Sailplane" reported in September 1930 about the current use of titanine: "… Three coats are sufficient to tighten the covering and forms a lasting, firm wing skin with the lowest weight increase. It is weather proof and durable … Lindbergh and Chamberlain crossed the Atlantic in their titanine coated airplanes. Cobham, Hinkler, Barnard, Pinedo and Franco performed their famous flights with titanine coated machines. Even the wings of the largest airplane in the world, the large flying boat, is varnished with titanine." What the Englishmen also guaranteed in 1930, was fire-resistance of their dried lacquer. Titanine failed to provide proof, however, during the fire of the Do X in Lisbon.

In the winter of 1932/33, during the complete overhaul in the hangar in Altenrhein, and after the German tour, the wings were given new coverings. Afterward, it received its last coat of paint. Otto Eitel wrote about it: "After the second fabric covering, there were three coats of titanine (dope 2) in red and two coats with aluminum 3P nitro vernish. The tension as well as the waterproofing is satisfactory with both coverings. On the upper side of the wings, which are more exposed to the weather, the aluminum coat, or aluminum powder, dissolves over time and the red base color shimmers through. Therefore, the wings should be re-coated with titanine from time to time." In conclusion, Otto Eitel gives a recommendation for a sustainable preservation of the boat under the water line: "One base coat with diamond gray oil paint. Let the base coat dry out (8 to 10 days). Two finishing coats with Inertol. All coats painted on by hand and not sprayed!"

In files recently discovered in Switzerland, extensive hints were also found about the first coat of paint for the Do X 2. In the protocol of "Inspection – Weighing" of the Do X 2 from August 1, 1931, a note under "1. Finish Coat" reads: "… for wings with ailerons and compensation surfaces as well as wing shafts: two coats of aluminum-titanine. Upper and lower tail plane, elevator with compensation surfaces, vertical stabilizer with rudder and compensation surfaces with tail unit supports: spray two coats of aluminum-titanine. Boat floor and boat sides-water line: paint one coat of diamond gray, spray one coat of KZ tar lacquer and KZ silver. Sponson floor and sides: paint one coat of diamond gray, spray one coat of tar lacquer and KZ silver. Boat sides and deck: spray two coats of berlac-silver. Engine nacelles with shaft: spray two coats of berlac-silver. Paint boat interior, cockpit, command room, toilets front and rear, kitchen and hallway, B and C decks gray and white." Before the paint finish, all fabric-covered surfaces of the wing unit and the rudder are already coated three times with titanine.

Do X 2 with a greenish protective coating on the duralumin plates.

The "Prodomo" system. Seating furniture by Walter Knoll, Stuttgart, in all rooms of the passenger deck on the Do X.

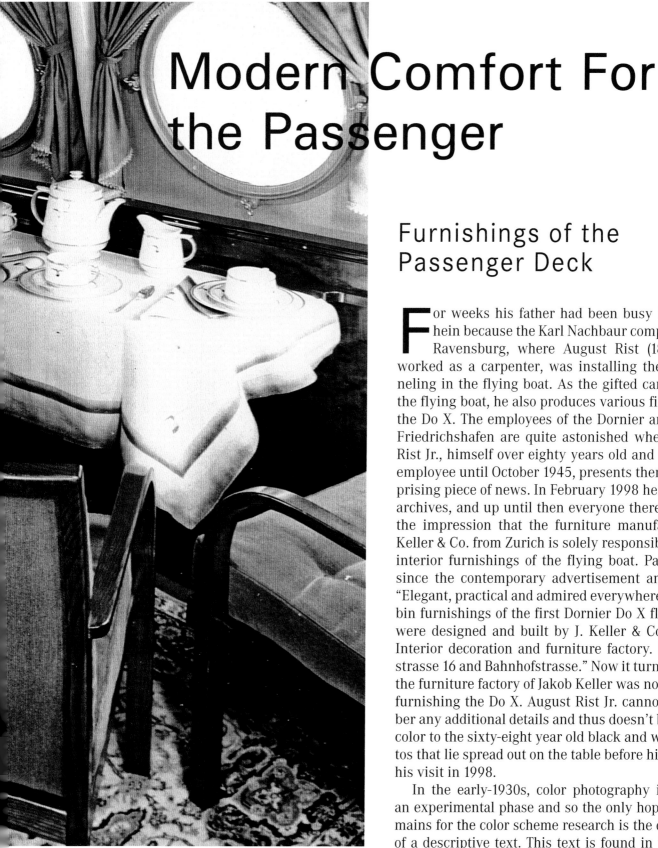

Modern Comfort For the Passenger

Furnishings of the Passenger Deck

For weeks his father had been busy in Altenrhein because the Karl Nachbaur company from Ravensburg, where August Rist (1882-1955) worked as a carpenter, was installing the wall paneling in the flying boat. As the gifted carpenter of the flying boat, he also produces various fixtures for the Do X. The employees of the Dornier archives in Friedrichshafen are quite astonished when August Rist Jr., himself over eighty years old and a Dornier employee until October 1945, presents them the surprising piece of news. In February 1998 he visits the archives, and up until then everyone there is under the impression that the furniture manufacturer J. Keller & Co. from Zurich is solely responsible for the interior furnishings of the flying boat. Particularly since the contemporary advertisement announces: "Elegant, practical and admired everywhere – the cabin furnishings of the first Dornier Do X flying boat were designed and built by J. Keller & Co. Zurich. Interior decoration and furniture factory. St. Peterstrasse 16 and Bahnhofstrasse." Now it turns out that the furniture factory of Jakob Keller was not alone in furnishing the Do X. August Rist Jr. cannot remember any additional details and thus doesn't bring any color to the sixty-eight year old black and white photos that lie spread out on the table before him during his visit in 1998.

In the early-1930s, color photography is still in an experimental phase and so the only hope that remains for the color scheme research is the discovery of a descriptive text. This text is found in the Fachblatt für Holzarbeiter (Eng: 'Woodworker's Journal'), published by the Deutscher Holzarbeiterverband (German Woodworker's Association), and headlined the November 1930 issue on page 241 with a complete report on the topic. The article: "The Interior Design in the Do X Flying Boat" with a copy of the blueprint and six interior photos originates from Emil Rau (1878-1969), interior designer for Jakob Keller in Zurich and creative mind behind the Do X interior. His report is seen as the source of all later descriptions since Rau puts it to paper during the installation phase in Altenrhein in August and September 1930.

The planning begins with the "guidelines for furnishing the cabin space of the Do X flying boat." In the beginning of October 1929, Emil Rau holds four pages of typewritten text in his hands. With the call for bids to design the interior space of the world's largest aircraft, a project begins for Rau that will occupy him for well over three years. His sits at his desk at Jakob Keller on the corner of Peterstrasse and Bahnhofstrasse in Zurich and a letter from Altenrhein demands his full attention. The "incorporated company for Dornier-Flugzeuge, Altenrhein" or "DoFlug" invites the most renowned furniture shop in Switzerland, J. Keller & Co., to bid on providing the furnishings of the passenger deck for sixty-six passengers. Rau doesn't seem to think that it is a difficult task. Many of Switzerland's classy hotels carry the signature furnishings of Jakob Keller & Co. and thus his as well. After some deliberation, he produces a colorful gouache of an interior design, which radiates the ambiance of a passenger liner. Unfortunately, only a black and white photo of it is preserved. Rau's design from December 1929 already shows fundamental elements of later interior furnishings of the Do X 1a.

Emil Rau, Creative Mind Behind the Do X's Interior

Georg Emil Rau is employed by Jakob Keller beginning in 1910. First, as foreman of the furniture factory Keller, and then as interior designer with J. Keller & Co. during the Do X project. He was born on May 17th, 1878 in Stuttgart, the son of master carpenter Johann Georg Rau and his wife Salomé, born Eppler, and is baptized Evangelical Lutheran. Later in his professional life, Rau will no longer use his first given name "Georg." Beginning in 1892, Emil Rau spent three years learning the carpentry profession in his father's workshop. He works in his father's business until 1900 and finds carpentry jobs in Stuttgart, then in Mannheim, and then again in Stuttgart until 1909. During this period he puts off his master's examination. On March 7, 1903, Emil Rau marries for the first time in Stuttgart. Moving from Stuttgart, Rau, who in the meantime becomes a widower, registers in Zurich on January 18, 1910 where he marries again on April 9, 1910. In his registration, he lists his profession as: "foreman at the Keller furniture factory." After the outbreak of the World War, Rau returns to the warring German Empire in June 1915 and arrives in Ravensburg with the regional command of the 54th Infantry Brigade on November 5, 1915. After only three months of training for the front, the military is probably aware of his special skills. The German side desperately needs woodworking specialists for the increasingly industrial fabrication of airplanes. In 1916, these are constructions made from shaped wood, wire and airplane fabrics with flange-mounted engines. The Do X special edition of the Swiss Aero-Revue from 1931, page 86, reads: "… It was no ordinary task, when J. Keller & Co. in Zurich received the order to furnish the passenger cabin of the flying boat. One of their employees, Mr. Emil Rau, was more confident with this kind of thing since he led the carpentry work in a large aeronautical operation during the war years." In 1916, in Ravensburg, and on Lake Constance near Friedrichshafen, there are various operations that work in cooperation with the factories of the Graf Zeppelin for the production of airplanes and airships. One of these workshops, the carpenter's shop of Karl Nachbaur in Ravensburg, is involved in the cabin construction in 1930. It is possible that Emil Rau later uses his contacts there.

A few days after November 11, 1918, when weapons fell silent in Europe, Rau travels back to Switzerland. A widower once more, he can return to his position at the Keller furniture factory. On June 17, 1920 he marries for a third time. On June 22, 1923, Emil Rau files a petition of citizenship for himself and his wife at the City Council of Zurich. We have to thank the subsequent acceptance procedure for the amount a lot of biographical data for Emil Rau. In the files obtained from Zurich public records, the "reports by the following departments about the citizenship applicants" are especially enlightening. For example, the tax office lists 8,900 Francs of taxed income for 1923, which Rau earns as managing director at Jakob Keller. On January 30, 1924, the married couple successfully attained citizenship in the city of Zurich.

In 1928, Emil Rau publishes an amazing handbook for woodworkers and cabinetmakers. He uses his wealth of experience handling wood and presents the diversity of wood species. On thirty-nine pages of text, Rau describes trees from ash to zelkova, their occurrence, appearance, and uses as well as the specific weight of the wood. The highlight of the 15.5x11cm paperback bound in linen are the ninety-six wood samples printed in color and sized 7x10cm. Thus, it had a real practical value.

We now focus our attention back to the advertisement text for furnishing the Do X's passenger cabin from October 4, 1929. The first point of the "principle requirements" states: "Emphasis must be placed on the lowest weight possible." Rau refers to this in his description in the Fachblatt für den Holzarbeiter (Eng: 'Woodworker's Journal'):

"If the technical originality and large proportions of this flying giant in Altenrhein has already evoked admiration from all sides, then one would hope that its interior design will be noticed with interest in our industry circles.

It is no ordinary task to manage a minimum of weight with an artistic effect and still provide the best in solidity. Beforehand, let it be said that the company responsible, J. Keller Co. in Zurich, has still fallen substantially short of the already extremely closely calculated weight – but the pleasant cooperation with the leading figures at the factory contributed a lot. The ground plan shows the distribution of individual rooms, which together claim a length of around 23m (half of the fuselage length). From the entrance, arranged on both sides in the front third, there is room toward the front for sixteen passengers, half of which can be transformed into a sleeping compartment. Yellowish-brown, striped taffeta is used as the wall material, the furniture is upholstered with colorful horsehair fabric, the small curtains of green rep. The thick, beige-colored carpet increases comfort and, along with other objectively

The first design idea from Emil Rau. Fine like a luxury liner. Black and white photo of a color gouache from December 1929. (Staatsarchiv St. Gallen)

used insulating materials, reduces a large part of the engine sound. An 80cm high parapet panel, polished here in walnut, leads through all rooms and hides the technical installations. Small folding tables, each with two benches, are also arranged everywhere. Further ahead lies a very cozy smoking cabin outfitted with zebrano panels, eight leather chairs and a bouclé rug together with adjacent bar niche, in which a steward caters to the refreshment needs of the passengers.

Moving backward from the entrance, one enters the large lounge through a cloakroom alcove situated on both sides. Almost 7m long and 3.5m wide and separated by only two ribs, this room calculated for twenty-six passengers represents superbly in its beautiful golden ambiance. The walls are covered by polished cherry tree panels with yellow-ground chintzed craquelé with Chinese patterns; the front and rear seating groups are covered with plain green velour, the center seats with plain red velour.

Green curtains enliven the walls with portholes. Here too, like in all rooms, the floor is covered with a soft, plain carpet. The rearmost section is arranged the same way as the front passenger room, but the benches here have striped velour covers and the woodwork is finished with polished mahogany. The kitchen and two restrooms complete the passenger cabin … The quickly advancing technology of our time will still prompt some new construction, even in the interior design, as it has done in this case. Maybe aircraft and airship construction will assume the role to convince the traditional carpenter how wasteful he is with 'wood' throughout his life."

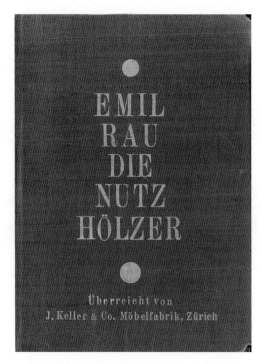

A look into the upholstery room of the furniture factory of Jakob Keller & Co. In the early-1930s the business is taken over by Ernst Hohl Senior. (Archive Ernst Hohl Culture Foundation, Zurich)

Die Nutzhölzer (English: Timber) the useful book by Emil Rau. J. Keller & Co. uses it for their own image advertising. (Archive Ernst Hohl Culture Foundation, Zurich)

Material thriftiness was not solely due to the weight problem of the Do X 1, but also the ongoing cost situation from the rudder, which strains the nerves of those involved at the time. Claude Dornier's cost estimate for the construction of the Do X flying boat totaled 1,470,000 Reichsmarks in 1925. At the time of the report from Emil Rau – after the installation of new engines, corresponding alterations and with the furnishing of the Do X 1 – the total has climbed to 3,966,595 Reichsmarks. With well over 1.5 million Reichsmarks over the agreed upon purchase price of 2,370,000 Reichsmarks, the German Reich will no longer cooperate. Emil Rau bears the brunt of the quarrels directly. Cuts will be made across the board for both Italian flying boats, whose furnishings are provided by J. Keller & Co. with Rau as site manager in Altenrhein. This results in a cabin configuration reduced to twenty-four passengers and an abundance of spartan aura. For Emil Rau, these activities, which last well into 1932, are the downside of the Dornier Do X project. On December 4, 1940, Emil Rau officially changes his job title from foreman to interior designer. After the death of his wife on

April 9, 1954, Emil Rau lives out the rest of his life in the Buchenhof old age home on Kreuzbühlstrasse 16 from March 1961 and eventually dies on August 29, 1969 in Bertschikon. It isn't until 2010 that some hand-colored furnishing plans of the Do X 1 and 2 are rediscovered. They come from the inventory files of the DoFlug factory in Altenrhein and are guarded by the Dornier Foundation for Aerospace (DSLR) in Friedrichshafen. They are published here for the first time.

Particularly striking is the colorful design with the modern colors and shapes of Art Déco. The creative connection of sophisticated forms, precious materials and strong colors is eye-catching with this first design. The colorfully planned execution would have cost a substantial amount of money, which was not available in the Do X budget in 1930. Implementation of the interior furnishings would have turned out considerably more puristic. The "prodomo" seating furniture by Walter Knoll & Co., in particular, which is linked to the Bauhaus style to some degree, will have relieved the budget through their cost-efficient production and corresponding price.

Port side of the smoking room with electrical lighter for cigars and cigarettes found in the middle above the little table. In a flying boat in which smoking was strictly prohibited.

Probably the first design for the cabin layout of the Do X 1 by Emil Rau. Implementation turned out considerably more spartan. (Archive DSLR)

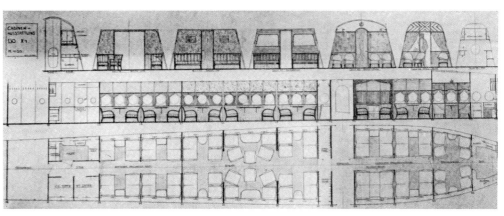

Master plan of the cabin furnishings by Emil Rau. It corresponds to the installations and equipment of the Do X 1a in the summer and fall of 1930.

A Marine Painter Documents the Do X in Color

We must thank a painter of the sea and of ships for the very special images of the Do X's interior furnishings. Claus Bergen (1885-1964), an academically trained painter from Munich, enjoyed an outstanding reputation in naval circles. His large-scale painting of the Battle of Jutland and the images of his self-experienced war patrol with the U-53 submarine under lieutenant commander Hans Rose (1885-1969) make him one of the most renowned German marine painters of the 1920s.

Claus Bergen is fascinated by Lindbergh's Atlantic crossing and the successful flight in an east-west

Elizabeth and Claus Bergen in the artist's studio in Munich, 1930. On the easel, the last battle of the small cruiser SMS Emden against the Australian light cruiser HMAS Sydney on November 9, 1914.

direction by Köhl, von Hünefeld and Fitzmaurice, and paints motifs relating to aviation subjects. Influenced by his travels in America and an important exhibition in the USA, he calls for "American Motifs." He names his oil paintings on canvas "Lindbergh" and "Bremen" and presents both aircraft images for the first time in the traditional Munich art exhibition in the Glaspalast beginning on June 1, 1928. After his journey with the luxury yacht Amida over the stormy Atlantic in mid-April 1929, Claus Bergen – "the best living marine painter on the European continent" – shows his paintings in the Gainsborough Galleries in New York from May 9th to 30th, 1929.

In contrast to many of his colleagues, the marine painter with aviation ambitions is doing well financially in the 1920s. But the effects of the global financial crisis of the 1930s gnaws at the substance of the married couple, Claus and Elizabeth Bergen, whose financial livelihood depends solely on the sale of paintings. Paintings from Bergen's studio find hardly any buyers and especially not at his usually high prices. A larger commission by the Berlin publisher Velhagen & Klasing comes at just the right time for the artist. In the fall of 1930 he is to deliver some illustrations for the well-known monthly magazine of the publishing house, the Monatshefte.

After the conversion to twelve water-cooled Curtiss Conqueror engines and the complete installation of the furnishings for the passenger deck, the date for the Do X's ferry flight to the USA stands firm for the beginning of November. Paul Oskar Höcker (1865-1944), editor of the Monatshefte and acquaintance of Do X commander Friedrich Christiansen is to be on board for one stage of the flight in Europe. For the written text he needs color illustrations that show the flying boat from the inside and out. Since Bergen had previously carried out some assignments for the Berliner, Höcker invites him to travel from Munich to Altenrhein on Lake Constance in early October 1930 to produce the necessary sketches and color impressions. His tempera paintings of the interior, in particular, are especially informative today because, apart from this, there are only black and white photos of the interior. That Claus

Claus Bergen titled this colorful gouache "Do X startbereit" (Eng: 'Do X Ready For Take-off'), which was created after his visit in Altenrhein. (Claus Friedrich Bergen, VG Bildkunst 2011)

Bergen would run into Emil Rau during his work in and around the flying boat, is inevitable. They were intrigued by one another and thus the artist is able to place some illustrations for advertisements of Jakob Keller & Co., in other words, sell.

Five tempera illustrations appear in color print in the January 1931 edition of Velhagen & Klasings Monatshefte. After the conversion in the early-1930s, originals painted on hardboard sized 35x40cm or 37x49cm disappear from Claus Bergen in a portfolio with the label "Dornier" and don't reappear until after his death in 1964 in his estate. Today, a total of eight original Do X themed paintings by Claus Bergen are kept, or rather hidden, in a recently unknown provisional art warehouse near the Lenggries in Upper Bavaria, and are not accessible to the public.

Advertisement for Jakob Keller & Co. from the Do X special edition of the Swiss AERO REVUE from 1931.

Artist's view into the lounge of the Do X 1a. The only authentic source from 1930 for the color scheme of flying boat's furnishings. (ClausFriedrich Bergen, VG Bildkunst 2011)

The most well known Do X painting by Claus Bergen is faring somewhat better. It shows the flying boat flying over a fast steamer à la Columbus on the Atlantic – an encounter that never actually took place. The Leipzig newspaper Illustrierte Zeitung, who commissioned Bergen to produce a four-colored panorama page, titled it "The Flying Boat Belongs to the Future." The motif is immensely popular at that time and so it is also printed in both special editions of the Swiss Aero Revue from 1931 and 1932. Bergen titled his 72x102cm tempera painting on paperboard much more pragmatically "The Do X in Flight Over the Atlantic." Those who would like to see this painting today have to travel to Bremerhaven. It hangs on permanent loan from the Bavarian Municipality

of Lenggreis in the "Shipping of the Industrial Age" section of the German Shipping Museum near the giant model of the steamship Bremen.

Two other sources for the interior design of the flying boat are found in the archives of Dornier GmbH (now EADS) in Friedrichshafen. Shortly before the ferry flight of the Do X to the USA, the interior furnishings are documented in the form of an inventory list. These lists from October 15, 1930 clearly convey the actual state of the furnishings in November 1930 together with a contemporary text from Erich Tilgenkamp (1898-1966) in the 1931 special edition of the Aero Revue. Dr. Erich Tilgenkamp, then already a well-known aviation journalist from Switzerland and on board the flight to Lisbon as chief

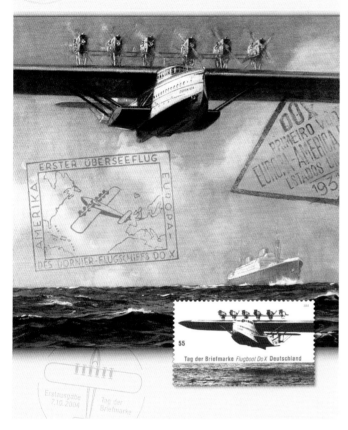

The 2004 annual edition of postal philately for loyal customers. In the background is the painting by Claus Bergen from the Shipping Museum in Bremerhaven. (Claus Friedrich Bergen, VG Bildkunst 2011)

press officer, describes the passenger area of the flying boat quite vividly. His report begins, as it has with every ship since the steamship period, in the front with the collision room and the final collision bulkhead. Up to the bulkhead, the flying boat is very much a ship in its function and equipped for possible risks on the water. There the crew stows part of its nautical equipment: the 95m long manila anchor line for the 100kg ground anchor with stock as well as the anchor winch with brake and hand crank. To enter the collision room from within there is a lockable manhole in the bar and from the outside a deck hatch on the foredeck. A large part of the flying boat's sea equipment is made up of: two sea anchors with rope, thimble and bridle, two sailcloth bail buckets,

a rubber dinghy for fifteen people with paddles, a set of leak protection materials, boat hooks, A Klepper "Wanderer" folding boat for two people, and more.

A Detailed Inventory List From 1930

Erich Tilgenkamp then describes the cabin on the main deck. The details are completed here, in parentheses, from the mentioned inventory list:

"… the entire length of the amidships main beam of 23.5m is divided into eleven rooms, whose partitioning is essentially given by the framework ribs of the hull. All the way in the front in the bow, a cute little bar is furnished with built-in cabinets, a refrigerator, sink, etc., where passengers can victoriously combat any possible momentary "weakness" with their favorite cocktail or the obligatory whiskey (bar room: two body; one wall cabinet; one bouclé rug, plain with ozite underlay).

Then, there is the smoking room which is covered in cedar wood and furnished with leather armchairs. Here, any fire risk is eliminated by using electrical lighters and good ventilation (smoking cabin: six window curtains; eight leather armchairs; one bouclé rug with ozite underlay). Behind the door of the smoking room there are two passenger rooms with sixteen seats and four tables that can be transformed into sleeping quarters by porters on demand (front passenger room: twelve curtains, rep; four benches between ribs #44 and #47 and four benches between ribs #47 and #50; four pillows as an intermediate layer for sleeping arrangements and four wedge cushions; runner, 70cm wide in moquette tapestry with ozite underlay, a path lengthwise and four paths between the benches; two pairs of curtains on the corridor for the sleeping cabin; two pairs of curtains for the skylights on rib #47). A door concludes these rooms toward the exit with entrance doors on both sides above the sponsons.

View from the front sleeping cabin facing the smoking lounge. In reality, the curtains were meant to maintain discretion. (Photo: DSLR

Corner of the smoking lounge with special wall lamps and a cabin clock. (Photo: DSLR)

Corner of the front passenger cabin behind the smoking lounge with a peak into the next section without curtains. (Photo: DSLR)

Two women are occupied with the sleeping arrangements in the front passenger cabin. Gouache impression by Claus Bergen. (Claus Friedrich Bergen, VG Bild-kunst 2011)

Front passenger cabin with wedge cushions. It can be converted into a sleeping compartment. (Photo: DSLR)

The passenger is taken aback upon entering the elegant, wide, seven-meters-long guest lounge, more a tasteful restaurant than an airplane cabin. The passenger cabin, 24m long by 3.2m average width and 2m height, is furnished in a cozy and modern fashion with seating for sixty-six passengers. If the passenger goes from the entrance toward the rear, he first has the opportunity to discard items in one of two cloakrooms (cloakroom: forty hat and jacket hooks; two umbrella holders and two umbrella bowls; one moquette rug with ozite underlay) and then heads into the large lounge with three sections. A joyful, colorful mood dominates here. A French craquelé material with chinoiserie pattern enlivens the walls with its mannekens, its colors repeat in pastel tones of the plain velour of the seating furniture: in the center lounge red, in both outer lounges green. Doors and parapet panels are in polished cherry tree wood. Coquettish green curtains make the portholes (twenty-eight on each side, 0.42m outer diameter) seem

Lounge of the Do X 1a with Persian rugs and view toward the stern. According to recent research, the photos of the interior furnishings were taken in October 1930 in the assembly hall in Altenrhein. (Photo: DSLR)

Folding table with a typewriter in the lounge. Surely a conveniently contrived photo. If there was even a typewriter on board the Do X, then it was only in the radio or navigation room on the command deck.

somewhat bigger than they really are (large lounge: twenty curtains, decoration material; four benches with velour cover, green; eight armchairs with velour cover, green, eight armchairs with velour cover red; two small armchairs with velour cover red; one entire carpet surface in moquette tapestry, plain brown-gray with ozite underlay). The following two small cabins are set up for eight people each (rear passenger cabin: twelve curtains, rep; eight benches covered with velour; runner, 70cm wide in moquette with ozite underlay, one path lengthwise and four paths between the benches). Farther back on the right is the electric kitchen with water tank, boiler, preparation table and sink unit, cupboard for supplies and tableware. Near it on the left lie two toilets and washrooms (three portholes, 0.23m openings, on each side can be opened, two other closed in baggage

compartment)."So ends Erich Tilgenkamp's description. One material term should still be explained though. Back then it was called "… with ozite underlay." Today this is relatively unknown. The ozite carpet underlay: "A practical luxury for the practical housewife" as the contemporary advertisement announces, is indeed practical but also a luxury. The ad from 1929 continues: "Ozite is a new elastic, felt underlay that gives your carpet luxurious softness and depth. Every step is dampened to silence. Your carpet's life expectancy doubles at the same time because it eliminates friction with the floor." Furthermore, the buyer had to look out for the orange-colored edging of the felt underlay since this was the mark of the original product. The designers of the Do X used ozite underlays to dampen walking on the metal floors.

Fluggasträume (Gesellschaftszimmer) im Dornier - Flugschiff Do X

The living room ambiance with Persian rugs in an airplane still fascinates as much as it did then. Awuko photo postcard #62489 of the interior furnishings of the Do X 1a.

Rear passenger section of the Do X. Elizabeth Bergen probably sat as the model for the woman in fur. Gouache from Claus Bergen for Velhagen & Klasings Monatshefte. (Claus Friedrich Bergen, VG Bildkunst 2011)

Do X Seating Comfort On "Prodomo" Chairs By Walter Knoll

The seating furniture of the Do X has a very interesting story. For the largest and most modern aircraft in the world, "prodomo" armchairs from the upholstered furniture factory Walter Knoll & Co. in Stuttgart were a perfect fit. Improved seating comfort through elastic, steel band springs in the seat and backing of prodomo armchairs allows either light upholstery to be applied or joined with press buttons to the wood or metal frame. After the introduction of the system in 1928, prodomo furniture conquers the market.

Walter Knoll (1877-1971) and his brother Wilhelm take over the "Wilhelm Knoll Leather Chair Factory" from their father in 1907. After residing in the USA for several years, Walter Knoll returns to Stuttgart and founds his own upholstered furniture factory in 1925. By the end of 1930, Walter Knoll manufactures and sells 21,779 pieces of upholstered furniture, 8,300 of which are prodomo models. Eighteen armchairs and twenty two-seaters, also called benches, fly on the Do X and the company's published advertisement "The world flying boat Do X is furnished with prodomo armchairs" enhances the image of the seating system and the company significantly. One exception is the eight club armchairs covered in leather in the flying boat's smoking cabin. They come from Jakob Keller & Co.

Walter Knoll emphasizes the importance of color and formal diversity of the materials used in prodomo chair covers. They are woven according to in-house designs and several patterns are immediately used in the Do X flying boat. Both Italian-made flying boats, Do X 2 and Do X 3, also fly with prodomo armchairs and benches. Alongside some other renowned designers of the prodomo line, the Austrian architect Franz Schuster (1892-1971) is one of the preferred furniture designers at Walter Knoll at the end of the 1920s. The seat designs of the Do X are attributed to him: "... recise edges and smooth curves alternate with one another, wood passing through on the sides functions as a supporting element." The prodomo furniture is comfortable, inexpensive to manufacture and leaves considerable room for designers to experiment. With the colorful variety of cover materials, Walter Knoll accommodates a large customer base and prodomo armchairs catch on within a short time at home and abroad. The company Walter Knoll AG & Co. KG in Herrenberg, south of Stuttgart, is still a fine address for exclusive seating furniture.

What Else Is On Board the Do X?

Light in the flying boat, especially on the passenger deck, accounts for about twenty-eight round deck lamps each at 20cm diameter with chrome-plated base and polished pressed glass. To counter the feared "fire on board" there are seventeen Tetra hand-held fire extinguishers spread throughout the deck of the Do X for fighting incipient fires. The amount of fire extinguishers alone shows the respect paid to this worse case scenario. Tetra extinguishers, with the poisonous extinguishing agent carbon tetrachloride on a pillow of compressed air and a turning valve, are among the top sellers for fighting gasoline fires at that time. However, those who don't want to be killed by inhaling the hydrochloric acid vapors created during the extinguishing must leave the fire area immediately. This explains the small hand extinguishers containing only 0.5 liter in the passenger rooms of the flying boat. This kind of extinguisher was banned in the 1940s due to the many deadly accidents involving Tetra extinguishers.

Some of the installation details on the furnishings list give information about the weight saving installations of the space-defining elements. Primarily, veneered plywood is used for the partition walls, doors and paneling as well as fabric covered, partly arched wood frames for the wall and ceiling lining. Tilgenkamp also notes something fundamental: "When an architect is distressed about construction costs that can't be exceeded, a difficult task exists apart from the construction itself: the relatively low upper limit of the estimated structural weight. While some assignments are concerned about money, the Do X is concerned about weight. We are certain that after finishing the job, the weight restrictions will be strictly maintained, pleasing not only the business but also the builders in Altenrhein." Incidentally, the two Persian rugs in the lounge, one 12m long, 70cm wide bouclé runner and three Billian clocks by the Zurich manufacturer (one in the smoking room and two in the passenger rooms) were all on borrowed for the Do X. Otherwise they decorate the executive offices of DoFlug AG in Altenrhein.

Only Half As Much
– The Furnishings of the Do X 2

The building contract for the two Italian flying boats lands on Claude Dornier's desk sometime in 1928. In the beginning of 1929, the Do X 2 has progressed quite far and the Italian customer receives the description of the cabin furnishings on the main deck by mail. They differ considerably from the Do X 1a. The description reads: "… two furnished travel cabins, each for eight passengers, a salon with eight armchairs, a kitchen, a sleeping room for the captain and pilots, a sleeping room with four hammocks for the crew and two lavatories for passengers (women and men) as well as two lavatories for the crew. In the two travel cabins, a total of eight benches are installed, each with two seats. These benches are upholstered over steel springs and have seat, backing and head cushions. For sick bags and newspapers, pockets are sewn onto the armrests. Two opposing benches can be arranged into two horizontal daybeds by pulling out the seat cushions. A ceiling lamp is provided for every four passengers. The folding tables attached to the wall can be attached to the ceiling. Baggage nets are installed above the benches for holding smaller pieces of luggage. The wall coverings below the windows are made of durable wood, and they are washable. The upper wall contains a fabric covering.

In the salon, two round tables with eight armchairs are fastened to the floor so that every seat can be reached without trouble. Table and chairs are made from the finest rattan. The tabletop is made of wood. The wall coverings are designed like those in the travel cabins, only in different colors. A ceiling lamp is installed above every table for the room ligh-

Until now the only known photo of the Do X 2's furnishings according to the description from January 29, 1929.

ting. On one side of the kitchen, a cupboard is installed to hold the kitchenware, while table tops and shelves attached to the walls help for serving and discarding meals.

In the sleeping room for the captain and pilots, a bed is installed on the port side and starboard side. Near each bed is a small bin for clothing and laundry, which also serves as a seat. For the crew, a total of four hammocks are provided – two on each side of the room, one stacked above the other."

A contemporary photo documents the installation of these furnishings. But apparently they did not please the Italians. A whole series of design drawings by Emil Rau for the redesign of the Do X 2 seems to match the layout of the Do X 1a. His plans from December 1930 have very little in common with the first description from Manzell on January 29, 1929. Which interior layout the Do X 2 will grace after the ferry flight over the Alps to its future home port La Spezia-Cadimare is still an unanswered question.

The arc to today, concerning the furnishings of the Do X, spans a remarkable story that can be read on the Internet. In 2009, Do X specialist and author Jörg-M. Hormann receives a particularly tough nut to crack from Atelier Brückner in Stuttgart, who set up the new Dornier Museum in Friedrichshafen. On July 14, 2009, the Nordwest Zeitung reports: "Do X Airplane Chairs Made in Rastede." "Where can we find two Do X armchairs?" The interior designers of the new Dornier Museum in Friedrichshafen turned to Do X specialist Jörg-Michael Hormann from Rastede with this question. A life-size replica of the Do X passenger cabin was developed for the museum on Lake Constance, which opened on July 24, 2009. The twelve-engine flying boat, the largest aircraft of its time and a technical sensation of aviation from 1929 to 1933, is a very special topic in the new museum. Claude Dornier and his Do X inspired people in the late-1920s, and on its German tour in the summer of 1932, hundreds of thousands saw it fly by or visited it at its stopovers in Norderney, Wilhelmshaven and Bremen. During an air raid on Berlin in 1944, the flying boat, with its complete, very luxurious furnishings, was destroyed. It was too large to be evacua-

Until now the only known photo of the Do X 2's furnishings according to the description from January 29, 1929.

ted from the German Museum's aviation collection. And now, two of the Do X armchairs had to be found. Eighty years after installing the furnishings into the flying boat in the Swiss town of Altenrhein, the chances of finding these original armchairs somewhere were low. The first search attempt was at the address of the former manufacturer in Zurich. The furniture factory of J. Keller & Co of course no longer exists, but a legal succession states: "Why are you just getting to this now? Three years ago, we completely emptied our warehouse of designs and blueprints due to a lack of space! I believe some things from the Do X were also present." These are moments that museum staff fear the most. But what's the use. Searching for something similar or recreating them remain the only solutions to the problem, and due to the limited time, the decision was made to build a replica of the armchairs. But who can do this? And, above all, it must be done in close consultation. The model is a black and white photo and a single concrete amount of literature. The chairs have a backrest height of exactly 80cm. 'Well Mr. Hormann, make it then!' Due to limited time and tight coordination, Hormann considered a carpenter and an upholsterer in Rastrede. Dieter Kieler and Ralf Oltmanns were truly amazed over this quite unusual job, but from a handcraft standpoint it did not seem all that complicated. There was, however, a need for thorough discussion about the details regarding measurements, form and colors. Dieter Kieler built a 1:1 model and Ralf Oltmanns took care of the appropriate cover fabric. And then: 'Only the look of the armchair on the photo counts.' It didn't matter whether the legs were unusually short and the upholstery was adorned with too many buttons. In the museum, no one will sit down on the ensemble because the alarms will go off immediately."

Open cupboards bursting with activity. A look into the galley of the Do X 1a, which was equipped exclusively with electrical devices. (Photo: DSLR)

Grandiose dining was hardly possible on the filigree folding tables in the salon of the Do X. (Photo: DSLR)

Fine Porcelain For the Flying Boat From Altenrhein

With the foreseeable completion of his Do X 1, the furnishing question hangs in the air for Claude Dornier. The designers have nothing to use for comparison. The only guide can be the features and operation of passenger spaces in airships, like the zeppelins. Developing something lightweight and cost efficient is new territory for those involved in the creative process.

The flying boat is not intended to be a luxury restaurant for sixty-six passengers, even though this rumor is spread by some contemporary reports and especially by the well-known photos of the passenger deck furnishings with a view into the salon. On November 5, 1930, the Do X begins its flight around the world. The priority of this experimental flight, or official ferry flight, was to bring the Do X over the Atlantic in order to begin a flying boat era in the USA. Dornier in Friedrichshafen has high hopes for the utilization of the flying boat under license, under patent use or even as a charter for commercial air services in the "New World." Claude Dornier has also been contractually involved with U.S. automaker General Motors, who want to get in on airplane manufacturing. The global economic crisis ruins these plans in the early-1930s.

More than three years beforehand, everything looked different. Lucrative transatlantic trade is the focus of aircraft transport strategists. At Deutsche Luft Hansa AG in Berlin, profitability calculations for a commercial trans-oceanic airline using Do X flying boats were already being generated in May 1927. Erhard Milch (1892-1972), director of Deutsche Luft Hansa at the time, has a plan in place to realize this vision with six flying boats and the appropriate personel at an expense of almost twenty million Reichsmark. The Dornier people in Manzell followed this thinking with great interest. Dornier wants to demonstrate what the comforts of future air travel will look like in their giant aircraft. In the summer of 1930, a well-designed passenger deck is built according to contemporary taste in the middle of the three-story fuselage of the Do X. It is ever so elegant,

like the former airship cabin of the LZ 127 Graf Zeppelin. Gentlemen who represent the manufacturer of fine porcelain, from which the passengers of the Graf Zeppelin dine, inquire about the kitchenware of the flying boat.

Here's the story: While reading a newspaper on vacation, Michael Heinrich, co-owner of the porcelain factory Heinrich & Co in Selb, Bavaria, learns about the installation of a kitchen on board the LZ 127. In his mind's eye he envisions the chain of events: where there is cooking, there is also serving … and for that, one needs porcelain … preferably from him … dining service on Heinrich porcelain! He immediately travels to Friedrichshafen and introduces his designs. It doesn't take long for him to convince the men from Luftschiffbau Zeppelin, who have already chosen a heavy weight hotel porcelain. His light and primarily contemporary household porcelain brings him the exclusive, prestigious contract, as the commemorative volume for 50th anniversary of the Heinrich porcelain company notes in 1946. During the furnishing of the Graf Zeppelin airship too, builders are skimpy about every kilogram. In 1929 a new inquiry comes from Lake Constance, this time from DoFlug AG. With mixed feelings, Michael Heinrich demonstrates a sense of family and sends the order to his in-laws, former co-owners of Heinrich & Co, Johann Adolf Gräf (1869-1926) and Friedrich Krippner (1875-1930). After Adolf Gräf's death, the porcelain factory Gräf & Krippner (G&K) has economic problems and urgently needs family assistance.

Retired from Heinrich in 1906, Gräf and Krippner operate their own factory across from the main building of the Heinrich porcelain factory in Selb. From just two kilns and a cobalt oven, the Gräf & Krippner porcelain factory was created. The main focus of production is hotel ware, coffee and dinner service. But even the Do X contract from Altenrhein can't really help. Heinrich & Co. buys the porcelain factory from Gräf & Krippner in July 1929, changes its porcelain mark and continues to produce until 1932. The Gräf & Krippner brand comes to an end as a result of the global economic crisis. Michael Heinrich closes the factory, while production in the main factory continues. This small company history digression is important because the production of the Do X porcelain falls right in this time of upheaval, which is reflected by the different porcelain marks.

First Porcelain From Gräf & Krippner

Featuring the decoration design by Marcel Dornier (1893-1988), Claude Dornier's youngest brother, and the logo for DoFlug AG also designed by him, Gräf & Krippner make their first delivery to Altenrhein in September 1930. It is coffee and dinner service made of porcelain that is quite dissimilar to standard porcelain for gastronomy. It involves an exclusively decorated form series from the available manufacture of G&K. Compared to the quality of more sophisticated household service, the Do X porcelain is downright luxurious. "… The body is exceptionally thin-walled and furnished with an etched gold rim and gold staffage. The pointed handle and the slightly stepped walls of cups and plates are totally consistent with the stylish form designs of household porcelain in the 1920s … With its tiered plate rims and cup walls, which are accented by decorative lines, and its angular, curvy handles, the service is reminiscent of the fashionable porcelain of Art Deco." Susanne Träger writes this in her exhibition catalog Around the World In 80 Cups, describing the model line A for the coffee and mocha service of the Do X porcelain.

The A porcelain differs in many details from the B model line, which conforms more to the functionality of hotel porcelain. Stackability or the special lids and the round handle construction with thumb rest are typical with the B porcelain. This model line takes the shape of a coffee or tea service. All parts of the Do X dinner service have characteristics of the B porcelain. It differs from common hotel porcelain in the strength of its body. The B porcelain's form is not the usual minimum double, but as thin as possible and simply weight-minimized. There are no differences in decoration between A and B. The name designation of A and B porcelain is only a linguistic auxiliary construction since the G&K design names of this form series is still unknown. The archives of Gräf & und Krippner are lost.

Coffee cup with saucer from the Do X porcelain's model line A.

Filigree cup with cover from model line B.

The mocha cup from the Do X porcelain has a height of 4cm, in contrast to the coffee cup with 5.7cm.

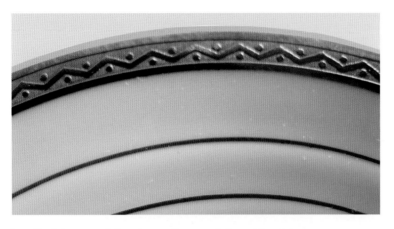

Detail of the use of line decoration on plates without logo.

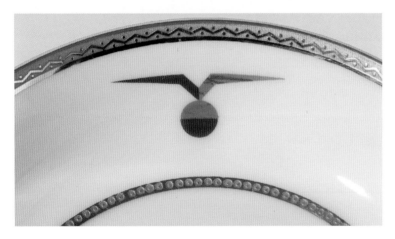

DoFlug logo and decorative strips on the Do X porcelain were designed by Marcel Dornier. (Photo: Hermann Historica)

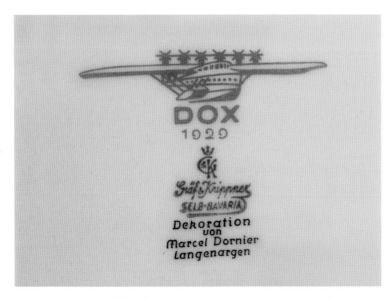

First backstamp of the Do X porcelain produced until 1930, here on the underside of a plate.

The Do X porcelain marking is made using the underglaze technique with three back stamps on all pieces. Large parts of the first Do X porcelain delivery still show the G&K back stamp of the 1920s. The green stamp (1st form) depicts G & K as ciphers overlapping one another underneath a crown, and below it, Gräf & Krippner written in cursive and SELB-BAVARIA in block letters, connected by a swerved line. Above it in gold is the stylized flying boat and DOX in capitals with the year of its first flight: 1929. Below the G&K backstamp, four lines of black type read: "Decoration, by, Marcel Dornier, Langenargen." Backstamps with Marcel Dornier above and the golden Do X below also exist.

This does not fit on the bottom of a cup and only "DOX 1929" remains from the golden flying boat. If the lavish decoration of salmon and gold lines on smaller plates does not leave enough space toward the rim, G&K also does without the DoFlug AG logo. The stylized bird's wings above a globe, in gold-red orange (RAL 2001) color variation, are found on most service pieces. One interpretation of the logo is that it is the view of the horizon through the porthole of a flying boat, with the wings of a high-wing aircraft symbolized by two stylized bird's wings. Both constructional elements of Dornier aircraft.

Some of the details about the first delivery are owed to the foresight of Horst Merz, pilot and commander of the Do X in spring 1933. The flight captain of Luft Hansa has a complete G&K coffee and dinner service delivered to his home in September 1930, and it has been kept by his daughter until today.

In 2009 she is able to clarify some facts that had been a source of irritation for years. "What was still left of our Do X tableware after the war, was decoratively placed on a table in our house in the 1970s and photographed for the Dornier company. By the way, the silverware there was not part of the Do X tableware."

Joachim Wachtel shows this same picture in his book ‚Claude Dornier, ein Leben für die Luftfahrt' (Eng: 'Claude Dornier: A Life of Aviation') from 1989. On page 172, deep and flat

Second form of the backstamp in the period from 1930 to 1932, here on the bottom of a cup.

Last form of the backstamp from 1931, with the anniversary laurel. (Photo: Hermann Historica)

dinner plates and voluminous lid tureens are pictured. The flying boat is indeed equipped with a small kitchen for limited food preparation, but the tables with such large service pieces on the filigree folding tables of the passenger deck seems pretty adventurous.

Just like the Graf Zeppelin porcelain from Heinrich & Co, Gräf & Krippner produce its Do X porcelain not just exclusively for Dornier, but also for the general porcelain market. In well-run specialist shops, anyone can stock up. Despite bombing during the war, sporadic pieces of porcelain that were able to survive until today without damages appear over and over again, which cannot be said for the large mass of the original furnishings of the flying boat from the fall of 1930.

Backstamp of the first form on the bottom of an eggcup. (Photo: Hermann Historica)

The "set table" at the home of Horst Merz in the 1970s. Promotional photo for Dornier GmbH. (Photo: Works Archives Dornier GmbH, EADS)

But DoFlug said thank you on September 24, 1930 and confirmed receipt of the porcelain with a letter to the management of the Gräf & Krippner porcelain factory: "… If we were also to assume that you, because of the special experiences that you have made in delivering porcelain for the airship Graf Zeppelin, would deliver something first-class, then we are pleasantly surprised in every way about the successful solution to the task assigned to you to create a suitable porcelain for our intentions." Printed as a facsimile in a full-page G&K advertisement in the first Do X special edition of the Swiss AERO REVUE from 1931. The use of the G&K backstamp for the 25th anniversary of the company is interesting here, as it appears in a later delivery of the Do X porcelain. The year 1931, the 25th anniversary of the company founded in 1906, is purely a brand anniversary since G&K had already merged with Heinrich & Co. in 1929.

On November 5, 1930, the Do X's ferry flight to the USA begins. The flying boat is supposed to travel to Lisbon with some stopovers in Europe to present the largest aircraft in the world. After a short rebuilding phase and furnishing for the Atlantic crossing, Claude Dornier plans to let the Do X fly to New York via the Azores and Bermuda. The time of the year for the operation, with bad weather throughout Europe and poor flying conditions over the central Atlantic, proves the skeptics right. It won't work, but for entirely different reasons than what is read in the press.

The Tableware Disaster on the Gironde

The following describes the fate of the first set of porcelain on the flying boat. On Monday morning November 17, 1930, during its European leg, the Do X lies on the Gironde near Bordeaux. Sightseeing flights with extra passengers who have arrived from Paris are scheduled for the day. At 11:39 am, the Do X takes off for a third time that day toward the Lac d'Hourtin Navy station. There are only six passengers on board.

After a tour over Bordeaux, the weather worsens. The clouds hang so deep that the destination can't be approached. After returning to the take-off stretch on the Gironde near Pouillac there is a problem for the splashdown and for pilot Horst Merz:

"… What a horrible surprise. The wind changes suddenly and is blowing exactly opposite to the very strong currents of the Gironde. The old song of the sea pilots begins. How should I land in these condi-

Details of the porcelain Do X coffee cup.
(Photo: Hermann Historica)

tions? Against the current or against the wind? I decide to splashdown with a tail wind against the current.

I set the machine down softly only to be caught by a tail wind in the same moment and we are forced forward into the water. In a fraction of a second, she took a square hook to the port side. The force of the rotation caused a small disorder. The machine had to withstand an enormous amount of pressure during this extraordinary test of strength. Immediate inspection revealed that nothing on or in the flying boat suffered damage other than our beautiful porcelain, which flew as debris by the shovel load through the small porthole in the kitchen into the yellow flow of the Gironde."

A serious mistake for the porcelain as other pilots later criticize: "It is always landed against the wind, no matter which way the current flows!" The tableware disaster on the Gironde is among the reasons why porcelain of the first shipment to the Do X with the first form of G&K's backstamp is very rare today.

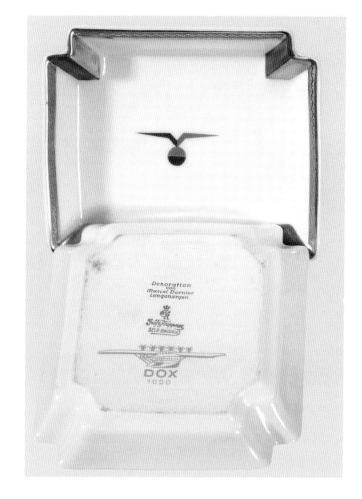

All of the known copies of the Do X porcelain ashtrays have the backstamp of the first shipment by Gräf & Krippner from 1930. (Photo: Hermann Historica)

Soon there will be warm sausages! Folding table set with glasses, plates, silverware and mustard pot. This kind of glassware was also on board the Zeppelin airships. (Photo: DSLR)

A replacement has to be delivered by the porcelain factory as soon as possible since the cost-saving planners at Dornier didn't order large quantities. The various parts of porcelain are reproduced with a new G&K backstamp, which takes weeks. After the takeover by Heinrich & Co in 1930, this second shipment, primarily the coffee service, has the new backstamp (2nd form): a green stamp in underglaze featuring a striding lion on a pedestal with a crown on its head and a star above its paw, and under it Gräf & Krippner written in cursive as well as SELB BAVARIA in block letters. The other stamps are identical to parts of the first shipment, where the Marcel Dornier stamp appears on top and the DOX stamp on bottom. An arbitrariness of space takes place during the production in order to place as many relatively large-sized stamps on occasionally cramped space. When and where the replacement porcelain of the second shipment reaches the new world on the flying boat's odyssey is

unclear because all plans surrounding the events of the flying boat are disrupted. Presumably, it doesn't arrive on board until June 1931 in Natal, Brazil.

After the Do X arrives in Lisbon, shortly before the flyover to the shipyard in Cadiz to prepare it for the Atlantic crossing, the portside of the flying boat's wings burns off on November 29, 1930. The accident with a dry tarp, which ignites on the hot exhaust of an auxiliary motor, has grave consequences. On one hand, it shows that the wing panel covering, contrary to all assurances by the linen and paint manufacturer is not fire-resistant. On the other hand, the repair and resulting time delays create costs that would have nearly spelled the end of the Do X ferry flight during the intense effects of the global economic crisis.

The route changes born out of necessity turn the planned three-week ferry flight with an Atlantic crossing into a half-year odyssey.

On June 5, 1931, the Do X splashes down before the Brasilian port city Natal. The South Atlantic has been flown over and the furniture and all dismantled installations come back on board during a fourteen day stopover. They manage to get it there stowed in boxes in the hold of a cargo steamer. For the planned onward flights, first to Rio de Janeiro and from there to New York, the Do X transforms itself from "flying fuel tank" back into a commercial aircraft with the help of its crew. Meanwhile, the G&K porcelain from the second shipment had to have arrived in Natal. It is desperately needed now because under the direction of the Syndicato Condor, the South American offshoot of Deutsche Luft Hansa, a passsenger flight operation will include service on board. The leg from Rio de Janeiro to New York from August 5th to 27th, 1931 constitutes the future of air transport services that Claude Dornier hopes for with his flying boat. This includes flying scheduled day trips with paying and alternating passengers as well as airmail on board to be shipped and delivered. In-flight service is of course also a part of it, which steward Krause is responsible for from Rio. In Sao Luiz, he even wangles a complete dinner for the passengers. There is roasted chicken with peas, potatoes, carrots, fruit salad and coffee, which receives considerable approval. Whether it is served on fine Do X dinner service from Gräf & Krippner, is still not clear.

The last shipment of porcelain takes place after the flying boat returns to Berlin in June 1932. During the first leg of the Germany tour, paying passengers are allowed on board and in-flight service is provided to them. This service is limited, however, to alcoholic drinks and coffee or tea. The dinnerware has indeed been produced by G&K in 1931, but it stays on the ground and doesn't travel with the Do X. The porcelain manufactured during the brand's anniversary year 1931, contains a special G&K backstamp (3rd form). The familiar lion of the second form is surrounded by two laurel branches and a round shield with the number 25 where the laurels meet, in green underglaze. As the Do X comes to an end as a means of air travel, after an interlude lasting a few days under management of Deutsche Luft Hansa in the spring of 1933, the Do X porcelain is lost without a trace. Tableware that has survived almost eighty years until today after the "German Century" with its devastating war is a true rarity. For decades it was very quiet around the Do X porcelain. There were only a few places where the porcelain could be seen up close: the early Dornier Museum in the Neues Schloss in Meersburg on Lake Constance, which opened in 1970, and the Altenrhein Flight Museum on the Swiss shores of Lake Constance. Black and white decoration photos from 1930, which show tables set in the salon of the flying boat and photos of the bar and the kitchen, also document the porcelain's variety in specialist literature.

Original and rare. Mustard pots with decorated saucers and a toothpick dispenser from the Do X porcelain. (Photo: Nachlass Keppeler)

An Exciting Year For Do X Porcelain

1997 is an important year for Do X porcelain. In the spring, the German Porcelain Museum in Selb presents the special exhibit Around the World in 80 Cups, which also shows pieces from the Do X porcelain. The highlight of the pieces shown turns out to be very interesting. Richard Heinrich, family member of the porcelain dynasty Heinrich from Selb, Bavaria, makes the porcelain from his private collection available on loan.

In the fall, two lots of a porcelain bundle from the 35th auction of the Herman Historica auction house in Munich draw the attention of interested Dornier people. Cups, saucers and lunch plates of a "six piece tea service" and a "six piece mocha service" from the estate of Do X commander Friedrich Christiansen come up for auction on October 25, 1997. Acquired by a representative of Deutsche Aerospace AG (DASA), the porcelain remains in Munich in a storage cupboard of the company, which becomes the European Aeronautic Defence and Space Company (EADS) in 2000. Meersburg receives complementing pieces from this purchase on loan and EADS makes the porcelain available on loan for some special exhibitions. Most recently for the exhibition From Zeppelin to Airbus – Aviation in Northwest Germany in the 20th Century, which also used the Do X as a central theme. In the summer and fall of 2008, Northern Germany marvels at the rare porcelain in Emden and on Norderney. Around the same time, the planning for the new Dornier Museum in Friedrichshafen results in reconsidering the museum landscape on Lake Constance. EADS closes its Dornier Museum in the Neues Schloss, much to the disappointment of the City of Meeresburg, and hands the inventory over to the new Dornier Museum at the airport in Friedrichshafen. The new museum opens in 2009 and it is a hit with its Do X porcelain. Again it is the Herman Historica auction house in Munich

Model line B of the Do X porcelain. Details of the coffee pot.

that announces a remarkable shipment for its 57th spring auction. Almost 150 pieces of Do X porcelain from the USA are to be auctioned in Munich. The highlight is stated in the estate of Dr. Erich Tilgenkamp (1898-1966). The Swiss journalist and aviation author is the press chief on the crew of the Do X on the European leg from Lake Constance to Lisbon in November 1930. But in the auction hall on April 28, 2009 around 4:00pm there is no sign of crackling excitement. Lots 5718 and 5720 with seventy-nine porcelain pieces comes to a total price of 15,500 Euros and is sold to a bidder without a fight. Vendors and auctioneers decide to halve the delivered bundle and spread it over two auctions. The first round is rather frustrating for both. Customs alone has already collected 6,000 Euro with the shipment from the USA and now the auction doesn't go above the initial bid. A bargain for the buyer, who had sent a stalking horse into the hall.

Assortment of Do X dinner service pieces from the estate of Erich Tilgenkamp, the press officer of the Do X's European leg. (Photo: Hermann Historica)

Do X plate variations in stacks. View of the Tilgenkamp bundle during the auction in Munich. (Photo: Hermann Historica)

Coffee pot and sugar bowl from the model line A. In the center a Do X porcelain coffee pot from the model line B. (Photo: Hermann Historica)

Many forms of the Do X porcelain in the Munich auction, such as plates, bowls, serving plates, saucers or lidded tureens from the "Tilgenkamp bundle," ultimately prove the existence of the dinner service, which probably never flew on the Do X.

One inconsistency with the description of a cup type from the Do X porcelain is corrected in 2009. With the "Christiansen bundle" from 1997, and occasionally appearing in other collections, is the Do X mocha cup. Of course mocha can also be enjoyed from the delicate Lady Curzon cup (recreated stack cup of the B model line for the popular turtle soup), but the genuine Do X mocha cup has a different appearance. It is the scaled-down format of the Do X coffee cup. In the 1984 book from Lutz Tittel, 100 Jahre Claude Dornier, Metallflugzeugbau 1914-1969 (Eng: '100 Years of Claude Dornier, Metal Aircraft Construction 1914-1969'), coffee and mocha cups are pictured next to one another on page 68 for comparison. One of these mocha cups, with matching saucer, runs through an Ebay auction at the end of September 2009 and finds

a new home for 370 Euro. The previous owner, a porcelain collector from Friedrichshafen, had managed to grab the absolutely rare ensemble at a flea market in Lindau a few years ago.

But it gets even better. After the opening of the Dornier Museum in Friedrichshafen on July 23, 2009, with the presentation of the reproduction of the Do X cabin segment and the former porcelain exhibits from Meersburg, visitors' interest in the topic increases. Some of them remember seeing pieces of the porcelain in their household cupboards. One ensemble beats all others by far. A Do X porcelain tray with three cups and four saucers, creamer, sugar bowl and coffee pots with lids, all in excellent condition, amazes the museum personnel. All pieces were manufactured by Gräf & Krippner in 1931 and belong to the same model line B. It's a true museum ensemble, which was purchased for the Dornier Museum at a reasonable price by the Dornier Foundation for Aerospace (DSLR). During the special exhibition Dawn of a New World – The Do X and Transatlantic Travel in 2011, the ensemble is presented to the public for the first time.

Cup comparison between coffee and mocha cups of the Do X porcelain.

On all Do X porcelain cups, the DoFlug logo is only visible to right-handed users. Here a mocha cup with logo visible to left-handers.

A unique tray with harmonious ensemble of Do X porcelain from model line B. From the collection of the Dornier Museum in Friedrichshafen.

Unusual tableware pieces from the Do X porcelain. Reversible cup, usable as an eggcup or for other purposes, always with an upright logo. In the middle, the rare table vase with Do X decoration. (Photo: Hermann Historica)

Now to the second act of the "Tilgenkamp bundle" auction. The bidding begins on the remaining two lots of Do X porcelain on October 8, 2009 in the fall auction by Hermann Historica. For lot 831, with forty-seven pieces, the bidding begins with 9,000 Euros and ends at 15,000 Euros for the already

Backstamp from 1930 on the bottom of the Do X table vase.

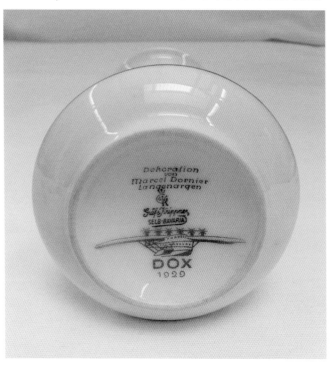

experienced, and again present, stalking horse. Apparently frightened off by the employees and the unexpected bid amount, she misses the immediately following lot 832. Consisting of twenty pieces with coffee pots, teapots, sugar bowls and more remarkable service pieces, the bidding begins at 5,500 Euros. The hammer falls at 12,500 Euros. The lot goes to a telephone bidder who is unknown to this day. Four of the five lots from the "Tilgenkamp bundle" go to the buyers from Munich, which is comforting for the interested observers. The Do X porcelain is back from the USA, remains in Munich and, in accordance with the constellation of things, is available to the Dornier Museum in Friedrichshafen for exhibition purposes.

Again the USA comes into play in this matter. Drury Wood, former Dornier test pilot of the Do 31, which was designed to take-off and land vertically, reports from his home in Oregon about his experiences with the experimental airplane in the late-1960s. A delighted reader of his article introduces herself on the telephone as the daughter of Alfons Keppler (1895-1947), the former business director of DoFlug. In the conversation, Keppler's daughter tells of her father's estate, which is divided among his three daughters and also includes some pieces of the Do X porcelain. In a nutshell, twelve pieces of her porcelain find a new exhibition site in the Aviation Museum of Günter Leonhardt in Laatzen (near Hannover). The hope is that this information awakens the discovery instinct for Do X porcelain that is still slumbering out there somewhere.

"Cold Splendor" of a Menu

The Do X's famous food and drink menu has a chilly beginning. Its food selection only offers a "cold plate." It is probably put together from the food offerings of various companies who had to be involved during the round-the-world flight of the Do X 1a. The compilation suggests that it involves business offers to DoFlug in order to use the Do X for their own image propaganda. The food on the menu has cost DoFlug nothing, and, in exchange, the exaggerated company credits of the suppliers are too prominent. With some, a lot of research is required today to find out what each company actually supplied then. Bahlsen cookies, Maggi and Wrigley's chewing gum are among the few known companies. For the "fine wines" on the drink menu, those of quality and renown are also represented. On contemporary photos from the bar, the noticeable placement can be partly read. The frequent mention of the outstanding selection in the bar from various travel impressions of Do X flights suggests that ample provisions are always looked after here. So of course it is also mentioned that on the flight from Cuba to Miami, during prohibition in the U.S., all supplies were reluctantly left behind, much to the joy of ground personnel in Antilla, Cuba.

The flag symbolism on the front side of the food and drink menus is irritating at first glance. The flags of Switzerland and the USA as the first and last of the journey are logical. Even the imperial merchant flag with the black-red-gold of the Weimar Republic, as a result of fierce flag disputes in the years before the flight of the Do X 1a, has its reason. The German Reich has ordered and paid for the Do X and thus shows fanciers the ownership situation. The Dutch colors still make sense since the first flight on the way to the new world goes to Amsterdam on November 5, 1930. But what is with the Scandinavian colors? Invalid planning outpaces the printing date of the cover for the Do X drink menu. After the installation of the new engine unit, testing is planned with a flight via Travemünde to Denmark, Sweden, Norway and a return flight over the Müggelsee near Berlin. Nothing comes of it, though, because the delivery of the Curtiss engines and the installation and conversion of the engine system is constantly delayed. Once the oil cooler problems are cleared in October 1930, the flight to the USA has to begin immediately in order to fulfill the contract with General Motors. For the so-called European leg, the flags are correct: England, Spain, Portugal again. But in the potpourri of problems for the Do X 1a in November 1930, the food and drink menus are of little concern.

Cold splendor. The only form of the food and drink menu on board the Do X 1a, and an original bottle of Kessler sparkling wine with its original label from 1930.

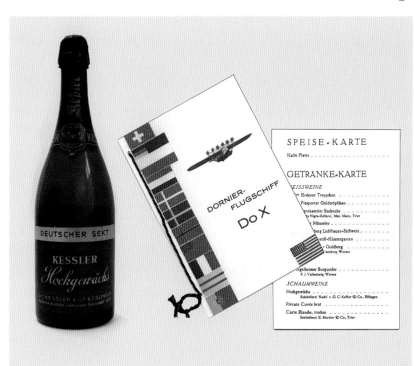

Do X Porcelain Data

Coffee and Mocha Service From Model Line A

Position	Form	Decor sequence from top to bottom or from the inside to the outside (plates)	Height mm	B x L mm	ø mm	Weight g	Stamp ▲■●
01	Coffee cup large (table setting)	Outside: WS 3, Lr 3, Kr. (handle: gold), Inside: Jb., logo	57-58	104	86-92		■
02a	Saucer large(table setting)	1.TfS. Lg., 3 TfS, Lr 3, Jb. (no Logo) ■	21	152	110-114		●
02b	Saucer large	1 TfS., 3 TfS Lr 3, Jb. (no logo) ●	21	152	ca. 114		
03	Lunch plate (table setting)	3 TfS Lr 3, Jb. (no logo)	20	203	ca. 232		
04	Mocha cup small	Outside:WS 3, Lr 3, wide Lg. (handle: gold) Inside: Jb., logo	40	72	ca. 40		▲
05	Saucer small	1.TfS Lg., Lr. 3, Jb. (no logo)	17	106	ca. 60		▲
06	Coffee pot	Lg., Jb., logo, WS 4, Bb. handle: golden, spout edge with golden line and end drops	265				
06b	Lid	Knob: gold, Lg.2, Jb.					
07	Creamer	Outside: Lg., Jb., logo (both sides), WS 4, Bb., handle: gold, spout edge with golden line and end drops	125-130	60-90	264		●
08	Sugar bowl	Lg., Jb., logo, WS 4, Bb. two golden handles	120				
08b	Lid	Knob: gold Lg.2, Zb					
09	Bowl small (candies, etc.)	Outside, Lg., inside: Jb., without logo, Lr	25	70	30		▲

Simple, thin-walled bodies furnished with etched gold rims and gold staffage. The pointed, gold-colored handle and slightly stepped walls of pots, cups and plates fits the fashionable form design of household porcelain from the 1920s. The stepped plate shoulders and cup walls are accented by line decoration in gold and red. The prominent, gold plated lid knob is also concise. With its curvy, angular handles, the service is reminiscent of the fashionable porcelain designs of Art Deco.

Tea or Coffee Service From Model Line B

Position	Form	Decor sequence from top to bottom or from the inside to the outside (plates)	Height mm	B x L mm	ø mm	Weight g	Stamp ▲■●
15	Stackable cups (table setting 1 or 2)	Jb., logo (only front side with handle to the right), Bb. handle: golden with thumb rest	40		56	44-45	■
16 a	Saucer (table setting 1)	TfS 1, Lr., logo, Jb. ▲			110		
16 b	Saucer (table setting 2)	1.TfS Lg., 2.TfS Lr., no logo, Jb. ■			110	58-68	
17 a	Lunch plate (table setting 1)	TfS 1, Bb., logo, Zb (also dessert plate)			180		●
17 b	Lunch plate (table setting 2)	TfS 1, Bb., no logo, Zb			180		
18 a	Pot	Jb., logo (both sides), Bb., WS 1, Lr., Lg., handle: golden with thumb rest, spout gold plated on top side	145		110 top		
18 b	Lid	Knob: red tip, 2 x profiled white-gold, Lr.	55		90		
19	Creamer large	Jb., logo (both sides), Bb., Lr., Lg., handle: golden with thumb rest	115		73 top		
20 a	Sugar bowl large	Jb., logo (both sides), Bb., Lr., Lg., two handles: golden with thumb rests	72		100 top		
20 b	Lid sugar bowl	Knob: red tip, 2 x profiled white-gold, Lr	40		75		■
21 a	Small pot	Jb., logo (both sides), Bb., WS 1, Lr., Lg., handle: golden with thumb rest, spout	ca. 110		70-90	228-246	▲
21 b	Lid (serving set)	Knob: red tip, 2 x profiled white-gold, Lr.	40		60	36-42	▲
22	Creamer small (serving set)	Jb., logo (both sides), Bb., Lr., Lg. handle: golden with thumb rest	73		55	60-76	▲
23 a	Sugar bowl small	Jb., logo (both sides), Bb., Lr., Lg., two handles: golden with thumb rest	60		80-92	160	■
23 b	Lid	Knob: red tip, 2 x profiled white-gold, Lr	40		62	46	

One and a half-fold body with etched gold rims and gold staffage. Round, gold-colored handle with white thumb rest, decorated with two short, red end lines. Bulbous, downward proceeding lines. The one stepped teller shoulders and cup walls are accented by line decoration. The alternating white and gold profiled lid knob with red tip is concise.

Dinner Service Model Line B Only

Position	Form	Decor sequence from top to bottom or from the inside to the outside (plates)	Height mm	B x L mm	ø mm	Weight g	Stamp ■ ●
							▲
25	Dinner plate	TfS 1, Bb., logo, Zb	25		255	458	●
26	Soup plate	TfS 1, Bb., logo, Zb	35		250	418	●
27	Breakfast plate (lunch plate)	TfS 1, Bb., logo, Zb	20		203	234	●
28	Dessert plate	TfS 1, Bb., logo, Zb			180		
29	Dessert bowl	Bb., logo, Zb			130		
30 a	Lidded tureen large	Lg., Jb., logo (both sides), Bb., base, (Lr, until 1930) Lg., two handles with thumb rest	200 m. D.		260		
30 b	Lid	Knob: red tip, 2 x profiled white-gold, Lr.3, Zb					
31 a	Lidded tureen small	Lg., Jb., logo (both sides), Bb., base, (Lr, until 1930) Lg., two handles with thumb rest	200 m. D.		260		
31 b	Lid	Knob: red tip, 2 x profiled white-gold, Lr.3, Zb					
32	Bowl	Inside: Bb., logo. Jb.			235		
33	Sauce boat 1tlg	Lg on the rim, Jb., logo (both sides under the spout) Bb., Lg., base: oval bowl attached with Jb., two handles: golden, with white thumb rest	100	230 x 150			
34	Platter round	Inside: Bb., logo. Zb			300		
35	Serving tray oval	Inside: Bb., logo. Zb	30	220 x 250			
36	Serving tray oval	Inside: Bb., logo. Zb	30	220 x 300		640	▲

Exclusive household porcelain with etched gold and gold staffage. Round, gold-colored handles with white thumb rests, decorated with two short, red end lines. The one-stepped plate shoulders are accented by line decoration. Prominent are the alternating white-gold, profiled lid knobs with red tips and the logo found on every piece.

Tableware

Position	Form	Decor sequence from top to bottom or from the inside to the outside (plates)	Height mm	B x L mm	ø mm	Weight g	Stamp ▲ ■ ●
45	Eggcup/drinking cup	Eggcup: rim, Bb., logo, Lr., Jb. (backstamp on inside ▲) Drinking cup: Jb., logo, Lr., Bb., porcelain rim (seen from the front with each use, the logo is situated in the top part and is upside down on the back side of lower part).	105		27-70,1	122	▲
46	Table vase	Rim, WS 2 with Lg., WS 1 with Lr., Belly: Jb., logo, Bb., base: Lg	160-165		35-90	206-212	▲
47 a	Lidded container	Lid topview: logo, Jb., Lg. Container: Bb., Lr.	40		67	234	
47 b	Lid	TfS 1, Bb., Logo, Zb			180		
48	Ashtray	Logo, Jb., corners alternate gold and red	15	114 x 104		104	▲
49	Tray	Lengthwise from handle to handle: Jb., logo, Lr., Bb., tray surface, Bb., Lr., logo, Zb	20	440 x 268		1495	■
50 a	Mustard pot	Pot edge with painted rim and pot with decorated saucer. Jb., logo (one side, with handle to the right), Bb., Lr., Lg.(wide), one handle: gold with thumb rest, saucer Jb.					▲
50 b	Lid	Knob: red tip, 2 x profiled white-gold, Lr, spoon bay	200 m. D.		260		
51	Toothpick dispenser	Horizontal cylindrical dispenser with Jb. on the top ends and logo on the side surfaces, grip holes toward the top and stand with Lg.(wide)					▲

Household porcelain with etched gold rims and gold staffage of various shapes and functions.

Etched Gold Rim Decor

Jagged Band = Jb.

Beaded Band = Bb.

Logo

Lines

Gradation in

Red = Lr.
Gold = Lg.

wall = WS
Shoulder
of plate = Tf

Backstamps

1. until 1930 ▲   2. 1931 ■   3. from 1932 ●

Typical Combinations of Backstamps

Plate First Layout until Nov. 1930	Cup 2nd Layout 1931	Plate Layouts after 1932

People stood in line at the airshow in Altenrhein to catch a glimpse inside the flying boat. (Staatsarchiv St. Gallen)

A Sensation The World Over

Over 50,000 Visitors See the Do X at Air Shows

On the 24th and 25th of August, 1929, people marvel at the Do X, which is on display for the first time. They have already heard a great deal about to the giant aircraft, and some of the residents on the shores of Lake Constance have even seen it in the sky. Most recently on August 23rd when the 20th test flight takes place, lasting fourteen minutes. But on this weekend the Do X is there to be touched, in the true sense of the word. The organizer of the Altenrhein Air Show is the eastern Swiss company Aero-Gesellschaft

St. Gallen. Tens of thousands of visitors come to get a close look at the flying boat. On scaffolding with platforms and galleries, visitors can peak inside through windows and portholes. There is not much to see since furnishing of the passenger cabin doesn't take place until the summer of 1930. With only a view of uncovered duralumin ribs and walls, the well over 50,000 visitors have to be content without experiencing the Do X take-off and fly. The flying boat stays the weekend in the large assembly hall in Altenrhein.

The first official flight, with over thirty reporters, begins on September 30, 1929 as test flight number 31 of the Do X 1. With Lady Drumond-Hay, representative of Hearst Press, and other illustrious members of the press on board, the flying boat does a thirty-seven-minute tour over Lake Constance. The English

Admission ticket for the air show in Altenrhein. If the ticket number is any indication of the volume of visitors, there must have been huge crowds.

There were only a few posters at that time with the Do X as the subject. This one for the Altenrhein Air Show on August 24th and 25th, 1929 was the first one ever.

False design. Awuco Do X themed postcards with cross sectional view of the flying boat. Generations of graphic artists use it as a template.

Lady, well known in aviation circles those days, gives Dornier an excellent reason to be especially accommodating to her. The press empire of U.S. tycoon William Randolph Hearst has confirmed its utmost support for Claude Dornier's "flying boat idea" and have granted him 100,000 Reichsmark.Around this time, the first series of photo postcards, with Do X as the subject, begin to appear. The graphical art and publishing firm A. Weber & Co. (Awuco) from Stuttgart produces them. Authorized by DoFlug AG, the cards are in a 14x9cm format and have a violet, oval company postal marking on the backside: "Dornier Flugzeuge AG (asterisk) Altenrhein (Rorschach), Switzerland." Number 61282 of this first series "Longitudinal Section of the Dornier Do X Flying Boat With Twelve 500HP Engines" shows a drawing by the graphic artist Römer from Munich. It is created after a description of the planned design of the passenger deck and doesn't match the real thing from 1930 in any way. Profile illustrators of the Do X still follow this template today and go by a false basis.

Over Lake Constance With 169 People On Board

October 21, 1929 is a Monday. Lake Constance lies under an overcast sky with light waves and a wind of two to three meters per second. The barometer reads 720.3mm. The ground temperature is 7.5° C and 9.5° C 300m above sea level. The Do X will fly at this altitude today when it sets a special record.

On the list of test flights, we have arrived at number 42, and take-off is scheduled for around midday. But beforehand, the flying boat, equipped with light straw benches, must be weighed for the trimming. It weighs 30,541kg with equipment, furnishings, trim ballast, etc. Fuel and oil for the engines accounts for 2,224kg. Equipment for the film crew and the press is 181kg. The rest is passenger weight and brings the take-off weight to 44,768 metric tons. During this important flight, there are extra crewmembers on board for tests and for information and are included in the weight with 1,352kg. That's an average weight of 75kg for eighteen people. The press is made up of

twenty-four people and weighs 1,825kg. The report for determining the take-off weight reads: "Factory employees as passengers: 8,645 kg."

In total, 169 people are on board to experience the record flight. In addition to the crew and members of the press, 120 factory employees also fly over Lake Constance. This number not only includes the employees from the factory in Altenrhein, but also their wives and children, some of whom are little tykes having their fun as stowaways.

The flying boat still has no type certification, which will not be issued by the DVL until February 1930, and no air service permit. This is merely an official acceptance flight, which is supposed to confirm that the contractually required flight performances have taken place. Incidentally, this is subject to a repeat flights for measured performance values. Proof has still not been provided by this time. With such requirements, registering an official record flight with 170 people on board would have been doomed to failure in Germany, where they police the skies to prevent such things. But on October 21, 1929, we are in Switzerland. The elated passengers, almost all of whom know one another well, are brought out to the flying boat on motorboats from the shipyard. They are about to experience an impromptu record flight which will not be broken until decades later. After take-off, the Do X circles over Lake Constance for forty minutes at a maximum altitude of 400 meters. Chroniclers report about the apparently overheated, heavily smoking rear engine row.

In December 1929, the Siemens Zeitschrift reads: "… The record-breaking flight by the Do X, with 169 passengers and nearly an hour of flight time, does not, by far, represent the upper limit of the capabilities of air travel. Calculating for an average weight per person of 80kg, and an hourly weight demand of 1,400kg for the operating materials, results in a total load of fifteen metric tons. But actually, during test flights, a total flight weight of 51.3 tonnes had been carried – an additional eight tonnes added to the empty weight of twenty-eight tonnes. That means that an additional 100 people could have flown, or that the 169 people, which included a nineteen-man crew, could have flown for six hours." This theoretical calculation is quite clear compared to what the people at Siemens will have to hear about the continuous output of their engines.

"L'Avion géant Do X a survolé le Lac de Constance avec 169 passagers!!! L'hydravion en vol, au dessus du lac." Text on the backside of an adhesive label on a French press photo.

Over the next few days, national and international news attention for the Do X reaches its first peak. Here are some examples from the Leipziger Neueste Nachrichten: "The Dornier flight makes a great impression overseas. It is almost impossible to describe the enormous impression the record-breaking flight over Lake Constance by Dornier's giant flying boat, the Do X, has made in England. The morning news devotes long descriptions, editorials and critiques by authorities on the subject to the results. People admire the achievement and, with true English self-restraint, look for the lesson to be learned from the German feat for the future development of aviation. The editorial article of the Daily Express points out the purposefulness, in particular, with which Germany looks to gain domination of the skies. Word for word, it reads: "Germany has scored another remarkable triumph in the air. We shall much mistake the significance of this achievement if we think of it merely as one more triumph of German engineering. It is the triumph of national psychology; it is the crowning expression of that determination to be foremost in the air, which has captured the imagination of the German people, and is dragging them from the abyss of defeat to a wholesome self-respect. There is nothing of the old pre-war bombast and blunder in this new spirit. It is simply that Germany, debarred from military aviation by the Treaty of Versailles, means to make herself the headquarters of commercial flying in Europe and the leader in all its developments. We salute this resolution as an example to be followed. Germany has built the finest airship and sent it safely round the world. She has now launched a flying boat that promises to open an entirely new chapter in the history of aviation. That is the result of a capable and tenacious people becoming filled with the consciousness that its future is in the air."

Hamburger Fremdenblatt: "… All of England presently speaks of the first hugely successful flight of the Dornier flying boat. Several English engineers, who are well respected in aviation circles, had doubted that it would be possible for the Do X, despite its massive weight, to lift off the surface of the water. Therefore, the reaction to yesterday's flight is a feeling of speechless surprise. The headline writers in the press are falling over themselves with superlative phrases like 'A Triumph of German Technology,' 'The Leviathan of the Sky in Flight,' 'The German Wonder Ship of the Future,' etc."

The Chemnitzer Tageblatt: "Italy Congratulates. During a reception held in the Kurgarten Hotel, the leader of the Italian aviation commission, Undersecretary Balbo, who was present for the test flights of the Do X, again expressed his enthusiasm for the Do X flying boat, which has exceeded his highest expectations, a Berlin correspondent reports. Germany can be proud to have created such a marvel of technology. To the same end, Balbo also sent a long congratulatory telegram to the head of the aviation department at the Ministry of Transportation, Ernst Brandenburg." Balbo's enthusiasm is understandable. But he has withstood sharp criticism in Italy. The purchase order of two Do X flying boats, which takes place on his initiative, generates a powerful political storm there. Every proof of performance by the Do X confirms his decision and he happily awaits the completion of the Do X 2 and 3, which come into existence parallel to the "Wonder Ship of the Future" in Altenrhein's airplane hangar.

Radio Broadcast From the Flying Boat

"For your friendly cooperation – from the flight coverage of the Do X, a greeting card, which may be considered a rarity due to its postmark." Wise foresight by the card writer from 1929. His postcard from the Do X, with two postmarks "Südfunk on board the Do X" and Austrian postage, is among the rare postal items of Do X philately. His postcard greeting is for a co-worker at Süddeutscher Rundfunk AG (SÜRAG) from Mannheim. The affectionate colleague thinks of her despite the storm, which the 17th of November 1929 brings for him and SÜRAG, also known as "Südfunk." He is participating in a radio-technical experiment – a live report from an airplane, and this time from the airborne Do X. Quite adventurous considering radio transmissions have only existed in Germany since October 29, 1923 and the radio-technical conquest of airspace with an airplane as a medium was just pioneered in the late-1920s.

Preparations begin weeks beforehand. In 1929, the technical operation and broadcast authority of all eight German master transmitters on the medium wave is incumbent upon the German Reichspost and Telegraph Authority (RPTV), which became Deutsche Reichspost (DRP) in December 1924. The initiative to offer the growing number of listeners something special comes from the Reichspost. Regional broadcasters are responsible for the program content and planning, and this time Südfunk is called in and commissioned by RPM because the events surrounding the Do X lie within its transmission range. The programs of almost all German radio stations promise a very special listening experience for Sunday, November 17, 1929. For the best broadcasting time slot back then, after Sunday lunch, between 1:00pm and 2:00pm, the announcement in the program schedule reads: "News coverage from the large Do X flying boat. Followed by broadcast attempts from on board the flying boat, landscape descriptions, interviews with builders and pilots, and a colorful entertainment program from on board the flying boat. Directed by Rolf Formis. Broadcaster on board the flying boat: Dr. Holzbauer – Broadcaster on land: Dr. Cassimir. Broadcast from Stuttgart."

Rolf Formis (1896-1935) is responsible for the set up of the broadcast station and the radio technology of the planned reportage. Formis is among the pioneers of German radio and amateur radio. He introduces, for example, DE numbers (DE = German receiving stations) for radio amateurs beginning in June 1925. In 1929 he runs Südfunk's remote receiving station, Solitude. Beginning in September 1934, after the Nazis seize power, he operates a self-built short wave sender that spreads poignant propaganda against the National Socialists. His underground transmitter is located in Hotel Záhofií on the banks of the Moldau, near Stechovice, Czechoslovakia. He is murdered there on January 23, 1935 by an SD commando sent from Berlin. Rolf Formis's fate hardly touches anyone in Nazi-drunk Germany and even today he is almost forgotten.

By the late-1920s, Südfunk has made a name for itself beyond the borders of its listening range as a specialist for flight coverage. The outstanding "Zeppelin News Service" from August and September 1929 still echoes in the ears of listeners. The reports from Tokyo, Los Angeles or Lakehurst, NJ about the LZ 127 Graf Zeppelin airship during its round-the-world flight are organized by Rolf Formis with the help of his remote receiving station, Solitude. Two months later, equal expectations from curious listeners accompany his Do X reports.

Rolf Formis, 1929. Organizer of the Südfunk reportage manages the remote receiving station Solitude of SÜRAG in Stuttgart.

With the transmission location on the ground, there are still no technical problems with the live coverage. The palm-sized, box-shaped carbon microphone for recording audio hangs in its mount and stands with a tripod on a head-high, wooden podium in front of the large assembly hangar in Altenrhein. Claude Dornier and other people involved with the Do X will surely be questioned here. Unfortunately, a recording of the live coverage has still not been found in the archives, which is probably due to the quality of the source. For the reportage in the air, Formis chose a problematic spot for the microphone. It hangs in the cockpit of the Do X with its splendid view. At the beginning of the broadcast, the Do X lies ready for take-off on the buoy and waits with the crew on board for the passengers and the start signal.

Music is now a part of radio too, and the same holds true then as it does now: without music, you only have half the listening enjoyment. The Dornier company band makes sure that there is no shortage of it on this rather fresh Sunday in November 1929. They also sing the new Do X March by Leo Bürkle. The contemporary text to the Markdorf music director's march offers verses to keep listeners smiling: "Do X, you work of German strength, shine through the skies in proud glory. To the hero of the magic on the Swabian Sea, Doctor Dornier, the master, thy honor is due. The twelve engines rattle and clatter, the propellers hum like newborns, the pilot at the wheel boldly and bravely flies the whale at full throttle."

At quarter past one, the passengers are taken in motorboats from the shipyard to the flying boat. But engine ignition is delayed unexpectedly. They start up poorly and have to warm up before the water take-off can finally take place at four minutes past two. According to noted flight data, the flight travels over a distance of 98km, lasts thirty minutes and flies up and down the coast of Lake Constance on the Swiss side. The DoFlug people in Altenrhein prepared the Do X for its big live radio performance one day earlier, Saturday, with three starts and landings as well as short test flights. But the cast off from the buoy and the starting of the twelve engines with compressed air does not come off perfectly. It is too cold on this Sunday, as Dornier chief pilot Richard Wagner sits behind the steering wheel on the left pilot chair.

And how does the radio experience that was promised to the listeners fare? This is documented in the Bayerische Radio Zeitung. Two weeks later they describe "an unsuccessful reportage." With a very direct assessment on page 11 of its 49th issue from December 1st, they relate the events in Altenrhein and on the flight over land that day: "… the Stuttgart sender did not miss the opportunity to include the giant Do X flying boat in their reports. Unfortunately, though, the success of this attempt was thoroughly unsatisfactory. All German senders (with a few exceptions), Austrian and Swiss senders, and even in London, were connected to the transmission. On board the aircraft there was a complete transmitter installation, which delivered its transmission to the various senders through an intermediate ground station. The technical direction of the company, which was well built according to his layout, lay in the hands of Rolf Formis, who had also managed the Zeppelin news service. This time, he seems to have neglected to have the actual transmission sufficiently tested since what there was to hear was more than deplorable. The ground station announcer, Dr. Heinrich Cassimir, failed in his ability to give a clear picture using lively description, and the failure of the transmission from on board the flying boat

Berichterstattung vom

Groß-Flugschiff Do X

13.00
(1.00)

Anschließend Sendeversuche von Bord
des fliegenden Schiffes. Landschafts-
schilderung, Unterredung mit den Er-
bauern und Führern des Schiffes,
buntes Unterhaltungsprogramm von
Bord des Schiffes.

Leitung Rolf Formis
Sprecher im fliegenden Schiff: Dr. Holz-
bauer - Sprecher auf der Landstation:
Dr. Casimir

Übertragung von Stuttgart

"News Coverage From the Giant Do X Flying Boat." Program section from the Bayerische Radio Zeitung, Nr.47 Page III, on the 17th of November 1929.

Reporter in action: "... failed in his ability to give a clear picture using lively description ..." harsh critique for Heinrich Cassimir, announcer from the ground station. (Photo: DSLR)

completed the technical shortcomings. Be it that the motor noise covered up the announcer's voice, or that the modulation of the airborne sender was defective, whatever the case, the results were despicable. The technical inadequacy of this test was even more regrettable when the broadcaster on board the flying boat, Dr. Holzbauer, the head of Süddeutscher Rundfunk's conference site in Mannheim, seemed to grow excellently into his role as reporter, as far as one could gather from the barely understandable fragments. Before organizing a broadcast for almost all of Central Europe, the feasibility of implementing this must first be made clearer."

Attempts to cover up the engine noise during the flight's live report were unsuccessful. The connection between the ground and the Do X's radio equipment, however, worked just fine. The rather strong transmitter installed on board by Formis also did its job. With the corresponding amplification of the ground station, several Sunday strollers in Stuttgart's market place also hear the "failed reportage." Big loudspeakers from Siemens, set up by Südfunk, let the Do X motor noise be heard over the ether in fragments.

The First Philatelic Items of the Do X

Even though the reportage doesn't offer something sustainable, this cannot be said of a parallel action on the same subject. Aerophilatelists regard the reportage flight of November 1929 as the first postal flight of the Do X. The official blessing by the German Reichspost, with a corresponding announcement in the official journal of the Reichspost Ministry, is indeed missing, but all later catalogs of Do X philately begin with the postal marking: "Südfunk on board the Do X," the first series on long list of postal items.

The postcards, postal stationery and picture postcards transported on the flight receive two special markings. According to information from today, letters are not included. The first, a circular marking with a diameter of 29mm, is a flight confirmation mark with the text: "Südfunk on board the Do X (star)" and the date "17 XI 29 13-14." The second special marking is a double circle mark with a 38mm diameter and the writing "Südfunk on board the Do X" as well as a stylistic silhouette of the flying boat in the center. It appears in black and red ink.

When Günter Harms, oft quoted editor of the most important Do X post catalog, writes, "… the first documentation of promotional postal items for the Do X flying boat took place on 11/17/1929 during the 77th test flight. Private, single and double circled postal markings with the writing 'Südfunk on board' distinguish these private postal drops over Rorschach, Switzerland and Gaissau, Austria as well as the postal delivery in Friedrichshafen," it is only half of the truth. The Reichspost most likely initiated the actions, so there were no private markings. Officially, the post remains a secret because the future of the Do X is hardly predictable. One year later, this is a different story. The Do X will become an aid to the postal service and receives its own sworn-in postmaster, Wilhelm Niemann.

A December 1929 announcement in the Sieger Neuheiten Dienst, Zeppelin Post, sent to subscribers in irregular intervals by Hermann Ernst Sieger (1902-1954), includes the following hint which documents the role of the Reichspost: "… furthermore, the Do X had a big flight on 11/17, which we all know was also broadcast by all German radio senders and several foreign senders. Thanks to the kindness of the organizing authorities (organized for the radio listeners by the Post), it was possible for me to give a card commemorating the mail drop to each of my subscribers. Mail was dropped over Rorschach (Switzerland), Gaissau (Austria) and Friedrichshafen (Württemberg). Now, this mail did not come from the Zeppelin, but I didn't want to pass on this unique opportunity to deliver mail to my subscribers from the world famous giant airplane. Furthermore, such a postal delivery can no longer be provided since it probably won't continue to be transported. This flight was organized for radio on behalf of the Post." Incidentally, a Sieger-Südfunk card at that time costs three Reichsmark.

But what happened on board the Do X between 1:00pm and 2:00pm on that Sunday, November 17, 1929? As already mentioned, the men from radio are quite preoccupied with themselves, with the exception of Dr. Heinrich Cassimir, who has already finished his announcing duties on the ground. He finds the time to write a postcard to his parents in Karlsruhe:

"Dropped on 11/17/29. My dear parents! Greetings from the airborne Do X! Heinrich."

On the short flight, shipyard personnel on board from Altenrhein stamp the postal items to be delivered with two different markings. Beautifully placed next to the postage stamp, the official postal marking with date is considered the flight confirmation mark. The other, somewhat bigger marking with the Do X in the center is placed on postcards and postal stationery where there is space available for a special postal marking. Apparently, two varieties of the special postal marking were used at the same time since there are markings in black and also red ink, used without any kind of recognizable system.

The piles of marked postal items are dropped in heavy pouches, neatly sorted according to Swiss and Austrian postage terms, over Rorschach and Staad in Switzerland, as well as Gaissau in Austria. This is what the evidence suggests at least. Whether it was really handled this way, is still questionable. Reasonably targeted postal drops from an airplane at almost 200km/h in uncertain November weather conditions seem somewhat risky. In a skillfully handled airship, pinpoint drops are possible. But in an airplane?

For direct delivery with the appropriate post offices, a courier doesn't have to go far from the Dornier compound in Altenrhein. The Swiss post offices in Staad and Rorschach are only three and seven miles away, respectively, so that the postal clerk in Rorschach stamps his postmark just after 2:00pm. In the village of Gaissau, Austria, the post office is located directly behind the border only three kilometers from Altenrhein. The longest way is over Lake Constance to Friedrichshafen, where the "Südfunk" items are handed over and postmarked between 6:00pm and 7:00pm. Some items don't make it to mail boxes until November 20th.

Of the known postal items today, the striking number of Sieger-Südfunk stationery is remarkable. In December 1922, Hermann Ernst Sieger founds his postage stamp office in Lorch, Württemberg, which still provides philatelists with stamps and other postal items today. The business enjoys worldwide renown, especially as a specialist for "Zeppelinpost." For the Südfunk campaign on the Do X, Hermann Ernst Sieger delivered a large quantity of postal stationery commemorating the special flight so his subscribers could have them marked.

The quantity of marked Sieger postcards, all with identical handwriting, suggests that Hermann Ernst Sieger was on site and organized his postal stationery. Also on the card is the rare special marking "Südfunk on board the Do X" in black ink, implicitly approved by the Reichspost.

One of the "Sieger cards" prepared with a Swiss postmark from 2:00pm in Rorschach. The flight confirmation marking in the middle notes the time of the reportage. The allegedly rare Südfunk marking in red ink. Why in red, and why the even rarer black, is still an unresolved issue.

Hermann Ernst Sieger. The initiator of the Liechtenstein Post Museum led the way for German aerophilatelists.

The Do X over Manhattan shortly before landing in New York Harbor on August 27, 1931. (Photo: Dornier GmbH, EADS)

Adventure Instead of Travel – Over the Atlantic and Back

During the "Südfunk" operation in November 1929, the Reichspost, as instigator, still remains in the background. Upon further observation of the events in Altenrhein, international flight operations with airmail transport are put on the back burner. The engine problem has to be solved – reasonable air service on the Do X is only possible with stronger engines. Twelve new water-cooled Curtiss Conqueror engines roar over Lake Constance after take-off on August 4, 1930. All technical problems seem to be dealt with, and the plans for the Do X's flight out into the world are on the table again. Flying the Do X to the USA is a priority because the license agreement with General Motors must be fulfilled. Claude Dornier wants to see his flying boat on its way as soon as possible. He sees airmail delivery as a source of revenue for the ferry flight costs, which DMB has to pay. Organizing this nationally and internationally in just a few weeks is a difficult task that will not be solved satisfactorily. The chronology of the Do X 1a flight is very well documented on postal stationery – through Europe, on the African west coast, over the South Atlantic to Rio de Janeiro, to New York and back over the Atlantic to Berlin.

The official story of the Do X as a "postal service aid" begins on October 29, 1930 with the swearing in of Wilhelm Niemann as head official at the main post office in Friedrichshafen. On this Wednesday, the navigation officer of the flying boat becomes the first German postmaster of the flying boat. For

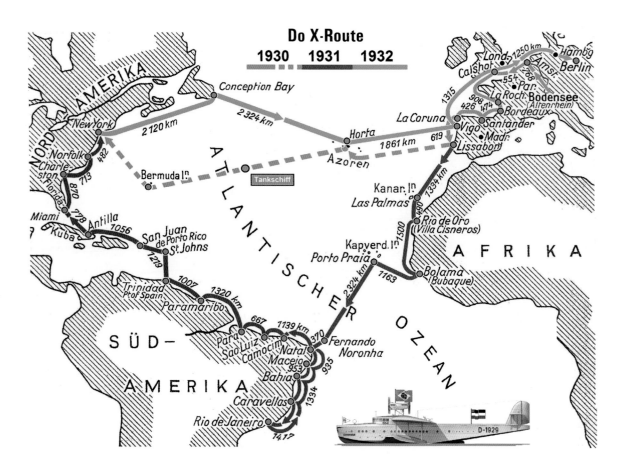

postal activities of the Do X's airborne post office, Wilhelm Niemann's records can be evaluated. To this day, his correspondence, reports and accounts have attracted little interest in the historical depiction of Do X mail. After several years of life in the shadows of aerophilately, Rolf Schneider from Essen comments on the topic in November 1969. In his treatise The Do X Story, he describes the history of Do X mail. As he himself describes, he didn't want to write a catalog. This is made up for, on the basis of his statements, by Günter Harms from Bremen in 1981. Neither of these authors was familiar with Nieman's records. They are published for the first time in 2004 by Jörg-M. Hormann. The first German postage stamp with the Do X as motif appears in October of that year.

On the date of its arrival, and in line with the anniversary edition by the Deutsche Post, Jörg-M. Hormann published his book A Boat Flies Out Into the World, which is quoted here.

The European Leg and Airmail Problems

Deutsche Reichspost and Dornier Metallbauten GmbH reach an agreement on a postal contract that guarantees Dornier suitable revenues from the airmail business with the Do X. It's not until October 21, 1930, just ten days before the planned flight to the USA, that the Reichpost Ministry announces the postal operation in issue #92 of its official register. Under the rubric of operating services, the RPM rules under #382/1930. America flight of the Do X: "The Dornier Do X flying boat will likely fly to America in early November. This flight shall be used to transport normal letters and postcards to recipients of any desired destination under the following conditions: 1. Individual weights of letters may not exceed 20g; 2. on the mailing, the sender must specify the route indicator "to America with the Do X flying boat"; 3. the fee for a letter is 6RM and 4RM for a postcard." Incidentally, the mailings cannot be individually thrown into mailboxes somewhere, and have to be sent in a separate, prepaid envelope to the post office in Friedrichshafen. The envelope must read: "Mailing for the America flight of the Do X flying boat – Friedrichshafen Post Office (Lake Constance)."

The first deadline for Do X mail at the Friedrichshafen post office, October 30, 1930, is delayed twice. The first reason is the short leadtime and a looming lack of interest in the Do X mail service. The postmark deadline is thus changed to November 8, 1930, 11:00pm. The second deadline change takes place after the flight delay due to the wing unit fire in Lisbon. The Reichspost confirms the collection of mail in Friedrichshafen and its transport to the flying boat in Lisbon

Mail from Danzig. Front and back sides of a letter from Horst Merz to his wife for the Atlantic flight of the Do X. (Photo: Johannes E. Palmer)

He diligently writes letters home. Horst Merz, Lufthansa flight captain and pilot of the Do X. (Staatsarchiv St. Gallen 1664a)

until the scheduled start of the Atlantic overflight in January 1931.

Ordinance #382 from October 21, 1930 further reads: "… 6. in addition to the postmark date, mailings will also get a special postal marking from the post office in Friedrichshafen that reads 'First Transatlantic Flight Europe-America of the Do X Flying Boat';

7. A postal service station will be set up on board the flying boat to accept airmail shipments during the flight under the same conditions. These shipments will receive the postmark of the service station with the specification 'Dornier Do X flying boat – D 1929' and the special postal marking."

This is the extent of good will by the people at the Reichspost. Originally, the issuance of a special postal stamp is planned for the flight, but the Reichspost denies its approval. Seventy-five years go by before the Deutsche Post commemorates the flying boat with a special stamp in October 2004.

After Wilhelm Niemann is sworn in at the post office in Friedrichshafen in late-October 1930 (on a side note, Do X commander Friedrich Christiansen also gets sworn in) he acknowledges the receipt of two round in-flight postmark stampers and two rectangular special stampers as well as an impressive number of stamp sheets for the on board post office worth 10,000 Reichsmark.

The stamps listed here are with Michel numbers for the German Reich collection area because only these eleven different stamps are handed out from the Do X postal service station until the entire inventory is used up, as we shall see later. Only high stamp values make sense – 50 Pfennigs and up – with the defined postage of six Reichsmark for a letter and four Reichsmark for a postcard. There are few valid and high postage face values at this time. The following stamps are the first on board: "Bauwerke" with prices of one, two and three Marks (Mi. #364 to #366); "Luftpost Steinadler" with prices from 50 Pfennigs and up (Mi. #381 to #384); "Luftpost Zeppelin" for two and three Reichsmark (Mi. #423 and #424) as well as "Luftpost Zeppelin, 1. Südamerikafahrt" for two and three Marks (Mi. #438 and #439). Together with the delivery of collected mail in Friedrichshafen for transport to America on the Do X, the post office sends more stamps on behalf of DMB to Lisbon in January 1931. The listed selection costs 6,000 Reichsmarks. Niemann has a total of 16,000 Reichsmarks

worth of stamps to sell in his airborne post office. An invoice from October 10, 1931 documents the use of stamps and how many remain.

"Do X Ferry Flight" is the title of Niemann's fourth report from November 1, 1930 and is intended for the beginning of the ocean crossing, with the first leg from Altenrhein to Amsterdam. In the text he notes: "… Regarding the postal service station, it should be mentioned that the sale of stamps and possession of stampers have been assigned to me. Dornier sees such great earning potential in the mailing business that they sent 500 letters to their own address alone … hopefully there is a good rate, 4/5 of the proceeds go to Dornier." Six Reichsmarks postage for a letter and four Reichsmarks for a postcard is the result of negotiations with the Reichspost. Dornier actually only pays 1.20 Reichsmark for each of their own letters and hopes for further added value from the continuing sale of internal stationery to aerophilatelists, collectors of airmail stationery. The thrifty and careful people at Dornier go even further. They deliver envelopes addressed to the flying boat postmaster Wilhelm Niemann with four different imprinted Dornier company addresses, with the specification to postmark and cancel the stamps shortly before the Do X would fly over the Atlantic. Postmarked letters would have been lost for Dornier if the operation were to end before the ocean crossing. This doesn't apply to just the 500 letters that Niemann mentions in his report. The postmaster had to stick postage stamps from the on board inventory on a total of 1,924 letters from Dornier Metallbauten GmbH, as his later statement from October 10, 1931 in New York shows.

The Flight to the USA Begins

On November 5, 1930, at 10:30am, the journey of the flying boat begins with a take-off from Lake Constance. Twenty months later it would end with a splashdown on the Müggelsee near Berlin. It is a trying time for all the wishes and hopes that were result from the careful planning. Hardly anything turns out as expected, and this applies especially to the Do X postal service. The first dilemma begins with the departure. Because notification of the special letter and postcard transport occurs only ten days before the planned take-off, a considerable amount of mail for the flying boat does not accumulate at the post office in Friedrichshafen. The lunacy of six Reichsmark postage for a letter, in a time of global economic crisis, reduces the good intentions of the surely interested aerophilatelists to only a few hundred items. The signers of the postal contract between Dornier and the Reichspost didn't expect larger quantities of normal mail for South and North America anyway. This was probably one reason for the "enthusiast postage" too. To make the best of the situation, all that remains is to extend the delivery deadline in Friedrichshafen from October 30th to November 8th. After this, the letters and postcards are to be brought to Lisbon by train. Before the transatlantic flight, a longer stopover is planned in Cadiz for the Do X's engine conversion.

With European countries on the first stage, negotiating postal contracts for direct mail delivery on the Do X were also unsuccessful. Some countries, like Holland and Portugal, stall for a while, others reject it flatly, like England and Spain, while the authorities argue with France before the Do X even starts. The impenetrable walls of the airmail monopoly surround the Do X in Europe. Because of these unsettled handling and delivery situations, the Do X mail to be delivered remains in the post office in Friedrichshafen during take-off on November 5, 1930. On a loosely related note, the Do X does not take-off from Friedrichshafen, but rather from Altenrhein. On its "Rhine flight" to Amsterdam, the flying boat transports no mail, no passengers and also no Claude Dornier with wife, as rumored in some places. Only the sixteen-man crew flies in the Do X to Amsterdam. Tens of thousands of people watch the flight from Lake Constance down along the Rhine. They welcome the flying boat at its stopovers with huge cheers. In Amsterdam they swarm to the dykes and stand in wind and drizzling rain on the rooftops of the city. They want to see the Do X. Shortly after this first flight stage, a story circulates of an alleged postal drop from the Do X, complete with a private in-flight postal marking. Tempers soon flare at DMB and the Reichspost. Niemann is prompted by his employer to address the accusations. On October 6, 1931, he

writes from New York to DMB: "… During the flight from Altenrhein to Amsterdam, we transported no mail at all on board the Do X. The first airmail was accepted on board in Amsterdam, in accordance with an agreement between the Deutsche Reichspost Ministry and the Dutch Post Ministry, and, in fact, with Dutch postal stamps. During the flight from Amsterdam to Lisbon, only an occasional letter with German postal stamps was accepted, as the itemization in the list that I sent to you also reveals. On the entire flight from Altenrhein to Lisbon, not a single letter was handed over to any post office. According to my instructions from the Deutsche Reichspost Ministry, not a single mail drop was to take place on any of the flights from Altenrhein to New York.

With respect to the letter from Mr. Walter Bruckmann (Manilla an die Ina-Press, Den Haag, Holland), the proportions reveal that the Do X envelopes Zaandam, Halfweg and Bourg (Gironde) are fakes. The same also applies to the envelopes Mainz, Schaffhausen because only the crew was on board during the Rhine flight and they were instructed to make no letter drops."

Did Postmaster Niemann, with the crew status of first officer, have control over his people, in respect to secret postal drops in larger quantities? None of the handpicked troop who have committed themselves to the task of flying the Do X to America, would risk instant termination with a prohibited mail drop. Some have only been on board for a few days and are not yet 100% familiar with the operation of the flying boat. They have entirely different concerns.

Just like with the "Südfunk" items, the airdrop of individual mail or in airmail bags from the flying boat, is unlikely with a traveling speed of around 190km/h. Items thrown out of a porthole would land anywhere and nowhere. Pilot Horst Merz later confirms that he didn't fly a single postal route in any of his flights with the Do X, which entails approaching a target destination at particularly low altitudes and at reduced speeds. As Wilhelm Niemann mentions, Dutch mail in Amsterdam is the first to come aboard the Do X. The short-notice agreement with Holland for immediate delivery, hardly allows for wider public promotion of the postal service, and only because of a weather-caused, longer stopover in Amsterdam, from November 6th to 9th, do some airmail letters and a few airmail cards accrue.

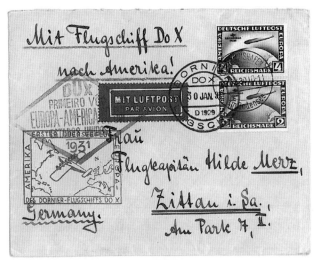

Mail prepared for delivery on board the Do X. A letter and postcard from Horst Merz in Lisbon to his wife with fondest regards. The flight confirmation marking for the Do X flight from Europe to Rio de Janeiro can be seen on the top of the envelope in red ink. (photos: Johannes E. Palmer)

Most of them are submitted on Friday, November 7th in Amsterdam. According to the agreement made, only mail to overseas addresses or addresses in Holland may be transported. Transport to other European countries is prohibited. This Amsterdam mail flies along to the Canary Islands, where Niemann assigns it for further transport.

On January 31, 1931, the Do X lands in the new harbor of Las Palmas. Why the Do X postmaster doesn't take care of the mail delivery until after the failed take-off and lengthy repair in Las Palmas, and just be-

fore the flight to Villa Cisneros on May 1st, remains unclear. Despite the special Do X postal marking, the Amsterdam mail did not cross the South Atlantic and goes to its addressees with the transit marking, "PUERTO DE LA LUZ (CANARIAS)-2. May 31."

Before the landing in Las Palmas, with Dutch mail, there are many problems to solve. The detour to Calshot, the water airport of the Royal Navy at Southampton, and a visit from the Prince of Wales are some of the pleasant experiences. The future English King flies the Do X a few laps over Calshot, after a cavalier takeoff by Clarence Schildhauer, who needs only twenty-five seconds to get off the water.

To Lisbon In Erratic Weather Conditions

The erratic weather in November 1930 interferes with the onward flight to Lisbon. Fog, rain, storms, everything that aviators feared in those days, accompanies the Do X along the Bay of Biscay on the French coast, and in Santander and La Coruna, Spain. And yet there are still crowds of people there to see the Do X. On November 27th they land in Lisbon. All mail forwarded from Friedrichshafen is loaded and the Atlantic crossing is finally set to begin after a short stopover in Cadiz. The installation of additional fuel tanks and removal of the furnishings from the passenger deck are planned here. The furniture, Do X porcelain and non-essential items are sent to Natal on a cargo ship for the overflight. On Saturday 11/29 around 2:40pm, the day before the flight to Cadiz, the port side wing panels burn off in Lisbon. A tarp laid out to dry is blown over the glowing-hot exhaust of an auxiliary motor. It burns and ignites the fabric-covered wing panels. The outdoor repair with replacement materials from Altenrhein lasts until the end of January 1931.

During the repair work in the submarine harbor of the navy arsenal, with foreign technicians and aircraft builders from Altenrhein on board, Commander Christiansen orders the relocation of mail to a local supplier of the flying boat. Dornier hires the HAPAG agency Marcus & Harting for the job and the post office in Friedrichshafen is supposed to send the accumulated mail there. But the officials at the Reichspost in Berlin have a problem with this arrangement. They express security concerns, which the command of the flying boat ignores. Ever since the official announcement of the transport on October 21, 1930, people had sent their Do X mail in a separate envelope to the post office in Friedrichshafen. Mail with the appropriate route indicator also comes in, which accumulates at other post offices in the German Reich, as well as foreign mail from supplier countries, including: Holland, Austria, Portugal, Switzerland, Liechtenstein, Hungary, the Free City of Danzig and the Saargebiet. A few letters from the USA and Russia are also included. Friedrichshafen collects all postal items for the flying boat and dispatches the airmail receipts. They receive the postmark "FRIEDRICHSHAFEN (Bodensee) b" with date, or the transit postmark for foreign mail as well as the special postal marking (flight confirmation marking).

The officials in Friedrichshafen step into action and process the accumulated mail as well as verify the date and time. The following datelines are well known today: a.) 13.11.30 10-11; b.) 21.11.30 10-11; c.) 28.11.30 10-11; d.) 15.-1.31 11-12; e.) 23.-1.31 14-15. The post office's grouped shipments go to the Marcus & Harting agency in Lisbon. When the flying boat receives the mail on January 29, 1931, there are a total of 1,303 letters and 1,778 postcards in mailbags from Friedrichshafen.

Now the Portuguese mail for immediate delivery is added too. In April 1932, in a short report to Maurice Dornier, who is responsible for public relations on board the Do X at that time, Wilhelm Niemann describes the handling of the Portuguese mail: "... we obtained the Portuguese mail after overcoming various difficulties (French airmail monopoly) in Lisbon. It should be noted here that the Portuguese postal authorities had also inadvertently ac-

Henry Kiel, DEBEG radio operator and radio officer of the Do X help Wilhelm Niemann with "on board mail matters." (Staatsarchiv St. Gallen 1668)

cepted some registered mail items. After the corresponding telegram exchange with the R.P.M. in Berlin, the registered mail notice was declared invalid and transported as normal mail, which the Portuguese postal authorities agreed to. In Las Palmas, on the Canary Islands, I delivered first mail on land. Letters and cards with Spanish postal stamps could not be accepted. Only the passengers or the crew could have German mail transported, after it postage was paid at the on board post office. In Guinea-Bissau and on Cape Verde, Portuguese delivery items were again allowed since these are Portuguese colonies and we had an agreement concerning this matter. Mail was also delivered to these two places." Niemann begins the biggest cancellation campaign of the entire trip on January 30-31, 1931, shortly before, and during, the flight from Lisbon to Las Palmas.

Radio Officer Henry Kiel helps him with it. They postmark the Portuguese mail and the mail from Friedrichshafen with the Do X stamper as a transit postmark. Furthermore, over a thousand DMB letters receive various free stamps from the on board

Decorated for a high-ranking visit. Flag dressing of the Do X on February 15, 1931 in the harbor of Las Palmas. Italo Balbo, Italy's Aviation Minister has announced that he is coming.

inventory. Niemann settles the postage with the Dornier company and then cancels the letters with the on board stamper as postmark. A large quantity of letters and postcards, among the items delivered from Friedrichshafen, are date stamped immediately in Lisbon. It's still not clear where these are, particularly the mail from the Soviet Union.

No Sunshine For the Do X on Gran Canaria

The journey over the South Atlantic should finally take place from Las Palmas. The plan is to jump over to the Cape Verde Islands and then fly over the South Atlantic to Natal. Because the take-off runway in the harbor of Las Palmas is too short for the heavily loaded Do X, it taxis under its own power to the Bay of Gando on Gran Canaria. During the unfortunate take-off on February 3, 1931, while traveling at speed of 130km/h, a groundswell wave crashes against the starboard sponson. The abrupt stall nearly breaks off the wings. The compli-

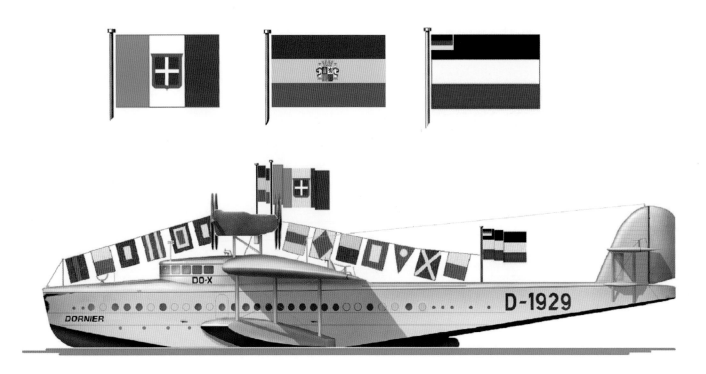

Provisional slipway in Puerto Luz on Gran Canaria. (Photo: Dornier GmbH, EADS)

cated repair on a provisional slipway in the harbor of Las Palmas will last almost three months. Shortly after the serious accident, Italo Balbo, the Italian Aviation Minister, visits the ailing Do X on February 15th in Las Palmas. Italy has ordered two Do X flying boats from Claude Dornier, which are already being built in Altenrhein. Balbo wants to take a look.

He recommends to the commanders that the Do X start the trip over the South Atlantic in Bolama on the eastern coast of Africa. That had worked excellently with his whole squadron in early February. Christiansen and his men are convinced and the Do X flies over the African Villa Cisneros to Bolama, right at the beginning of the rainy season on the equator. From Bolama, Guinea-Bissau, the overflight has to finally work out, thinks Wilhelm Niemann, and he marks another part of the DMB letters and cancels them with the Do X on-board stamper, with the dates May 1st and 3rd, 1931. The forthcoming attempts to lift off the water for the overflight of the fully fueled flying boat are useless. The hot, humid air will not carry the fifty tonnes of take-off weight, even under the powerful wings and twelve roaring engines.

With less fuel, the Do X takes off for Cape Verde off from Bubaque, an Island off the coast of Bolama. Pilot Horst Merz and seaplane specialist Rudolf Cramer von Clausbruch, who came aboard in Las Palmas, use the ground effect for the flight. Flying three to five meters above the smooth water surface brings almost 20% more distance and consumes less fuel. Driven by Claude Dornier's ultimatum from Friedrichshafen "Either start the Atlantic overflight from Cape Verde or come back!" they are forced to take-off from Porto Praia. Flying at only a few meters altitude, the Do X disappears quickly behind the horizon around midday on June 4, 1931. A Portuguese ship's captain observes this unique event and reports via radio: "The Do X has crashed!" In times of unreliable radio connections, his message is the only one that reaches Lake Constance. For Claude Dornier, it's one more sleepless night.

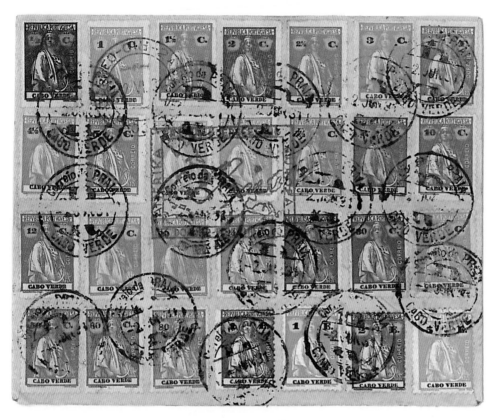

A postmark and marking for all the stopovers in Africa. A special collection by crewmembers. Here the letter from Horst Merz. (Photo: Johannes E. Palmer)

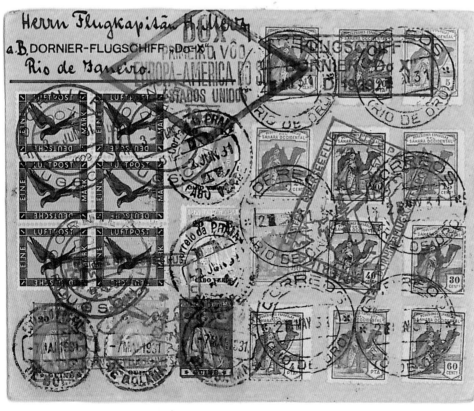

Over the South Atlantic and On To Rio de Janeiro

Reassuring news of the Do X's successful crossing of the South Atlantic with its thirteen-man crew comes from Natal, Brazil. The flying boat, having sprung a leak during takeoff at Cape Verde, taxis onto the beach there so that the damages can be inspected.

During the ten-day stopover that follows, the additional tanks that were installed in Lisbon are removed and the original ones built in again. In this time, Niemann processes the last DMB letters due to a written order from Friedrichshafen. According to his on-board mail statement, he postmarks another twenty-four letters at Dornier's expense. The cancellation date is interesting. The Do X postmaster turned the stamper back to June 3, 1931. Thus, he "produces" letters with a date just before the crossing of the South Atlantic. Niemann is actually unable to work on June 3rd. A severe case of malaria leaves him confined to bed. Made fit again by a massive quinine shot, he is able navigate the overflight. After the makeshift repair of the leak damage in Natal, the next stage to Rio de Janeiro begins.

On June 20th, at 1:00pm, the promenade of Rio's Botafogo Bay is full of people. The Do X splashes down to euphoric cheering. For weeks it is the topic of conversation and is makes headlines in the press. In Rio de Janeiro, all of the mail exits the boat. It weighs a total of 240kg and consists of about 8,500

After the overflight of the South Atlantic, on the beach in Natal. (Photo: Dornier GmbH, EADS)

Proud crew after the landing in Rio de Janeiro on June 20, 1931. (Photo: Dornier GmbH, EADS)

The Do X on-board postal marking for the stages in South America.

letters and an equally large amount of postcards. All mail receives a special Brazilian diamond shaped marking as well as a Rio arrival mark on the backside from June 22, 1931, and it continues on as normal mail to addressees around the world.

The Dornier internal mail remains together and is brought back on board the flying boat. The DMB letters for "Mr. Von Meister" with a New York address are sorted out by Wilhelm Niemann for the arrival confirmation in New York; they receive only the diamond marking on the front side as transit validation and no Rio arrival marking.

A sealed, registered parcel with other stamps valued at 6,000 Reichsmarks awaits the Do X's on-board post office in Rio de Janeiro. Wilhelm Niemann puts it away unopened since it doesn't require any postage stamps. On other South American stopovers

of the flying boat, plenty of mail goes in and out, but this mail comes on board with domestic postage stamps. Only a few passengers and crewmembers on the flight from Rio to New York have to pay postage for on board mail in Reichsmark, and the available supply is sufficient.

Syndicato Condor, the South American offshoot of Deutsche Luft Hansa, is a strong partner for all issues concerning the Do X in Brazil. Maintenance and repair of the flying boat are a part of this just as much as the services for the crew and organization of the postal operation. The Syndicate, whose director, Fritz Hammer, replaces Captain Friedrich Christiansen as commander of the next Do X flight to New York, delivers a special diamond-shaped stamper to the on-board post office.

With engines running in Botafogo Bay. (Photo: Dornier GmbH, EADS)

Another rush of visitors in Rio de Janeiro. (Photo: Dornier GmbH, EADS)

Weather-beaten coat of paint. The Do X went through a lot up
until Rio. (Photo: Dornier GmbH, EADS)

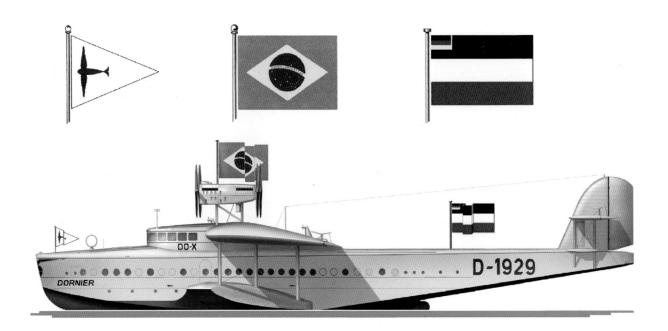

Flying flags like a merchant ship. The Do X in Rio de Janeiro on
June 20, 1931.

Before coming in to the shipyard. Makeshift repairs in Rio on damages to the bow. (Photo: Dornier GmbH, EADS)

The Brazilian President welcomes the Do X crew. (Photo: Dornier GmbH, EADS)

Telegram to the Berlin branch office of Dornier Metallbauten GmbH. Program before departure to the USA.

Clara Adams flies with the Do X from Rio to New York. (Photo: John Provan)

Backside of a greeting card from Clara Adams to the captain of the fast steamer Europa.

Telegram from Rio. Document of the competency dispute and problems in Rio de Janeiro. (Archive: DSLR)

The Do X off the coast of Rio de Janeiro. The front side of the greeting card from Clara Adams to the captain of the fast steamer Europa.

Advertisements for the transport of mail with the Do X are carried on fervently in Brazil, and thus a large quantity of airmail piles up in July 1931 until the deadline on August 1st. It consists of mail deliveries with addresses for all stopovers.

On August 5, 1931, the flying boat begins its flight to New York. With a total of sixteen stopovers on the South American east coast, the Caribbean and the USA, postal authorities give local mail from Brazil, Surinam, Trinidad and Antigua to the Do X for delivery. Brazilian airmail is provided with domestic postage and local postmarks. It receives the special diamond-shaped marking in black ink as a transit and confirmation marking, and the stamper is now part of the on-board post office's supply. Apparently, Niemann also nabs the red marking pad. Diamond markings in green and violet also appear – probably accidental slips in the on-board mail operation and have no further meaning. Otherwise, each marking color definitely has its own meaning. Black is for an official date marking, red for a special marking and green for postal information markings – this also applies in the postal operation of the Do X. Marking pads in the three colors are part of the on-board postal equipment.

Surprise in Surinam

The publicity that the Dornier company had envisioned finally happens in Surinam (Dutch Guiana). At least from a philatelic perspective. When the Do X lands in Paramaribo on August 18, 1931, the Dutch postal authorities present a surprise. Eleven days before the expected landing, they print out and issue a special edition of Surinam's complete airmail stamp catalog.

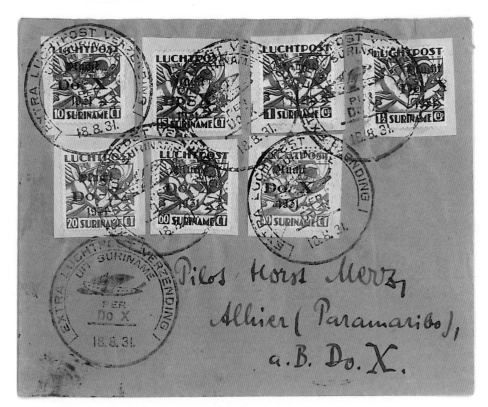

Letter from Horst Merz in Surinam to his wife. On the front side of the envelope, the official Surinam airmail postmark from August 18, 1931 can be seen, on the bottom of the back side, the oversized special marking from Antigua in blue ink. (Photo: Johannes E. Palmer)

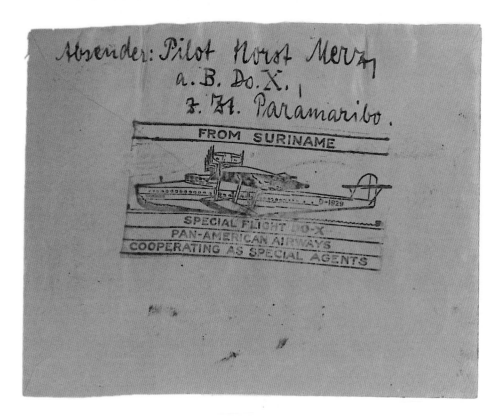

Medallion for the South America flight of the Do X. Created by the famous medallion artist Karl Goetz from Munich.

The last official mail in South America comes on board in Port of Spain. Apparently, European airmail restrictions do not apply in English Trinidad. Pan American Airways (PAA) plays an important role here, as it had already in Surinam. They make their ground staff available for the "German Wonder Ship of the Future" at airbases all over the Caribbean. They also deliver the very "American" flight confirmation marking for Surinam, Trinidad and Antigua, which go beyond all the normal dimensions and often only find space on the backside of postal stationery.

The opportunity to deliver mail on the flying boat ends with the landing in Miami on August 22nd. The especially restrictive American provisions and the airmail transport monopoly don't allow any room for exceptions. And especially not for foreigners. In Antilla in Cuba, Miami, Charleston and Norfolk there is only on-board mail for passengers and crew and a flight remembrance marking. All mail for further transport comes on board in New York, which the Do X reaches on August 27, 1931.

Left Alone In New York

All letters and postcards get a New York transit marking from August 27, 1931, 6:00pm, and are transported as normal mail to addressees. The DMB letters of course remain on board since they will now be sold to help finance the crew's stay. This applies in particular to the internal stationery addressed to: MR. VON MEISTER, 578 Madison Avenue, NEW YORK (City) U.S.A. Friedrich Wilhelm von Meister, general agent of Maybach Motorwerke in the USA and the point of contact for the Do X crew after arrival of the flying boat in the metropolis, soon puts a damper on the hopes of the Dornier people. In order to boost business, Niemann gives this DMB internal stationery addressed to "von Meister," with two cents postage on the backside of the envelope, to the U.S. Post Office on September 25, 1931. This was the point when there were no longer any arrival markings.

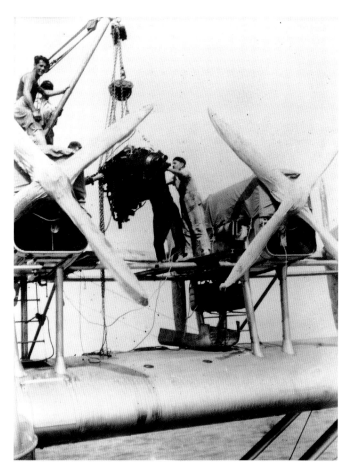

The only motor damage during the entire journey. Repairing a broken crankshaft in Para. (Photo: Dornier GmbH, EADS)

The imprint reads "Vluht Do. X 1931" in red and black ink respectively. The print run of the stamp values range between 5,270 for the ten cent stamp with black imprint and 4,200 pieces for the 1.50 guilder stamp with red imprint. All stamps not sold are immediately destroyed after the flying boat takes off and the authorities make contact. The frequency with which these stamps appear in mint condition today, leads one to doubt the assertion from that time.

The post office in Surinam cancels the mail items with a specially designed postmark stamper before they are given on board. The Do X is actually supposed to land in Paramaribo on August 10th, but is delayed with engine repairs for eight days in Para. For this reason, a part of the Do X mail already gets the special marking on the 10th and the rest on the 18th. The menacing Dutch leader of the post office in Paramaribo prohibits any courtesy cancellations, as Horst Merz later recalls.

The Do X above Manhattan. Brochure cover for the Do X's America flight from the Swiss Aero Revue.

Do X in front of the Manhattan skyline on the day of its arrival
in New York. (Photo: Dornier GmbH, EADS)

Welcome reception after arrival in New York with Clara Adams
as the only woman in the photo. (Photo: Dornier GmbH, EADS)

On the green grass of the White House. Welcomed by
U.S. President Hoover. (Photo: Dornier GmbH, EADS)

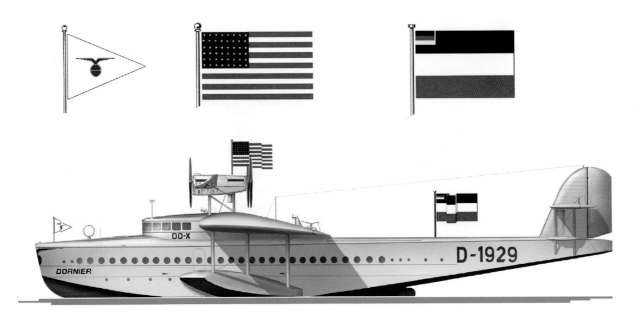

Do X flag dressing in the USA, 1931.

The Do X landed there a month beforehand. For the utilization of the letters by American interests, which seems particularly attractive to the initiators of the Dornier letters, American authentication must ultimately be on the stationery. Thus, the action costs a couple of more dollars postage.

On November 6th, the "bitter pill" then comes from Mr. von Meister from New York, and DMB in Friedrichshafen reacts twenty days later with the following message: "From your above mentioned letter we have regrettably seen that the Do X envelopes themselves are hardly sellable at a price of $2.75 each. Since we would also possibly be prepared to deliver them at a lower price, kindly ask for details of the price which, in your opinion, would enable the sale of all of the mail in a short time. We have taken note of your message that you have given the envelopes addressed to you back to the command of the Do X." Tough times for nice things that are not primarily necessary for living. All the more in the U.S. recession as a consequence of the global economic crisis after the Black Friday of October 1929. Even the hopes of chartering the Do X to American aviation companies like PAA or to the U.S. Navy are shattered in these economically bad times.

Nobody really knows how it will progress. And that goes for the on-board post office of the Do X too. In early November 1931, Wilhelm Niemann asks Friedrichshafen how the further operation should be shaped. DMB writes back to Niemann: "… We contacted the local post office to find out if the postage stamps there could be used on additional Do X flights. The post office thinks that with the possible charter of the aircraft, the on-board post office would no longer be allowed to operate. However, nothing would stand in the way of using the remaining postage stamps with a possible return flight or a flight conducted under our direction that would visit different countries." So the remaining stamps, worth 806 Reichsmarks, stay on board the docked Do X and probably the still unopened registered package too, with postage valued at 6,000 Reichsmarks.

For Wilhelm Niemann, the months in New York from September 1931 result in unanticipated difficulties. Within a few weeks, Curtiss has completed the planned maintenance changeover of the twelve engines and the flying boat. Now repaired and inspected, it is available for the long-desired charter

View from a skyscraper of the Do X. (Photo: Dornier GmbH, EADS)

business. For that the crew must stay in New York and stick together. The navigation officer of the Do X finds himself faced with this task since there is no commander of the flying ship at the time. Friedrich Christiansen returned from Rio to Germany for news coverage at the Ministry of Transportation, and South America commander Fritz Hammer and his pilot Cramer von Clausbruch are needed in Brazil. Now Niemann is supposed to take care of the daily expenses of the crew. The money is earned through souvenir sales and sightseeing revenues. For that he receives postcard books, pins, the special edition of the Aero Revue about the first leg of the Do X's journey and similar items sent from Germany. The main revenue hope, from a German perspective on the other side of the Atlantic, is still the DMB internal stationery. A fiasco for Niemann. Souvenir sales are slow to non-existent, and after the initial arrival euphoria, visitors marveling at the flying boat are absent. Soon the Do X will only be allowed to be viewed on the weekends instead of daily, as was planned.

Telegrams and letters pleading for badly needed money fall on deaf ears and the slow response from Friedrichshafen is demotivating. On November 16, 1931, the remaining crewmembers, who are living on credit, threaten to leave. It's over. In Germany, money is just as tight as it is in the one-time land of unlimited opportunities. The majority of the crew return to Germany on a steamship. All that remains for the Do X is winter storage at the Glenn Curtiss Airport.

Return Flight From New York To Berlin Over the Atlantic

In early 1932, the return flight to Germany looms. All charter and sales negotiations for the Do X in the USA have failed and in April the preparations for the return flight over the North Atlantic begin. There will be no mail accepted in New York because the U.S. postal authorities stand in the way. Only on-board mail can be brought to Germany. In order to save at least a part of the hoped-for mail revenue, Deutsche Flugschiff GmbH (DFG) has envelopes and postcards printed, which will include postmarks and special postal markings. They are to be offered to those interested for the price of postage plus a processing fee after the overflight. The DFG, a start-up company at the instigation of Dornier Metallbauten GmbH, originating on March 24, 1932, will operate the Do X in the future. With this, the Flugschiff company would become a beneficiary of the 4/5 share in revenue from the postal business. Despite discouraging experiences with the DMB internal stationery, a new attempt at philatelic Do X marketing defiantly begins.

When Flugschiff introduces its plans for Do X Atlantic flight stationery in the USA and Germany, there is definitely an interest for it. Wilhelm Niemann takes care of the internal stationery process, this time in the form of pre-printed DFG letter sheets

and postcards. With the rest of his stamp inventory, worth 806 Reichsmark, he would not get far. Now the postage stamp package from Rio de Janeiro serves its purpose.

It contains postage stamps worth 6,806RM, enough for around 680 letters, and about as many postcards. The Reichspost postage stamps of the on-board post office are quickly used up. With the large demand expected for DFG on-board postal stationery, Niemann falls back on the unloved bar stamper. Later interest for postmarked stationery with: AF-FRANCHISSEMENT PERCU, 6RM and 4RM, respectively, (postage paid) is limited. Postage stamps are missing on the mail. His cancellations with the Do X on-board postal stamper from 19 MAI 32 and 21 MAI 32 are well known. All postal items receive the diamond-shaped special marking: AMERICA EUROPA FLUGSCHIFF Do X (violet) as flight confirmation.

Four days after Pentecost, on Thursday morning of May 19, 1932 at 5:10am, the Do X takes off from Long Island Sound, 30km from New York City, with 51.1 tonnes in only fifty-three seconds. A successful take-off in ideal conditions gives hope for a smooth overflight. But on the first day, the North Atlantic shows its treacherousness. Thick fog prevents the approach of the actual target, Holyrood (St. John's) on Newfoundland, where the operating materials are stored and mailbags wait. After the involuntary stopover near Dildo in Trinity Bay, the flying boat splashes down in Holyrood's Conception Bay on May 20th. Now the Do X refuels for the overflight to Halskrause and full gasoline canisters are stacked in the passenger room.

One day before, the Department of Post and Telegraphs from Newfoundland publishes the following lines: "The Do X flying boat, which is set to arrive in St. John's today, will make the transport of mail to Europe possible. No more than 3,000 letters, each weighing under one ounce, will be delivered.

Its own postage stamps will be issued for $1.50, which are up for sale starting today at noon in the main post office. The deadline for Do X let-

On-board postal stamp marking during the return flight from New York to Berlin on May 22, 1932.

ters is immediately after special stamps sell out or at 10:00pm this evening, Thursday May 19th. G. Hodder, Deputy Minister."

The stamps, only available for purchase as a block of four (2,000 blocks were printed), cost six dollars per block and sell out in a short time. There are 8,000 Newfoundland airmail stamps with the red imprint: TRANS-ATLANTIC WEST TO EAST Per Dornier Do X May, 1932. One dollar and fifty cents (line) of course are not a substitute for the journey over the North Atlantic. The Newfoundland postal authorities leave 1,804 letters in closed mailbags on board. They are to be handed over in the Spanish port of Vigo for further transport in Europe. In sealed bags means no on-board Do X postmark and no special marking as flight confirmation. With this action, two allied airmail monopolies, the USA and Spain, use the German flying boat as a transport vehicle. A peculiarity still needs to be mentioned. The imprint on twenty or forty stamps is upside down. Specialists argue over the number of misprinted blocks of four. Was it five or ten blocks? A half a sheet or a whole? Of the 1,804 letters, 1,362 carry the postmark: ST.JOHNS,N'FLD. 1932 MAY19 7-PM and also 10-PM, with the advertisement: PREVENT FOREST FIRES-SAVE-OUR FORESTS in the line frames and to the right in the subsequent seven-fold line field. A delay by the flying boat brings an extension of the deadline and so 427 letters get the postmark with the date: 1932 MAY20 12-M.

The twelve Curtiss engines need one minute and fifty seconds to lift fifty-five tonnes off the water of Conception Bay. On May 21, 1932, at 8:40 in the morning, the Do X turns toward the open sea and disappears relatively quickly behind the horizon. Crossing the North Atlantic at an altitude of between three and five meters above the waves begins. After 2,260km of fuel saving ground effect flying, the Do X splashes down at night near Horta on the Azores. After stopovers in Vigo and Calshot near Southampton, the flying boat lands on the Müggelsee near Berlin on May 24, 1932 around 6:27pm. An excited crowd of Berliners greet the returning flying boat on the shores and in several boats on the water. Some postal clerks in the transit post office Berlin C turn up their noses when Niemann delivers the Do X on-board mail. They uncover a fly in the ointment, which can only be sanctioned by the Reichpost Ministry. The Graf Zeppelin airmail special marking "1. South

America Trip" (Mi. #438 and #439), widely used by the flying boat's postmaster, have not been valid since 6/30/1931. But the Reichspost turns a blind eye during the international Do X event. Postcards and letters of the last on-board mail receive their Berlin transit and arrival markings with a date of May 27, 1932. Thus concludes the history of the Do X flying boat's postal station.

Horst Merz sends on-board mail to his wife during the return flight too. (Photos: Johannes E. Palmer)

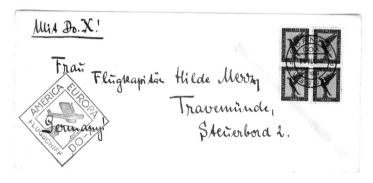

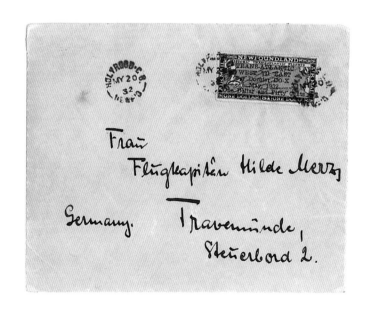

Cumbersome refueling from barrels in Holyrood,
Newfoundland. (Photo: Dornier GmbH, EADS)

Off the coast of Horta in the Azores at dawn. A few minutes
before takeoff towards Vigo on the Spanish west coast.
(Photo: Dornier GmbH, EADS)

Anchored in Vigo, the Cap Polonio on its way to Brazil sails near the Do X. (Photo: Dornier GmbH, EADS)

The Do X during its German tour, in Warnemünde on July 21, 1932. From left to right: Horst Merz, Friedrich Christiansen, Ernst Heinkel and Wilhelm Niemann. (Photo: L. Niemann)

The People and Personalities On Board and On the Ground

Claude Dornier, Creative Spirit Of the Flying Boat

Claude Honoré Désiré Dornier is the oldest son of Dauphin Dornier, born on May 14, 1884 in Kempten, Allgäu. His father had settled in Bavaria after the Franco-Prussian War of 1870/71 and tries to ensure a tolerable childhood for his eight children from two marriages as a sawmill owner, wine merchant, sanatorium operator and language teacher. This doesn't work out.

Financial distress, resulting from two bankruptcies and advanced physical decrepitude of the father's arthritis, leaves all of the children with bitter memories of their childhood. Claude Dornier experiences this for the first time as a mechanical engineering student in Munich. His father tells him that he can no longer pay for the cost of his studies. For Claude, who particularly values the funny side of life, mountain climbing and fencing at the Corpus Guestphalia fraternity, all of his hopes would crumble. But for his father as well, who now discovers that his oldest son has idled away the last few semesters of his studies. "College dropout, spiritual death, annihilation!" With this in mind, Claude finds a benefactor, who advances him 3,000 Marks up to the end of his studies. In a tour de force of asceticism and drawing work, he makes up for the missed work in a short time. He passes his diploma exams at the Technical University in Munich in 1907 and, from this time on, the family looks to him for help.

Claude Dornier, around 1935. (Dornier Museum)

He does what he can to help his siblings and parents make ends meet. After three jobs as a design engineer in Karlsruhe, Illingen and Kaiserslauten, Claude Dornier applies to Luftschiffbau Zeppelin GmbH in Friedrichshafen. The liberating invitation to interview comes months later:

"I saw light in the darkness of my existence." Starting on November 2, 1910, he is part of Graf Zeppelin's staff with its innovative operation. More than twenty-five years later, in a radio broadcast by the Reich broadcaster in Stuttgart, Claude Dornier, Honorary Doctor of Engineering, recounts the beginnings, the difficulties and the ascent of his own company: "When I came to Zeppelin as an engineer in 1910, I had already been through a lot. My introduction to airship construction began in the research department. After only a short time, Graf Zeppelin was already aware of me. My first big job was the design of a revolving airship hangar. The construction later received an award.

In 1913, Graf Zeppelin assigned me to design an airship for trans-oceanic service, but the outbreak of the World War brought this work to an end. At the end of 1914, he wanted me to build a large seaplane. Back then you still said aeroplane! The names airplane, seaplane or flying boat did not become customary until much later. When we began with this job, I certainly didn't think that I would be the first to build the first real flying boat. The job was enormously difficult because there was no foundation, and the fact that I envisioned building the water aircraft entirely out of metal didn't make coping with the assignment made any easier.

However, after all initial problems had been solved through hard work, the war again brought this work to an abrupt end. But in the following years, the old, wooden Zeppelin hangar in Seemoos was our highly competitive workplace, and we often didn't know if we would get paid. Today's "Dornier method" came about as a result of that endless effort. Then came the peace treaty, which was paralyzing to further work. So we had to turn our interests abroad. In 1922, we successfully founded a subsidiary company in Marina di Pisa, Italy. An order for a flying boat with six twin engines came from Spain. These were the first boats in the large family of Dornier Wals, whose performance became recognized throughout the world. There is no doubt that these flying boats were the foundation for us to slowly but surely increase exports in the following years. Furthermore, the sale of licenses abroad was important for further development. The resulting experiences were so broad that we could dare to tackle the construction of a flying boat with quite extraordinary dimensions in 1926. This flying boat, the Do X, was another milestone on the path of our ascent. It was often claimed that the Do X was ahead of its time. But over the last few years, the views on large flying boats has changed considerably. The thoughts I expressed years ago have prevailed more and more, and now no design engineer can do without the wealth of experience gained through the Do X or the Dornier method when considering the future development of large flying boat construction.

In 1932, I was able to acquire all of the company shares in our factory from the hands of the remaining partners. The economic situation of the following years improved a lot from the preceding low point. Aside from flying boats and seaplanes, new land plane models were now being developed too, which have made a great impact in the buildup of

The beginnings of Dornier Metallbauten GmbH in the See-moos shipyard near Friedrichshafen. (Dornier GmbH, EADS)

Claude Dornier and his chief engineer Albert Presser, in the middle, studying construction plans. (Dornier GmbH, EADS)

the German Luftwaffe, like the Do 179 fighter plane, for example."

The military armament, described as an "impro-ved economic situation" by Dornier, is a consequence of the political changeover of power in Germany, and makes the company of the German aviation industry one of the world's top aircraft manufacturers. Claude Dornier and his fellow enterprisers then experience National Socialism as driver of the defense economy. The devastating catastrophe of the Second World War and its consequences are a final turning point. After Claude Dornier dies on December 5, 1969 in Zug, Switzerland, his life's work, now in the hands of his family, aspires to new technological heights

with changing ambitions. In conjunction with practi-cal technology for aviation and astronautics, Dornier continues for another half century after 1945 before they too hear a nostalgic ring at the beginning of the twenty-first century.

Friedrich Christiansen, Ship's Captain as Commander

Friedrich Christiansen comes from a long-es-tablished captain's family from the tranquil seaside resort town Wyk and is among the fa-mous sons of the North Frisian island Föhr in Schles-wig Holstein. Wyk makes him an honorary citizen after Kaiser Wilhelm II honors him with the highest Prussian decoration for bravery, the Pour le Mérite, on December 11, 1917. Until 1980, Große Straße, lea-ding from the bell tower to Königstraße, is named Friedrich-Christiansen-Straße. And it probably would have remained so had he not had a prominent position during the twelve years of National Soci-alism, after which his name and achievements are discredited. Today, citizens and vacationers stroll down Große Straße again, and Friedrich Christian-sen is banned from the archives.

In August 1932 the situation is quite different. A contemporary chronicle describes it:

"A crisp August day. The otherwise quiet Wyk, the lovely little seaside resort town, is in a festive mood. The farmers drop their harvest work, and attention is drawn to the beach, where anything that has legs and time gathers in an expectant mood. The houses are decked with flags and decorated, and no one remem-bers ever seeing so many people on the beach. The Do X and "Fiede" are approaching. The fire department is deployed to establish order. The central path on the beach promenade is blocked off. The arrival is plan-ned for twelve o'clock. The accidentally transmitted message of a late departure from Flensburg creates a certain disappointment. The fire department is sent away for lunch since the arrival is not expected un-til one o'clock in the afternoon. But before noon, a roar fills the air. The Do X appears, barely visible at first, above the Oland hallig. A flurry of excitement on the beach. Where is the fire department? The roaring grows to a rumble, the giant bird grows ever larger over the home waters of its commander. The fire marshall is frantic, How will he get his men into position? 'Sound the fire alarm!' calls one of his trusted men. Then everything gets lost in the awesome sight and the eruption of joy by the otherwise peaceful island inhabitants and delighted crowd. Over Olhörn, where he sailed many times in his youth, Fiede guides his flagship at a low altitude over his birthplace. The next loop goes over the churchyard of St. Nikolai. The roar of propellers reverberates on the ancient walls of the dignified church, announcing a new era to the ancestors resting there. An islander returns home from distant travels over the oceans! The motors thunder over the green island once more, over Wyk, then the landing takes place in view of the crowded local beach." With four maneuver engines running along the promenade, the flying boat turns to the anchor buoy on the Wyk roads in front of the south beach and moors there. With his sailboat and a large flag on the mast, nine-year-old Harro Christiansen and an older friend appear at the buoy. Harro Christainsen recounts: "This maneuver was successful on the first try. When the giant bird headed to the buoy, I wasn't afraid because I'm familiar with handling painters and maneuvering ships; the only thing that's frightening is the tremendous engine noise. Unfortunately, the conning tower forbids us from going alongside the ship since the swell could have forced the mast of my boat through the wing panel covering. But later I got the opportunity to be taken on board to look around."

Discredited By National Socialism

Karin de la Roi-Frey, from Wyk, also speaks about the fascination that young people had in the flying ship and its commander, in her memoir 'Why Does a Girl Need a Desk?'

"Grandmother's son Otto is six years old in 1932 when he runs down to the sand wall on Wednesday, August 1st to witness one of the most impressive events in the history of Föhr, which will stay with him forever. They are all waiting for Friedrich Christiansen, the "Föhr lad," who has crossed the Atlantic with his Do X and has thus become known in all corners of the world. Over the course of his life, my

Friedrich Christiansen with his staff, as commander of the Wehrmacht in Holland.

father tells me again and again of the unbelievable moment when a low roar announces the arrival of the Do X, which is sighted in the sky shortly after by a cheering crowd … Besides this experience, my father, whose confirmation takes place during World War II, has a very personal memory of the Do X captain Christiansen. Father's already simple and thrifty home life has become even more frugal during these years and it isn't possible for my grandmother to sew a confirmation suit for her oldest, let alone buy one. It probably would have remained this way, had Friedrich Christiansen not existed, whose name is mentioned with a certain gratitude since then. When the Germans enter Holland, the former Do X commander is the commander of the Wehrmacht in occupied Holland and is responsible for the evacuation, eviction and 'cleansing' of certain areas, streets and houses. Friedrich Christiansen sends part of the property left behind by this to his home island and it is distributed to those in need. And so my father does get a confirmation suit. Not until many years later, after I hear this story for the first time and Friedrich-Christiansen-Straße is renamed to Große Straße due to the mistakes of the name giver, I dare to ask my father if he ever once thought about the boy who wore the suit before him."

In 1929, Captain Friedrich Christiansen steers his decorated freight and passenger motor ship, the Rio

Bravo of the Flensburg ocean line, on a long voyage over the mid-Atlantic. With freight, eighty-eight first class passengers and seventy-three crewmembers, the Rio Bravo has been commuting between Hamburg and Mexico (and/or Texas) about five times a year since 1924. England and Cuba are among the other stopovers on this voyage.

Going out to sea is a family tradition of the Christiansen men. Friedrich, who is born on December 12, 1879 in the family house near the bell tower in Wyk, is no exception. After attending secondary school and a private school, when Friedrich Christiansen is just fifteen years old, he joins the merchant marines as a cabin boy. He experiences his first trip to South America as a sixteen year old aboard the fully rigged ship Parchim. This is followed by the Hamburg Navigation School with his officer exam in 1900 and signing on as 2nd officer to the German Empire's five-mast ship, the Pruessen.

After more training, he passes the exam as a skipper on long voyages (patent AC) in 1904. "Krischan" as his good friends call him, discovers a love for all things technical. After he gets his 3b driver's license in 1913, he meets Carl Caspar, the later founder of Caspar Flugzeugbau in Travemünde-Priwall. At the time, Caspar is head of the Centrale für Aviatik and starts the Hansa-Flugzeugwerke in Hamburg. He arranges flying lessons for the seaman Friedrich Christiansen, taught by the flight pioneer Wilhelm Krumsiek in a 100hp Hansa Taube. On March 27, 1914, "Krischan" holds pilots license #707 in his hands. He becomes addicted to aviation. He signs off as a ship's officer in favor of "vague airplane projects," as he himself puts it. He begins to train pilots at this time and takes part in numerous competitions and airshows.

Becoming a Flying Hero
In the First World War

With the outbreak of World War I, the now thirty-five-year-old is called to the sea flight station Kiel-Holtenau where he trains pilots – back then he was one of the few pilots with flight experience over open water. Despite his above average age for a pilot on the front lines, he is pulled in the direction of the he-

ated war effort. In January 1915, he gets his transfer to the sea flight station Zeebrügge (Flanders). He remains stationed there until the war ends and climbs in rank from airman first class to highly decorated lieutenant with twenty-seven aerial victories. Christiansen becomes the tactical master of German marine aviation. But he is also a master of reconnaissance over the sea. Where he appears in the skies above the sea with his comrades Theo Osterkamp (1892-1975) and Gotthard Sachsenberg (1891-1961) remains uncontested in German air supremacy. "Our enemy, who was very cleverly led by Lieutenant Christiansen, displays great courage and intelligence during his operations. This officer is a seaman by trade, but also an accomplished pilot and an excellent marksman and sportsman," say the English of their successful opponent. With 440 sorties and 1,164 flying hours, Friedrich Christiansen advances to station commander of the sea flight station in Flanders on September 16, 1917.

Due to his aeronautical leadership qualities and his bravery, which are proven time and again, Kaiser Wilhelm II promotes him to Lieutenant Commander of the marine artillery.

Oberleutnant Friedrich Christiansen in 1918 – awarded the Pour le Mérite for bravery.

During the preparations for the Do X's ferry flight toward the USA. Friedrich Christiansen and Claude Dornier in Altenrhein.

The war is over. After an interlude at the marine brigade of Löwenfeld and in the Caspar aircraft factory on Priwall, Christiansen flies together with his war observer Wladika to Norway. With a machine, constructed according to his suggestions, he tracks down herring and sardine schools, which he then leads to the fishermen. Organizing something similar in the North Sea is unsuccessful, and so he returns to Christian seafaring – first, as captain of the mail steamer Nordfriesland and in 1924 as captain of the motor ship Rio Bravo.

His interest in aviation has not diminished, and when he learns of Claude Dornier's plans for the Do X, he travels to Friedrichshafen several times to catch up on the development and construction status. The two get to know one another and Dornier offers him, in consultation with the Ministry of Transportation, the command post. The nomination of "Krischan," the old sea dog, fascinates aviation people in particular. Internationally, the flying boat should be declared a sea going vessel. Friedrich Christiansen himself states: "This flying boat has been developed as an experimental and test boat for long-distance air transport. In this respect, obstacles still stand in the way of this air transport over countries and oceans when it is still particularly difficult to get permission to fly over foreign territories. Because the boat will fly primarily over the ocean, I asked

myself, can you avoid foreign territories? The seas belong to everyone. When you arrive at the coast in the three-mile-zone, you simply land in the water and navigate like a seafaring vessel into port. Of course, there is the provision that implies that any vessel that moves on the water under its own power is a ship. To continue this train of thought let me set up the ship's articles at the Hamburg Port Authority, which applies to every ship. I would hire my crew, as a captain signs on his people. With my ship's articles, I still have to be represented at the Hamburg Senate. The men before me are a bit bewildered, but then I reference the international maritime laws and demand that the flying boat have the same rights as other ships ... The Hamburg Port Authority has, in the past, helped me overcome major obstacles abroad through these ship's articles; when the aeronautical agreements make problems, I am just a ship, proven by the ship's articles."

Command Hierarchy Like On a Ship

All the important information about the flying boat and its crewmembers is recorded in the ship's articles, which is part of the ship's papers. Every crewmember also gets a seaman's record book. The port authority notes all personal and travel information it. The seaman's record book is maintained by flight mechanic Ernst Brombeis for the second Atlantic crossing. As a representative of Captain Christiansen, Wilhelm Niemann certifies the signing off of Brombeis on November 21, 1932 and the period of service during the Atlantic flight and the German tour from April 19, 1932 to November 14, 1932, lasting six months and twenty-five days.

The port authority confirms the pension insurance verification for Ernst Brombeis. Normally, the monthly pay is also stated in the seaman's record book, but this information is missing here. In addition to a rather low base pay, the crewmembers get a daily allowance and mileage allowance, which are scaled according to position and function. Some of the officers of the ship's command receive their salaries from their parent companies, like Newmann from the Hamburg-America Line, radio officer Kiel from DEBEG and pilot Merz from Luft Hansa. On board the Do X, Friedrich Christiansen organizes the hierarchy and duties like on a ship. Constant watch with an officer and two men are also a part of this, as is the appointment of Wilhelm Niemann as his proxy and first officer on board.

The next level of officers is equal, which applies to pilots, radio operators and mechanical engineers. Even if Horst Merz likes to portray it differently in later years, Commander and Captain Friedrich Christiansen has the say on board. Merz only flies under directive and not on all parts of the route. As we know, the Do X spends the majority of the time during its two-year journey, from November 5, 1930 to November 14, 1932, taxiing, moored on the water or on land. For the entire flight distance of 43,482km, the Do X needs around 258 hours, just about eleven days of pure flying time.

Horst Merz, Pilot of 8,000 Horsepower

Horst Merz in November 1930. (Staatsarchiv St. Gallen)

To mark his birthday in 1976, the public relations department of Dornier publishes a remarkable resume of the birthday boy:

"On December 2, 1976, flight captain, engineer, and Oberst Horst Merz celebrates his 85th birthday. His name will forever be connected with the pioneer flights of the twelve-engine Do X flying boat. Forty-five years ago, this first wide-bodied aircraft started one of the most spectacular flights ever over four continents and twice crossed the Atlantic Ocean, the southern and the northern route. At the wheel of the Do X: flight captain Horst Merz.

The biographical data of the birthday boy underlines an extraordinary pilot career from the pioneering days of aviation. Horst Merz is born on December 2, 1891 in Lehma (near Altenburg, Thuringia), the son of a royal Saxon forester. After his abitur (1912), Horst Merz wants to become a sailor, and he joins the Imperial Navy as a yearlong voluntary seaman. A medical examination quickly ends his dream of devoting himself completely to Christian seafaring. His eyes are not "seaworthy" enough, and so Horst Merz becomes a pilot, an inspired pilot and one of

the most distinguished flying boat pilots, but he always remains loyal to seafaring.

In 1913, Horst Merz begins his mechanical engineering studies in Danzig and also attends the men's pilot school of His Highness, Prince Sigismund von Preussen. In 1914, he is ordered to Fliegerersatzabteilung 4 as boatswain in Posen and receives his pilot's license at Albatros in Schneidemühl. During World War I, he flies reconnaissance flights on the eastern front for Hindenburg. After an emergency landing near Plock on the Vistula River, Merz is captured by the Russians. He attempts to escape the prison camp Krasnojarsk in central Siberia three times. He is caught twice but then makes it through to German lines in 1917 wearing a Russian uniform. In 1918, he receives fighter pilot training and is deployed to the fighter squadron in Flanders. In 1922, Horst Merz then goes into commercial aviation at the Danzig airline Danziger Aero Lloyd. He flies the five-seat passenger machine Fokker F II on the land route Danzig-Memel-Riga. Because the route can only be flown in the summer, he is able to continue his studies in the winter, and in 1925 he receives his diploma in mechanical engineering.

In 1924, Aero Lloyd awards a contract to Horst Merz to perform the first night test flights at sea.

Completely on his own, he flies the route Stettin-Copenhagen with a Dornier Delphin II flying boat under the most difficult conditions. In 1925 and 1926, Deutsche Luft Hansa, or more precisely Nordiske Flyg Reederiet under the Swedish flag, employs Horst Merz for passenger services across the sea. On the routes Danzig-Stockholm and Stettin-Stockholm, he flies the world-famous Dornier Wal flying boat. In 1927/1928, Deutsche Luft Hansa and the Imperial Navy in Warnemünde have the new Dornier flying boats, the twin-engine Superwal and the four-engined Superwal, tested for scheduled services by Merz.

Flight captain Horst Merz calls the years from 1929 to 1932 the high point of his aviation career at sea. As the pilot responsible for the Do X flying boat, he operates the giant plane on a unique demonstration flight from Lake Constance. The route includes Amsterdam, Calshot (England), Bordeaux, Santander (Spain), Lisbon, along the African west coast, the Atlantic crossing and along the South American coast to Rio. The return flight from New York via the Azores to Berlin, and the great Germany tour with over thirty splashdowns on German rivers and lakes are all piloted by Horst Merz. For this outstanding achievement in aviation, flight captain Horst Merz receives the Golden Lufthansa Pin for Atlantic Flight, and the Secretary of State Dr. Lewald Prize for promoting air services for Atlantic aviation."

His First Overflight Attempt Ends In the Atlantic Near Horta

An overflight attempt, in which Horst Merz is considerably involved, precedes the Atlantic crossing by the Do X. After Charles Lindbergh's legendary nonstop flight from New York to Paris on May 20, 1927, there is plenty of ambition on both sides of the Atlantic to be the next to fly across. The first German attempt to cross the Atlantic in an east to west direction belongs to the forgotten chapters of aviation history. With the serial number 286, Ernst Heinkel has a seaplane built in his Warnemünde airplane factory, and he plans a "big bang" with it. At his own cost, and risk, he builds his Heinkel He 6b, a low-wing aircraft with floats and a round glass cabin. Equipped with the strongest engines attainable for Heinkel back then, a Packard 3 A 250 with 880hp and crow-

Contemporary advertisement for Ernst Heinkels seaplane, with the He 6 in action.

After the failed takeoff off the coast of Horta, what's left of the Heinkel 6 hangs on a hook.

ded with fuel tanks, the machine should be able to fly over 4,000km uninterrupted. "On the other hand, the speed was not so important. Nevertheless, the machine reached 205km/h. Surprisingly, my airplane is to take off from Lisbon, stop over in the Azores during the first flight and then make it to Newfoundland, but then conquer the Atlantic without interruption," remarks Ernst Heinkel in his memoirs from 1955.

On October 12, 1927, Luft Hansa flight captian Horst Merz and his crew, consisting of on-board lookout Bock and radioman Rohde, takes off from Warnemünde in quiet stillness with the D-1220.

Afflicted by abundant mishaps they reach Lisbon via Brunsbüttel, Wilhelmshaven, Amsterdam and Vigo on October 18th. After waiting for better weather and necessary repairs, the flight to Horta on the Azores island of Faial takes place on November 4th, they happily arrive after nine hours and twenty-five minutes. Horst Merz then attempts to take off from the harbor several times. Against the Atlantic swells and with the heavily laden seaplane, he is unsuccessful. A last attempt to fly onward to Harbour Grace (Newfoundland) ends in a fiasco on November 13. Just as it lifts off the water, the D-1220 dips once more. A float cuts into the crest of a wave, gets ripped off and the He 6 somersaults. All crewmembers escape the closed cabin fast enough and are able to hold on to the floating debris until a motorboat rescues them. With that, Ernst Heinkels dream sinks off the coast of Horta with a huge financial loss. It is more than five months after the non-stop flight of Charles Lindbergh and five months before the first successful German east-west crossing by Köhl, von Hünefeld and Fitzmaurice.

Zero Altitude Flying With the Do X

Pilots and What They Experienced is the title of the book by Werner von Langsdorff, which is published in 1935. In it, Horst Merz describes the Atlantic crossing from Newfoundland to Vigo, Spain via the Azores from the perspective of a pilot seated on the left:

"On the evening of May 20, 1932, in the port of Holyrood, a difficult day lies behind us. We had to take 27,000 liters of fuel after all. It was difficult and time consuming because we only had two rowboats and only two to three of the many barrels could be

brought from the jetty to the flying boat anchored 100 meters away, where they were then emptied by hand pump. The work is often interrupted when the flying boat drifts in the gusty winds, and due to the stony ground, must return to its original position under its own engine power. Meanwhile, the entire vessel must be thoroughly inspected again because tomorrow counts!

Everyone inspects what he knows best one last time. My comrade Walter Diele and I test all of the steering with its rods, ropes and bearings since we pilots have to make sure it works properly. The radio operator gathers the weather reports. The engine mechanics give their engines extra special care because our flight depends on their smooth operation. Even if the breakdown of several engines doesn't affect the flying boat under normal conditions, we are, on the first part of the route anyway, dependent upon all engines, due to the very heavy take-off weight caused by the required quantity of fuel. Over the course of the day, everything is clearly reported to the commander and the gasoline delivery is completed at 9:30 in the evening.

A warm dinner on land should compensate for the efforts of this hard day of work and warm us up a bit. But what we get after waiting for hours is sparse and cold! Now we want to at least get on board and get some sleep. We make it as far as the jetty, where we discover that the owner of the boat has prudently taken the oars home with him. Another hour goes by and we stand freezing in the cold night before both are recovered. Needless to say that a few choice words are uttered here! When we finally crawl into our sleeping bags around 1:30, the mood is not exactly rosy.

Two hours later 'voyage-voyage!' echoes throughout the ship. Getting dressed and drinking coffee proceeds silently. This day of decision offers some difficult challenges: taking off with the unprecedented take-off weight, crossing the notorious Grand Banks of Newfoundland with its fog and icebergs, finding the 'needle in the haystack' Azores and finally the anticipated landing in darkness. But all thoughts are quickly cut off by the command: 'clear for maneuvering!' First, it is difficult to raise the anchor, which is stuck behind a rock. Then the engines don't want to start in the cold – it's only a few degrees above zero. Eventually they are all up and running and we taxi out of Conception Bay ahead of a strong south wind. We give the engines plenty of time to warm up and taxi far to the north because we have to take off to the south away from land and then turn within the bay with the heavy machine. Finally we reach the starting place. Turn! One last check of all the instruments and the steering. Go! Full throttle! Despite its 55.5 tonnes – actually, it's 57.5 tonnes, as we determine later in November when we return to Altenrhein and weigh it – the ship quickly comes to step and gains in speed. The cold, well-supporting air, the sharp wind and the quite steady low sea without swells are favorable conditions. I sit at the wheel extremely tense: an aircraft with this much weight has never taken off and flown, and my experiences only go up to fifty-two tonnes. I definitely believed that I would manage the take-off. What the ship will do in the air and especially in the turn, we had to wait and see. But I have full confidence here too.

The speedometer reads 120, 130, 140km/h. Just let her go on steadily, I think, until she wants to go out on her own because she can't fall in again at this weight! Finally, at 155km/h, a light tug on the pitch elevator, and we are free! Take-off duration is one minute and forty-six seconds. Now just press it properly and accelerate! Then up to thirty meters and into the turn. The machine is perfectly solid. We can breath our first sigh of relief! We are already on a north course and I can even reduce the engines a bit so that they no longer have to work at maximum load. When the tongue of land comes to an end on the starboard side, I slowly turn to the east. When we pass the headland, another critical moment arrives when we come into the downdraft winds, which almost pushes us back into the ocean with our low net force. Full throttle and clenched teeth! After a few seconds, we are through and stay on a southeast course along the Banks.

What do the next few hours have in store for us? Flying blind through the fog is out of the question with a load like this; climbing in altitude too. All that remains is flying low close to the water. And in the Newfoundland fog – a 50% chance of thick fog according to the month's report – not to mention the many fishing vessels and icebergs?! The sea is quite unsettling, and we fly one to two meters above it. But

we are able to spare the engines and save gasoline this way since the air closest to the water increases lift. The sky is cloudy; isolated showers dim the view. But we get through under the low lying clouds. Diele and I take turns at the wheel in short intervals. It is getting gradually warmer. Suddenly the clouds disappear and the sun shines through. And our location on the map is no longer a mystery. We have the Grand Banks of Newfoundland behind us and we haven't seen any fog, fishermen or icebergs! Now we can breath another sigh of relief!

Now everything is quite comfortable; inside and outside only bright sunshine! Hour by hour we move along on our course at two meters altitude. The horizon stands there as if engraved before our eyes. But we don't get bored. Twice we encounter whales that slowly wallow through the long Atlantic swell, and from time to time blow out spurts of water. I fly directly over one. And even though our twelve engines with at least 8,000hp thunder only a few meters over him, he is not bothered at all. A human form, sewn in a brown sailcloth like a clumsy wooden figure, floats in the waves – a flock of seagulls takes me off course a bit and then I discover it – a grave disposition and reminiscent of some of the absorbing narratives by Gorch Fock. A Danish barque sailing homeward at full sail makes all the sailors' hearts beat faster and they receive a lap of honor. Then we drearily continue our course. Finally, we see Flores and Corvo, the northwestern islands of the Azores archipelago.

Splashdown On the Atlantic At Night

It's already thick. For a quarter of an hour we fly through a thick fog. Then it stops. But it is replaced by night. We had hoped to reach the Azores earlier, but the cross winds were in no way favorable. We didn't choose our starting day according to the best weather

One of the first Luft Hansa Atlantic pins, which was awarded in 1932.

conditions, but set the departure day as May 19th from the get go, considering the New York mail deadline. Now the Do X will show that she can conquer the North Atlantic under unfavorable conditions too! Now it's dark and we have to fly higher because the surface of the water can no longer be seen. We turn the lights on and fly according to the instruments. Diele and I take turns more frequently. The very good longitudinal stability of the machine is an advantage for us. We read the lateral position and bank position according to the turn and bank indicator and the attitude indicator. Finally, the lights on the island of Faial are in sight, and we fly north along it in order to get a view of Horta's harbor lighthouse lying in the straight between Faial and Pico. But apparently that was obscured, so we fly further east, well clear of the island Pico with its 3,000 meter mountain.

We double back and we can make out Horta in the distance on the port side. At the same time, we are notified that the gasoline is running out. A precise check reveals that the supply is definitely not enough to reach Horta, which means gradually bringing the machine down onto the water with running engines. This is absolutely imperative because you can't see the water in darkness, so timely interception of the machine by an escort flight with turned-off or idle engines is impossible. The difficult decision has to be made to land here immediately, outside on the open Atlantic beyond the islands.

Horta reports wind and swells from the south, so I set the machine on a westerly course in order to land, not against, but along the swell, and prevent the machine from jumping out again and slamming against the next wave. Then I reduce the gas so that the machine gradually loses altitude at an even keel. Behind us, extreme tension prevails in the entire ship. Everyone knows that the next few minutes are crucial to the return flight! My eyes are glued to the instruments, and with slight steering movements, I improve the position of the machine. Diele looks out below on the starboard side to catch a glimpse of the water surface at the last moment. Time stands still. Meter by meter, the altimeter goes down. When it shows about twenty meters, I pull on the elevator just a bit. In the next instant, the heel touches the water! Gas out! The machine sets down in the water softly and without any impact and proceeds lengthwise to the swell. The most difficult part of the return flight

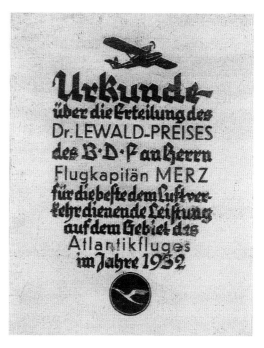

Certificate of the Lewald Prize for Horst Merz.

is over. In fifteen hours and twenty minutes we had conquered the Newfoundland-Azores route. We still have to taxi for four hours, driven by two engines. Soon the moon rises, which up until now has hid behind Mount Pico. Around midnight, we arrive at the port of Horta and moor on the same buoy that I did in November 1927 with my Heinkel D 1220."

After the fiasco with the Do X on the Danube in early May 1933 and his difficult position with Lufthansa, Horst Merz is reactivated by the Luftwaffe and is appointed the rank of colonel at the end of World War II. After the war he initially works for the company Siemens in Munich and then several years at Bölkow-Entwicklungen KG (later MBB) in Ottobrunn. During this time, he is active as joint engineer of helicopter development in Ottobrunn and prototype production at Waggon und Maschinenbau AG (WMD) in Donauwörth. He doesn't retire until 1966 at seventy-five years of age. One year before this, he is honored with the Chain of the Windrose for pioneers of aerospace by the International Committee of Aerospace Activities (ICAA).

He is appreciated for his "outstanding merits in promoting international aviation, which he demonstrated from 1930 to 1932 as the pilot responsible for the Do X flying boat on its Atlantic flights." With the Chain of the Windrose he is in good company with Wernher von Braun, Kurt H. Debus, Igo Etrich, James Fitzmaurice, Wolfgang von Gronau and John H. Glenn, to mention just a few of the aviation greats with this distinction. His contemporary, Rudolf Cramer von Clausbruch, with whom he competed for the South Atlantic crossing of the Do X on June 4, 1931, is also among the selected group of award winners. Horst Merz died on August 24, 1979 in Munich.

Wilhelm Niemann, Navigator and Postmaster of the Do X

Magdalena Niemann is probably the last contemporary witness to travel aboard the Do X and her first memory as a four-year-old is of an old man in uniform. In pouring rain, he helps her exit the Do X in Kiel. "So, my little one, uncle Fiede will help you!" still rings in her ears today. She tells of her father, Wilhelm Niemann, Navigation Officer of the Do X:

Wilhelm Niemann tries to keep the crew together in New York. (Photo: Lena Niemann)

"'Lena, you slept peacefully through the entire excitement!' Whenever my mother talks about the dreadfully beautiful scene that we experienced together as a family, which I slept through, I get goosebumps. On that Tuesday, July 26, 1932, around 1:40pm, the Do X is on one of the legs of its Germany tour and, at a few hundred meters altitude, it is on its way from Travemünde to Kiel with the Niemann family on board. My father is up in the navigation room and my mother is with me, the sleeping Lena, among the passengers. The passengers look out of the portside portholes somewhat skeptically at the green island Fehmarn with a menacing mountain of black-gray storm clouds hanging over it. But on the starboard side, the sun is shining on the unaffected Fehmarn Belt. The passengers of the well-staffed flying boat look curiously at a three-masted barque crossing under full sail. Apparently, the entire crew is whistled on deck and greets the passing Do X. 'That's the Niobe, the training sailboat of the Navy,' remarks one of the male travelers, and it slowly disappears from the field of view. No one could anticipate the tragedy that would take place in the next half an hour on the waters of the Belt. A sudden thunder squall capsizes and sinks the sailboat in only three minutes. It kills sixty-nine men of the crew, forty-seven of whom are young recruits, Navy career candidates who are having class below deck. A national disaster, which overshadows the day-to-day politics of the month. After landing in Kiel, my father learns of the incident and immediately volunteers to help the Navy search and rescue units. But there is nothing left to do.

My father can sympathize with what happened on the Fehmarn Belt. Born the son of a farmer in Ellingstedt near Schleswig on August 25, 1892, he loses his father at an early age. He dies in an accident with a horse and cart. His mother, alone with four children, dies one year later. After completing secondary school in 1908, he stands on his own two feet and, as the oldest of the Niemann siblings, who all grow up dispersed among relatives, he goes out to sea. He travels as a sailor trainee and a young seaman on various sailboats and steamships until the fall of 1913. In spring 1914, he passes his helmsman exam for long voyages in Flensburg. His first ship as an officer is the four-masted Ernst from Hamburg, whose voyage to Australia during the World War brings him into war captivity until 1919. From today's perspective, this is certainly a fortunate circumstance since officers do not lead a horrible existence in the Berryma prison camp near Syndey, as photos from a former acquaintance show. My father would have liked to have stayed in Australia as a farmer, but the soil was no good for it. Wilhelm Niemann makes his way back to Germany via Brazil, where he also hoped to make a living farming. In the jungle there, he meets a compatriot swinging in a hammock, which goes to show how small the world can be. She is the daughter of a sawmill owner from Schleswig, and helps him find a job as a lumberjack. But the burgeoning commercial shipping industry in Germany lures my father back to Hamburg where he climbs in rank from fourth to first officer on various steamships with the Hamburg-America Line.

During this time, he makes up for his abitur and passes the radio operator class II test and his license for skipper on long voyages in Elsfleth in 1923. He also meets my mother in this same year, another great story from his life. He actually wants to visit the captain of his steamship in Hamburg. But Captain Jakob is not home. He rings the neighbor to leave a message and who stands there in the door frame? My dear mother, who is struck by Cupid's arrow just as much as my father.

His professional interest in seafaring, navigation, communications, and later also in aviation, predestines him for great assignments in the stormy years of aviation between the great wars. The aviation department of his shipping company follows all air transport developments closely. In August 1927 they send my father to the Rohrbach airplane factory as a navigation and radio officer for an Atlantic flight enterprise, which, in the end, is never realized. Incidentally, the same applies to the planned flight of a Junkers G 24, I think it had the tail number D-1230, from the Azores to Newfoundland. After that, they send him to pilot training at the passenger aircraft school in Warnemünde in May 1928. In July of that year, I came into the world. His whole life, my father has been the kind of person who wants to be involved with performance and has never pushed forward to be in the spotlight. Others also noticed his professional competence and human qualities. The Deutsche Verkehrsfliegerschule (DVS), German Air Transport School, asks him to leave the Hamburg-America Line

for two years in order to lead the navigation and radio department of their branch office in Warnemünde. In Berlin he passes his class II aircraft radio test and obtains the aeronautical competency certificates Sea B1 and Land-A.

Work space of the navigation officer on the command deck of the Do X, in the navigation room behind the cockpit. (Dornier GmbH, EADS)

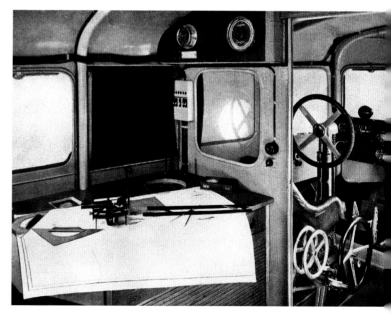

Claude Dornier and Wilhelm Niemann on the navigation table during the European tour. (Dornier GmbH, EADS)

Far left: Navigation officer Niemann confirms the entries in Ernst Bromeis's seaman's record book. Left: Master engine mechanic Ernst Brombeis.

When assembling a crew for his Do X, Claude Dornier inquires about a capable navigator with sea and aviation experience, and my father's name is mentioned immediately. Later, after the war, his brother tells a nice story that clearly depicts the family and hometown spirit of Wilhelm Niemann. In Warnemünde in 1929, he teaches the sons of the Bolivian president how to fly. After they both return home and talk about him enthusiastically, my father's desk telephone at DVS rings and the president personally asks him to come to Bolivia to build up an air force. After careful thought and consideration, together with my mother, he turns him down. The family council decides that Bolivia is too far away and can't be their new home.

On May 1, 1930, he returns to his post at the Hamburg-America Line and travels as first officer on the steamship Hohenstein for the South American route before his shipping company loans him to Dornier Metallbauten in Friedrichshafen to serve as navigation officer on Do X flights. From October 29, 1930 to November 1932 he functions as first officer on the flying boat and as stand-in for the commander, as navigation officer and as postmaster - or N.-O. "Do X," as he modestly abbreviated it.

In a letter from November 1, 1930, shortly before the start of the expedition with the flying boat, he describes his scope of duties on board: 'I have been assigned with navigation, including radio direction finder, all correspondence, the trimming of the ship, insurance matters, the control over the actual boat as well as all nautical tasks. I have also been sworn in as the flying boat's postmaster. Because my sphere of activity is quite extensive, the radio officer is available to me as an assistant.' Although his months with the crew and the flying boat in 1931 are not exactly easy, he experiences a lot. My parents didn't see one another for almost a whole year and my mother often told of her voyage to America on a steamship, their reunion in New York in the spring of 1932 and an impressive side trip to Canada before she had to return. In the months during the Germany tour, my parents of course saw one another often and the whole family traveled on board the Do X when it continued on. My mother was appalled to see a photo that she once received. The German Crown Prince invited the Do X crew to dinner and all the men sit in a large circle in formal attire, except for my father, who is wearing his beloved brown cardigan. When confronted by my mother, he only said: '… does it make me a different person then?' The Crown Prince was completely undisturbed, by the way.

In September 1933, my father becomes the head of the navigation department for the Deutsche Versuchsanstalt für Luftfahrt E.V., the German Research Institute for Aviation, in Berlin Adlershof. There he puts his real life experience in terrestrial, radio, and meteorological long-distance navigation to practical use. He wants to introduce the 400 degree circle to rotational measurements.

Today, we can imagine the outcry among traditional experts who wanted to hold on to the 360 degree system. My father countered the circus with slide rules and crooked values with a round, decimal logic. Fascinating, say the members of the German Society for Aeronautics, when my father presents them his findings in a speech in Berlin on January 22, 1935. They are all excited and want to take the difficult path to conversion. But fate had other plans for my father.

He plans a solo flight around the world for 1935. He begins with an exercise flight on March 21, 1935, during which he has to make an emergency landing near Beskow. Already on the ground, his machine responds uncontrollably with a jerk forward and he is fatally injured when his head slams into the compass on the instrument panel. That's how they reported his death to us anyway. My mother cannot attend the eulogy in Berlin with Milch and Christiansen, or the burial service in Hamburg. The pain of the great loss is too much to bear.

During my father's burial in Ohlsdorf, three airplanes circle over the cemetery with long black smoke ribbons and the words of the condolence telegram from the Crown Prince to my mother, '… you have had the love of a great man!' will remain a vivid memory."

Marcel Dornier, Logos and Fine Decor

During the unrest of the German Revolution in 1919, Claude Dornier, who has just lost his wife to the devastating flu pandemic and is left alone with two small boys, gets household help from his brother Marcel. In doing so, Marcel is able to pay Claude back somewhat for his protective hand over the years. Dauphin Marcel Dornier (1893-1988), painter and graphic artist, the youngest of the four Dornier siblings, experiences a tough adolescence after his care-free childhood and a rather frustrating schoo-

Marcel Dornier, around 1929.

ling period to become a penniless artist, which is supported by Claude as far as possible. His new endeavor at Luftschiffbau Zeppelin brings brother Claude a promotion. "Learn more at the Munich Academy!" says the ever helpful Claude to Marcel. "I can only give you 80 Marks a month!" Not much, but still enough to continue. Later, Marcel writes about himself: "I never knew what to do with my elbows. I always held them quietly by my side, maybe far too quietly and introspectively, and let the loud life pass me by."

Dornier – this name became a brand name in the international world of aviation – surely the sole merit of the nine-years-older brother Claude. But this is not the case. Marcel is able to make small, yet concise contributions to his brother's emerging enterprise. It's not only the company logos of Dornier Metallbauten GmbH and Dornier Flugzeuge AG,

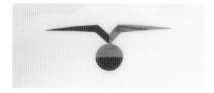

Logo of Dornier Flugzeuge AG, also in color on the porcelain of the Do X. Designed by Marcel Dornier in 1926.

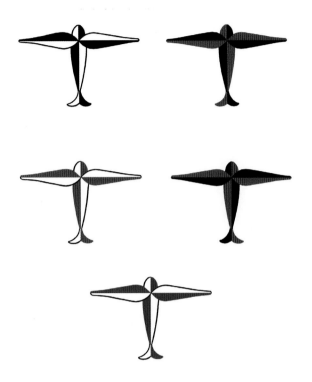

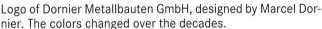

Logo of Dornier Metallbauten GmbH, designed by Marcel Dornier. The colors changed over the decades.

Advertisement example of Dornier Metallbauten GmbH by Marcel Dornier. (Dornier GmbH, EADS)

but also a multitude of promotional graphics that the artist implements for the needs of the business. Marcel Dornier later writes: "Advertising work and the design of passenger cabins kept me afloat from 1918 to 1926. The cabins of the Delphin flying boats and the Komet land machines, which I configured, were, to my knowledge, the first comfortable passenger cabins in aviation. The colorful coating of the airplanes, the comfort of the cabins, the installation of the seats, the wall treatments, the windows, doors and floor coverings, were all assigned to me by my brother. There was absolutely no standard! Every detail was a bother, sometimes it was the kind of mounting, sometimes the weight and the choice of materials. I could only overcome these challenges in cooperation with factory engineers. This was further complicated by the fact that my brother's taste, as well as mine, often deviated from the pure practical considerations of the technicians."

Marcel Dornier also commented on his brother's attitude toward aesthetic elements of his primarily technical, functional products, in other words, airplanes: "In his last years, my brother, the designer

of the Do X, the first giant flying boat, said to me, he would rather have become an architect than an engineer … My brother had an exceptional sense for beauty. Ugly things tormented him his entire life. The new auxiliary materials plastic, bakelite, cellophane, the wood-replacing building slabs and the like were unacceptable to him. As an architect, he would hardly have been able to resist these things. As an engineer, they didn't bother him. What my brother designed, he designed with authenticity and beauty." Certainly, with his brother in mind, and not in artistic conflict with his own opinions, Marcel Dornier designed several promotional materials for Dornier company advertisements.

Marcel Dornier designed posters, display elements, logos and interiors for Dornier products in the style of "New Objectivity." The décor of the Do X porcelain is also a part of it and other furnishings of the flying boat, such as table cloths, napkins, letter paper and others. Whether he also influenced the color layout of the Do X's interior furnishings is not completely clear. During the implementation and installation of the furnishings of the passenger deck in the summer and fall of 1930, he was already on the way to other shores. Disapproving of the political and societal developments in Germany, he moves to Switzerland with his wife in 1930, where he is allowed to live his life, and his artistic creativity unfolds over the next fifty years.

Chief Engineer, Albert Presser, Design Engineer of the Do X

"On March 23, 1935, Chief Engineer Albert Presser celebrates twenty years of uninterrupted activity in our factory (…)," reports the Dornier Post, the magazine for the operations of the Dornier Group, in issue #2 from January 1936. The column "Dornier Veterans" continues: "… His resume is the model of success gained through efficiency and tenacity. Our workmate Presser was born in Riedheim/Baden on June 10, 1880. After completing his three-year apprenticeship as a locksmith, he worked in this profession for several years in Straßburg, Freiburg and Singen. After completion of his military term of service, which he fulfilled from 1901 to 1903 with Infantry Regiment 114 in Constance, he attends the Stuttgart School of Architecture where he graduates with honors as a mechanical engineer after five semesters.

His work as engineer at various companies, most recently at Voith in Heidenheim, is interrupted by the outbreak of World War I. In the first days of mobilization, he heads to the battlefield with the Landwehr's Infantry Regiment 123 and takes part in the difficult fight on the front lines in the Vosges Mountains. After he is wounded and discharged from the hospital in March 1915, he is given leave upon request at the Dornier shipyard in Seemoos. At first, he works on the construction of the engine system of the first giant flying boat and later as machine operator during the testing of this model, in the hopes, as a member of the crew of the flying boat, to return to the front.

Dr. Dornier soon recognizes his extraordinary technical abilities, though, and appoints him to the design office, where he is assigned to the steering and tail unit department. Even if his wish to return to the front is unfounded, he has the satisfaction of knowing that the significance of his former actions for the national defense are recognized, not only by his war decorations, but also by being awarded the Prussian Cross of Merit."

During the relocation of the company to Lindau in 1917, he is assigned the general management of the technical office. In recognition of his service to the factory, Dr. Dornier appoints him chief engineer in 1923. As chief design engineer, Presser is significantly involved in new aircraft developments by Claude Dornier well into the Second World War. This applies to the planning of the Do X in particular.

Chief Engineer Albert Presser, right, and Claude Dornier having a discussion. (Dornier GmbH, EADS)

All hands on the passenger stairway! This photo of the complete crew of the Germany flight was taken in Hamburg. (Dornier GmbH, EADS)

Germany Tour of the Do X 1a

The jubilation in Germany over the successful return of the Do X knows no bounds. The events surrounding the flying boat and its crew on the Müggelsee in Berlin fills the newspaper headlines. Berliners are eager to the point of obtrusive and want to set foot on "their" flying boat and see it up close. "When can we see the Do X?" is a frequently asked question in the days following the landing, which is vigorously spread by the press and puts all persons involved, primarily the decision makers, under pressure. Shortly after the landing, a reporter from the Scherl Verlag asks Claude Dornier about his feelings at the moment: "... I can tell you that I am quite satisfied with the course of events – everything has unfolded nicely and according to plan. It was, however, quite bothersome that there were so many worries and sleepless nights – now everything has turned out well and I am happy about it. I was of course convinced of the success of my project, but there were also so many bitter disappointments. Someone just recently wrote that the Do X is utter nonsense and couldn't fly more than 500km. Today this person must stand corrected. This flight has taught me that its not just about the new boat, even though it is so well designed, but mainly about the crew, their spirit and their knowledge." These words by the designer of the Do X don't apply solely to the second successful Atlantic crossing, but also for the last three years. Existential financing concerns, the doubters and the inherent German ways of thinking, made the visionary's life sour, a man who's sense for viable and reliable technology extended far beyond the limits of convention.

During the all of the interviews, festivities and receptions in the first three days after May 24, 1932, Claude Dornier and Friedrich Christiansen have to hold important discussions in the background with the Ministry of Transportation. Since spring 1932, there have been efforts to release the Do X completely from Dornier. Behind this are the owners. The flying boat belongs to the German Reich, and Dornier Metallbauten GmbH is a restructuring case for

Hemmed in by recreational boaters from Berlin. After splashdown of the Do X on the Müggelsee on May 24, 1932. (Dornier GmbH, EADS)

All of Berlin wanted to see the Do X. Rush hour on Rübezahl on the southwest shore of the Müggelsee. (Dornier GmbH, EADS)

government coffers. For the transparency of the flying boat operation, the Reich demands that an operating company be founded. The events leading up to the resulting situation in June 1932 can be read in an audit report by the Deutsche Treuhand AG in 1934. It reads: "On behalf of the Reich's Aviation Minister, we reviewed the balance statement and the profit and loss statement at Deutsche Flugshiff Gesellschaft mbH for the 31st of March, 1933, and in particular the accounts for the expenditures accrued while chartering the state-owned Do X 1 flying boat to this company and the revenue generated … General. The company was founded, at the instigation of Dornier Metallbauten Gmbh (DMB), Friedrichshafen, on March 24, 1932 by both Berlin directors of DMB, Mr. Milatz and Schult-Frohlinde, for the purpose of operating of the Do X 1 flying boat. Capital was set at 20,000RM; the founders each assumed half of the capital with 25% to be paid in. The funds were made available to those named due to special contracts on the part of DMB. According to the contracts, the founders, as partners, were only trustees for DMB. The funds advanced (loans) were granted interest-free, with the obligation and the right to return the shares to DMB against the offset of loans."

That is the story of the founding of the Deutsche Flugschiff Gesellschaft. Now, after returning from the USA, a new contract with the owners must be made. The aviation department at the Ministry of Transportation was responsible for this. The Do X remains in Berlin until the conclusion of the new charter contract. After a technical review, preparations for visitors takes place. A pier suitable for the flying boat has to be rebuilt as quickly as possible. The spot on the yellow buoy, where the flying boat moors after the landing, is not suitable for visitors. After a few rainy days, the stampede to the Do X begins on June 6, 1932. The Berliners make the pilgrimage by foot, by bike, in special buses, by streetcar and boats of every kind and size to the Müggelsee. The popular excursion destination on the southwest shore of the lake, still called Rübezahl, is where the flying boat lies secu-

Königsberg is the easternmost point in Germany, and is one of the stops on the Do X's Germany tour. (Dornier GmbH, EADS)

rely moored for almost four weeks. There were no air tours for paying passengers in Berlin, in contrast to some other cities on the ensuing Germany tour. A carnival atmosphere surrounds the Do X, something the "veteran" Do Xers are already familiar with from their stopovers abroad. Thousands of people pass through the ship. Over the bridge, up on a sponson, through the door, look to the right, look to the left to the blocked-off passenger deck, oohs and aahs, and then the next curious people push in, through the opposite door, outside onto the second sponson and the second bridge and back. That was it! The Berliners and organizers think this is somewhat dissatisfying for the long stand in line. They have to come up with something new for the Do X's other stops.

Every visitor had to shell out fifty pfennigs for admission and the reduced price for the fun cost ten pfennigs. Fifty pfennigs (today about three Euro) is quite a deterrent price then. For many people du-

ring the deep recession, especially families, there was only a peak at the flying boat from the shore. This alone is enough. They are assured of seeing this grandiose flying boat in person and will now be able to tell their grandchildren about it. If we convert the 43,029.05 Marks of admission sales in Berlin to the possible visitor total, then close to one hundred thousand visitors see the sensation of June 1932.

The next stopover on the tour, now called "Germany tour," is Stettin. The announced take-off of the Do X, on June 23rd, again lures many Berliners to the shores of the Müggelsee. One low flying victory lap and Berlin is back to normal again. The first flight of the flying boat's Germany tour is only a hop, compared to the distances flown over the last few years. Two minutes from Berlin to Stettin at 159km/h, and this time without passengers. The Do X stays there for five days, from June 25th to the 29th, and then flies onward to Königsberg. This time there are passengers on board, as with almost all of the later legs of the tour. On June 30th, a Thursday, it flies along the Baltic Sea coast to Königsberg.

During the Do X's stopover in Flensburg, parliamentary elections take place that will shape the politically turbulent year of 1932. (Dornier GmbH, EADS)

When the roar of the engines rises, there is movement on the sandy beaches of Eastern Pomerania on this beautiful summer day. The Do X flies by at a moderate altitude and everyone cheers the flying boat with its proud crew. On the same day, a crowd of people develops in Königsberg to see it.

The unsatisfactory dock for the visitors in Berlin and the correct assumption to have a similar problem at all stopovers on the tour, leads to the construction of a special pier for the flying boat. In

Königsberg, the transportable lightweight construction made of metal pipes is used for the first time. The visitor comes over a mostly provisional dock to the sponsons. The steps of the dock climb up over the sides of the bow to the foredeck of the flying boat, and from here the cockpit can be viewed through the windows. On the other side, leading back down to the other sponson, the door to the passenger deck can be entered for a look around. From there, out through

the door, sometimes even out the rear emergency door, and back on land. This kind of circular course proves successful for the visitors. After acquiring the flying boat in April 1933, Luft Hansa is irritated when they discover that the dock installation is no longer a part of the equipment. The Flugschiff Gesellschaft sells it to them after the Germany tour.

During the period from June 6th to November 13th, 1932, close to 700,000 people come to see the flying boat and look around the cockpit and the passenger deck – a massive amount of people. Lining up and long waiting times are part of the ordeal in handling the stampede. Twenty-four stops in Germany, and ten days in Zurich, Switzerland, challenges the crewmembers. Although extra support staff is employed for ticket sales and ticket inspection, there is still plenty of daily work to prepare for the flights with paying passengers. Beginning in Stettin, the opportunity to fly on-board is provided, and the ticket prices are set according to distance. Between Königsberg and Danzig on July 6, 1932, the Do X had an almost full cabin – sixty passengers, at thirty Marks each, enjoy the excitement of a special flight.

Before take-off and after a landing, there are often thousands of spectators there to observe the maneuvers of the flying boat. Flight captain Horst Merz describes it: "… Before take-offs or after landings, we navigate to the buoy or to the dock without tug assistance, if possible, under our own power. Before take-off, everyone makes sure that they are clear about the things they are responsible for controlling. The pilot devotes particular care to the entire steering system and its many (and long) rods and cable pulls, which like to be used for hanging wet towels and the like. If everything is reported clear to the commander, he makes his way, with the pilot and the navigation officer, to the forecastle. The engineer is located in the engine room, the mechanics stand at their stations ready to start the engines. If the anchor is hoisted or the buoy lines are cleared for casting off, two engines, usually the ones front and center, are started and immediately given to the pilot, which means they are switched in the engine room to the throttle control of the pilot so that he can work with these engines. With the help of the water rudder and utilizing the torque of the laterally positioned engines, the machine can be maneuvered magnificently. As soon as the machine is free from the buoy and the waterway is open, the remaining engines are started. After warming up, they are individually slowed down by the lead engineer and given forward. Take-off can then commence as soon as all crewmembers have taken up their posts. The takeoff behavior of the machine is very good; it comes immediately up on the step and speeds up quickly to about 100km/h so that the cooling of the engines is ensured even in hot weather."

Coming to the step means that the hull of the ship lifts up out of the water to the cross step, near the center of the body, in order to overcome the suction of the streaming water with increasing speeds and to lift off with a slight tug on the wheel.

"… Despite the eye-level view of the pilot (around five meters at the moment of touching down), landing is relatively easy if you are first accustomed to the proportions and the large mass. After the landing, the engines are slowly cooled and then all but two

or four are turned off, each depending on the wind. The remaining engines bring the flying boat to the buoy, where they too are reduced to an idle, and the buoy pennant is taken either from the forecastle or the sponson and can be moored to the forecastle cleats. After this, the remaining engines can be turned off. During the Atlantic crossing, and with the many take-offs and landings during the first half of the Germany tour, the bottom of the Do X had to endure a lot. The outside of the flying boat's bottom, like with every ship from time to time, needed to be inspected, cleaned and repainted. The Do X's turn to be cleaned and brightened up occurred at the end of August."

After 70,000 visitors in Hamburg and various sightseeing flights, Horst Merz steers the flying boat toward the Priwall Peninsula near Travemünde on the Baltic Sea coast on August 27, 1932. There lies the new Flender airplane dock in the eight meters deep Pötenitzer Wiek. Now, for the first time, it will be loaded with the weight that the Lübeck/Flender factory built it for. In ten days, the experienced specialists and craftsmen of the Travemünde test site, to whom the dock belongs, finish the maintenance work on the Do X. On September 5th, the flying boat takes off from the Pötenitzer Wiek to resume its Germany tour. After a short stopover in Hamburg Altona, the Rhine is now the new target. The city hopping begins in Duisburg. At 635km, this will be the second longest flight distance of the year. Only the stretch from Mannheim to Zurich is longer, by 100km. Altona to Duisburg remains the longest flight in terms of time traveled. The flying boat needs four hours and twenty-six minutes in a strong headwind before it lands in Germany's largest inland port of Duisburg on September 6th.

The efforts by German cities to present themselves as a landing spots for the Do X, and to include a visitor program, begins long before the ferry flight to the USA. In the summer of 1930, a propaganda flight over the Atlantic to the USA is expected by the German public. Claude Dornier's intention to sell or to charter it in the States is of course unknown. Back then already, Albert Sonntag, first airport director of Bonn Hangelar, tried to get a visit by the flying boat with a landing on the Rhine. This disappointment is huge when the Do X only flies over Bonn on November 5, 1930 at around 2:00pm. After the return of the flying boat, Albert Sonntag begins to talk about a new chance.

On the Rhine. Flying along the Rhine, the Do X visits all of the big cities and is enthusiastically celebrated. (Dornier GmbH, EADS)

DFG director Milatz appears as the advance party in order to inspect the electricity and the shore conditions on the Rhine in Bonn. He approves of a landing there. Flying from Cologne, the flying boat arrives in Bonn on September 29, 1932 and anchors at Erste Fährgasse. Hours before the arrival, thousands line up along the shore in Bonn and Beuel. After around 20,000 visitors marvel at the interior furnishings on board the Do X and become intoxicated with flying boat elation, it leaves Bonn on October 3rd toward Koblenz.

Because the business figures of the Germany flight are known, a quick picture of the revenue and expenditure accounts are of interest. The rounded up revenue figures consist of: 293,000RM for tours, 21,000RM for flights, 1,400RM for lectures, and 916.71RM from transporting mail. The last figure refers to the flight from Zurich to Altenrhein on November 14, 1932, on which official mail is

transported. During the entire Germany tour, there is no postal transport. The Do X post office is dissolved by the Reichspost Ministry after landing in Berlin. The Reich was only able to register a meager profit of 850.55 Marks. So how was the 317,000RM in revenue spent? The biggest item was the cost for overhauling the flying boat's airframe and engines in the winter of 1932/33 in Altenrhein. Dornier Metallbauten GmbH charges the Flugschiff Gesellschaft almost 120,000RM for it. Other expenses from 1932 include salaries and wages as well as mileage and daily allowances for the crew, totaling 82,000RM, insurance with 29,500RM, fuel with 25,300RM, general operating costs with 23,000, ticket sales and ticket inspection costs with 10,400RM, auxiliary and replacement materials for the flying boat's airframe and engines with 8,800RM, auxiliary and replacement materials for the tours, including the tour dock with 7,600RM, traveling expenses for the advance party with 6,800, and last but not least 6,200RM tax on tour and flight income. All in all a break-even first year of business for the Deutsche Flugschiff company.

Victory Lap in Switzerland, the Do X in Zurich

The crowning conclusion to the Do X 1a's Germany tour is a visit to Zurich. Initiated by former Swissair director Walter Mittelholzer, whose excellent relationship with Claude Dornier comes into play, the Do X makes a twelve-day visit in Zurich before it will rest in the hangar in Altenrhein. It is Wednesday, November 2, 1932, 12:30pm when the Do X takes off from the waters of the Rhine near Mannheim. With a sixteen-man crew on board, the flight first goes to Ladenburg, where a lap of honor is flown over the place where Benz engines were inven-

ted. Heidelberg and Karlsruhe are also circled. The plan to appear over Stuttgart, though, is scrapped due to low-lying fog. The flight into Switzerland then goes over Kehl, Basel and along the Rhine to Lake Constance. Friedrichshafen, Altenrhein, Rorschach, Romanshorn, Constance, Winterthur and Dübendorf are other flyover targets on the route to Zurich. The original takeoff weight of 43.4 tonnes steadily decreases on the four hour and fifteen minute flight with the gasoline and oil consumption. When it splashes down on Lake Zurich, 723km have been flown.

On November 3rd, the Neue Zuricher Zeitung (NZZ) reads: "As the news spreads early in Zurich that the Do X will come to us for a long stopover after its round-the-world flight, many remembered how this promise was once given before the big flight, but then not fulfilled. They view this event with some doubt. Nevertheless, every time someone hears engine noise in the sky they look to make sure they don't miss the moment. Numerous flight fanatics have stood since late morning at the Alpenquai and have to practice patience since the giant bird won't be seen over the Allmend Fluntern until 4:40pm.

Mooring spot in Zurich for tours of the Do X. (Photo: Archiv Yachtwerft Faul)

Passengers come aboard. The
Do X on Lake Zurich. (Photo:
Dornier GmbH, EADS)

Lake Zurich, November 1932. Engine inspection before take-off of the next sightseeing flight. (Photo: Ortsmuseum Sust Horgen)

It then heads toward the Milchbuck, turns around there, flies over the city and turns over the lake to do another loop over the city. Next, it follows the lake shore until about Oberrieden, turns one last time toward the city and at 4:55pm it descends abruptly to the water, close enough to us in our motorboat that we are rocked about by its waves. The flying boat then glides over the lake in long cross and diagonal runs, constantly followed by several motorboats and rowboats, until it finally stops in front of the boathouse of the Zurich Yacht Club, where some more flights are planned for Friday … At 5:12pm the Do X moors, and barely two minutes later, our boat docks too. With a friendly welcome by the capable crew and officers, we climb aboard the Do X for a quick look after customs formalities are quickly taken care of. In addition to the representatives from the press, Walter Mittelholzer and the German Consulate Dr. Hellenthal take part in this visit. The Do X will remain in Zurich for ten days. On Friday, a few flights will be performed, and the rest of the time, it can be viewed by anyone interested. It goes without saying that the well-traveled crew will be warmly welcomed by us. Right after arrival they were invited to attend a performance in the theater."

During the Do X's stages along the Rhine on the Germany tour, there are no sightseeing flights for passengers. But on November 4th three sightseeing flights over Zurich and its surroundings are planned. After take-off from Lake Zurich, the first flight has to be cut short due to fog. But the weather clears up and the three flights with passengers can resume. A flowery account of one of the flights survives: "The Do X flying boat, which lures our curious citizens in droves to the shores all around our city lake, chose the most beautiful late-fall day to take the few passengers under its wings during its Zurich visit. The most beautiful of the three flights certainly belonged to the press (who were treated to amazing views of the city and countryside). This second flight, in the early afternoon, led our municipal and cantonal authorities and our magisterial guests through the golden skies of their territories. The skies were covered to some extent by an atmospheric haze, and before the take-off, the waterway had to be shut down due to possible obstacles. But the skies became noticeably brighter around mid-afternoon, and through the fading haze, far to the south, the Glärnisch massif was visible on the swaying floating bridge in front of the concert hall. The third flight, which carried about sixty-five passengers (on the first two, seventy and fifty-six, respectively, take part, not counting the crew of fourteen men), promised extraordinary enjoyment. And it delivered more than promised. With noise from twelve engines, though, one must make the best of it. But no one is here for chitchat in this roomy, comfortably padded salon (we're no longer allowed to say cabin). In fact, one no longer feels the need for it when the steel giant – looking daunting and imposing from the outside, but downright cozy and welcoming on the inside – thunders over the water and detaches from the runway after thirty-eight seconds (all technical respect for overcoming the weight so powerfully!), to now rise almost weightlessly hovering over the left shore, whose scenery, enlivened most delightfully by the autumnal colors, radiating the expression of loveliness full and warm, of our Lake Zurich landscape, conceded ungrudgingly and justly by strangers and locals, by poets and Baedekers.

The sun already stands far to the west, the shadow of the aircraft, becoming smaller with the increasing altitude of the flight and the growing vastness of the land underneath us, wanders vaguely on the diagonally shrinking, glistening surface of the water. Clean and neat, stripped almost of all the slags of reality, but also of the idyll of lively connectedness, the string of Lake Zurich villages flows by below. The church of Thalwil, the aircraft factory of A. Comte, prominent and unknown buildings: they are all made unreal and minimized in a toy jail. And the rhythm of the soaring, inland hills is graceful and sweet. But the colorful magic of their forests appear more extensive, wider and more illustrious, and turn from soft weary greens to intoxicating auburns and jubilant yellows. But above all, it is the magnificent spectacle of the Alps that enchants the viewer, with the pure silver of their snowy caps and the first golden afterglow filtering through. For the sake of this scenic homeland experience, its facilitator, the strange guests from our neighboring country, are welcome on our waters. The impressions fly past quickly – 170 to 180km/h is a ravenous pace. Over the back of the Etzel, one can just make out the bright contours of Glärnisch and the Scheerhorn, then the flying boat turns over the dam near Rapperswil and now the enraptured eye can fully take in autumn of the Zurich landscape, of the Bachtel and Pfannenstiel areas. But it also offers the opportunity to replicate the view, for the untrained eye, into the difficult to unravel, technical, and mechanical inner workings of this powerful steel eagle; on a

factory flight two years ago, before its fateful America journey, I had enough leisure time while we were in the air space of Lake Constance, traversing from Meersburg to Lindau-Bregenz and back, to climb up that neck-breaking little ladder in order to have my eardrums hammered by the thundering heartbeat of this monstrosity and my body shaken to its core. Back then I had not yet had the pleasure of nesting in the comfort of these upholstered rooms. Today, I would happily spend four and a half hours in this stable air vehicle, without having to suffer from the autumn cold.

But this time the flight only lasted twenty-five minutes. Long enough to collect an abundance of lasting impressions, long enough to savor our Lake Zurich scenery anew and to love it deeply. At 4:20pm the machine sets down on the water smoothly and safely, after an unforgettable sloping flight from the North over the city, whose sculpture, gold-plated by the evening sun, looks more and more impressive the closer the viewer is brought to the familiar squares, buildings and parks. And yet, there is consistently a new appeal from this perspective.

After this flight, the Do X is now moored at the boathouse of the yacht club in front of the concert hall so that no further passenger flights can take place; it only stands in the open to be viewed."

A newspaper advertisement reads: "The Do X flying boat will be made available for the general viewing of its cabin, etc., on Saturday, November 5th from 8:00am to 7:00pm and Sunday beginning at 10:00am. Admission: 1 franc, children 0.50 franc. The flying boat can only stay in Zurich until Tuesday. Therefore, we recommend visiting during the first few days. Tickets sold by Swissair, Walcheplatz, Zurich."

Over 52,000 people visit the flying boat from November 5th to 13th. In addition to the 3,316.78RM for sightseeing flights, 22,737RM is added to the revenue for admission proceeds, which also makes the stop in Zurich an economic success.

On Monday, November 14, the Do X takes off from Lake Zurich for its last two flights of 1932. The first flight, lasting thirty-six minutes over a distance of 102km, is another sightseeing flight with paying guests on board. After this, the return flight to Altenrhein lasts forty-seven minutes. On this flight, official mail with Swiss and Liechtenstein postage is transported.

HOTEL RIESEN-FÜRSTENHOF, KOBLENZ AM RHEIN

Horst Merz writes a letter to his wife. Apparently, he loved hotel envelopes. The special postal marking for the first Zurich-Altenrhein postal flight by the Do X can be seen in red ink. (Photo: Johannes E. Palmer)

This applies to letters, postcards and registered letters with Swiss and Liechtenstein postage stamps. The registered letter costs 1.05 Swiss francs and a normal letter, up to twenty grams, 75 centimes. On the 133km flight from Zurich to Altenrhein on November 14, 1932, the Do X transports exactly 2,678 postal items from Switzerland and 154 pieces from Liechtenstein in forty-seven minutes. They include a special oval and red marking that reads: "1.DO.X POSTFLUG I.D. SCHWEIZ ZÜRICH-ALTENRHEIN."

As proportionate earnings from the mail delivery, DFG registers a revenue of 1,078.48RM minus 161.77RM in agency commissions. This is quite a modest amount, compared to the revenue of 26,054.05RM from tours and sightseeing flights in Zurich alone.

The last flight of 1932 brings the Do X back to where she began her flight around the world two ye-

ars previously: to the aircraft hangar of DoFlug AG in Altenrhein. With the hangar roof over its head, a thorough technical inspection of the flying boat is carried out around the turn of the year, which includes the complete new covering of the wings with airplane linen. Exactly 119,207.39RM are spent on this, which is over a third of the profits from the admission fees. Wages, as well as mileage and daily allowances, insurance costs and gasoline used up the rest of the balance. Only a small profit of 850.55RM is left over from the 316,343.17RM in revenue from the Germany tour.

With Italian technicians and crewmembers, test flights of the Do X 2 and Do X 3 take place on Lake Constance. (Dornier GmbH, EADS)

Italy and Its Two Do X Flying Boats

The repairs after the Do X 1a accidents in Lisbon and the Bay of Gando make the flying boat a very special test plane. The Dornier technicians gain experiences that are very important for the two Italian Do X flying boats under construction in Altenrhein. In Lisbon, it was the construction of the wing skin panels and their quick replacement and installation. Because the two machines, ordered by the Italian Aviation Minister, are already in an advanced production phase in Altenrhein, the immediate transport of complete wing panels for the repair is arranged. Just getting there proved to be a problem, with time being a factor. At the time, Spain and Portugal think that different track widths of their train networks would have a positive affect on their national sovereignty. For the freight train from Altenrhein, with 3.6x2.8 meter sized wing panels set up on train cars, this peculiar kind of neighborly distrust means waiting for days and reloading on the border.

The time factor applies more so to the repair situation in Las Palmas. The transport of manufactured structural components and special tools goes by train to Genoa and from there by ship to Gran Canaria. During the accident in the Bay of Gando, a design flaw is found, which is corrected for the planned Atlantic operation by the Italian flying boats. The failed takeoff attempt in the Atlantic swell, during which the wings are nearly cut off from the fuselage, breaks the three upright ribs. They are a part of the supporting structure of the flying boat. The torn rib profiles consist of 1.8mm thick duralumin.

Do X 2 with protective coating during testing on Lake Constance near Altenrhein in May 1931. (Dornier GmbH, EADS)

Now 2.4mm steel profiles are installed, and in all three flying boats at the same time. The Do X 2 is in the last phase of it completion when Wilhelm Niemann reports about a particularly important visit to Germany on board the Do X on February 16, 1931: "… On Sunday (Note: February 15, 1931), the Italian Aviation Minister Balbo was here. The 28,000 tonne Italian steamship Conte Rosso came specifically to Las Palmas so that Balbo and all of his pilots and mechanics, around forty of them, could see the Do X. We picked up Balbo in the Woermann boat, brought him on board the Do X, showed him the damages and gave him the necessary explanations. Then there was a large reception in the city hall, where Balbo declared in his speech that he only came to Las Palmas to greet the Do X and its crew on their first Atlantic stage. The damages were minimal in his opinion and would be repaired. The machine was only damaged in the first place because the Atlantic could only be studied while on the Atlantic. The performance that the Do X had shown to this point proved to Balbo that the Do X idea was a huge advancement for aviation and shipping, and none of its significance for the future has been lost."

The command of the "ailing" Do X greets the three-hour visit by Balbo with mixed feelings. This is about the future of the Do X and the air force general can't even try out the flying boat. Balbo is among the committed advocates of the flying boat idea in Italy. Against resistance by the Italian public, he pushes through the ordering of two expensive Dornier Do X flying boats for four million Reichsmark altogether. To order airplanes from Germany, or rather Switzerland, is an inexplicable, political action, particularly with the catastrophic situation of their own aircraft industry. During the global economic crisis, every work place in Italy is supported. But dictator Benito Mussolini (1883-1945) and his fascists are already in power, and wipe out any public protests.

On May 16, 1931, twelve Fiat A22-RT engines bring the brand new Do X 2 to the step for the first time and lift it out of the waters of Lake Constance. Apart from the engine units, the three flying boats were identical in construction and assembly. Here lies another difficulty with testing, which should begin with an early first flight. The shaft radiators in the aerodynamically covered supports of the engine nacelles, cause considerable problems during the first of fourteen test flights on Lake Constance.

The interior furnishings, also designed by Emil Rau and supplied by Jakob Keller in Zurich, are significantly different from those in the Do X 1a. The entire bow is laid out as a cargo hold and toward the back there is a cabin with only twenty-four seats. Recently surfaced files and plans document the different interior layout as well as the different number and arrangement of portholes on the passenger deck. After three months of trials and test flights by Dornier head test pilot Richard Wagner, the ferry flight of the Do X 2 from Altenrhein to La Spezia succeeds with its fifteenth flight on August 28, 1931. The Do X 2 is named Umberto Maddalena after an Italian flying hero killed in an accident and carries the tail number "I-REDI." With an Italian crew, the flying boat climbs to an altitude of 2,600 meters over Lake Constance at 9:00am. Gaining more altitude, pilot Richard Wagner steers the Do X 2 toward Chur. Strongly shaken by gusty winds, the flyover of the 3,200 meter Splügen Pass is successful at 11:18am.

Test flights of the Do X 2 and 3 take place on Lake Constance with Italian technicians and crewmembers. (Dornier GmbH, EADS)

Souvenir photo of the flyover crew of the Do X 2 before the flight over the Alps on August 28, 1931. (Dornier GmbH, EADS)

Wagner has to keep his nerve on this flight because the flying boat has little reserve capacity at altitudes over 3,000 meters. "The down gusts were very unpleasant because they always caused a large loss in altitude and this demands a lot from Wagner at the wheel, which was not easy to hide from the Italian passengers. The experience shows that these kinds of Alpine flights can only be performed in perfect weather and good visibility since turning with the Do X flying at its ceiling between higher mountain peaks is critical," writes test manager Mitterwallner in his flight report. Shortly after 1:00pm, the Do X 2 splashes down in La Spezia and the Italians take possession. The subsequent tour along the Italian coast from September 16th to October 12th, 1931 is similar in many regards to the Germany tour of the Do X 1a in 1932. Public resentments have evaporated and almost 100,000 delighted people visit the Umberto Maddalena at its tour stopovers.

On May 13, 1932 the Do X 3 follows its flying boat sister to Italy, with the tail number "I-ABBN" and the name Allessandro Guidoni. It should be noted that at this same time in New York, the preparations for the Do X 1a's return flight to Germany are in full swing. With the Do X 3, Wagner experiences a completely problem-free crossing of the Alps, on the same flight path as the Do X 2. This flying boat even has an excess of power during its service ceiling of 3,200 meters, which ultimately calm his nerves considerably.

The Do X 2 after arrival in La Spezia-Cadimare. (Dornier GmbH, EADS)

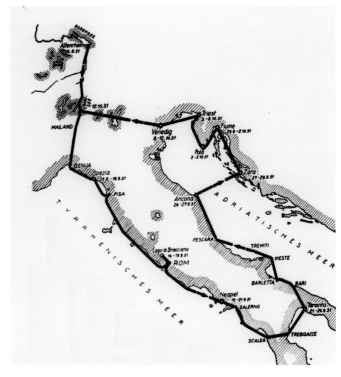

The Do X 2's Italian tour from September 16th and October 12th, 1931.

Both machines are handed over a short time later to the Italian Air Force. What happens to the Italian Do X flying boats in the custody of the Air Force, doesn't have to go through the rumor mill any longer. The story of both Italian flying boats has been worked on since summer 2011. Their "resumes" are documented in Italian archives with complete records. The question of their whereabouts, which is asked again and again, can now be definitively answered. The Do X 2 and Do X 3 flying boats were scrapped in 1937 in La Spezia-Cadimare.

In the summer of 1932, the astonished international aviation community gets to experience three flying boats in operation at the same time, and now the proponents of the flying boat can actually be satisfied. It appears to be the beginning of a new era. But during all of the rejoicing, a bitter realization also slowly spreads. It's too large for European air services, too small for transatlantic service, and too expensive to operate. Air transport strategists scratch Claude Dornier's Do X flying boat from their shopping lists.

The Do X 3 with the last official coat of paint in service.
(Dornier GmbH, EADS)

The Do X 2 in Fiume on September 30, 1931.

Waiting for the scrap yard. One of the Italian Do X flying boats as trailer on
Lago di Massacuccoli near Torre del Lago. (Dornier GmbH, EADS)

On a rail car at the DoFlug shipyard in Altenrhein, Switzerland. The Do X flying boat is managed by Luft Hansa while being equipped for the planned European tour in March 1933.

An Inglorious End To the Do X 1a On the Danube

O ver the winter of 1932/33, the Do X 1a receives a general overhaul in the airplane hangar in Altenrhein. Then the dice roll for the future of the Do X and a pivotal year in German history begins. After the sensational Germany tour of this first "jumbo" of commercial aviation in the summer and fall of 1932, big things are planned. Beginning in spring 1933, success is to be repeated with the motto "we are someone in the world again" and with the swastika as a good omen. Until then, the Deutsche Flugschiff Gesellschaft (DFG), a subsidiary of Dornier Metallbauten GmbH, operates the state-owned Do X.

With the establishment of the Reich's Commission for Aviation on January 30, 1933, which shortly afterward is called the Air Ministry and then the Reich's Aviation Ministry (RLM), a new political wind is blowing in the German skies. The National Socialists seize all airspace over the German Reich and all aviation activities shift to their policies. The Minister of Aviation Hermann Göring, later the Supreme Commander of the Luftwaffe, will soon repeat the sentence: "Everything that flies belongs to me!" The aviation department of the Ministry of Transportation, which stems from the "Systemzeit," as the Nazis disparagingly title the Weimar Republic period, is the nucleus of the explosively growing apparatus RLM. With Luft Hansa chairman Erhard Milch, Göring gets a secretary of state on his side who displays remarkable organization qualities.

DMB senses this immediately. With instructions from the commissioner of aviation in March 1933, operation of the Do X is handed over to Deutsche Luft Hansa. Beginning on April 30, 1933, the crane symbol is flaunted on the tail fin, and the lettering LUFT HANSA instead of DORNIER is written on the bow of the flying boat. Luft Hansa owns the Do X since early May with the tail number D-1929 listed in the German aviation registry. Luft Hansa announces the annual program for its flying boat: "... The Do X will undertake a European tour this summer. Flight captain Merz, who piloted the Do X twice over the Atlantic Ocean in the last two years, will be in charge of piloting the Do X on the planned European tour. A tentative flight path will include a southern route, which will travel from Lake Constance over the Lake Starnberg near Munich, down the Danube from Passau to Vienna and Budapest. After that, a flight to Switzerland is scheduled. Then, the twelve-engine giant will fly down the Rhine to Essen and from there probably pay a visit to the Scandinavian and Baltic Sea countries. After a flight over East Prussia and Danzig, the Do X will land in Berlin Wannsee. From Berlin, the route goes over the Elbe to the Rhine and then up along the Rhine over Worms, Karlsruhe and back to Friedrichshafen, where the landing will take place in the fall. Locally, there will be tours of the flying boat and sightseeing flights offering enough space for sixty-six passengers. The crew will consist of a total of sixteen men."

The new commissioning of the Do X is "settled" by commander and first pilot, flight captain of Luft Hansa and engineer Horst Merz within five days, according to some statements. After disembarking the hangar in Altenrhein and some test flights over Lake Constance, the Do X is checked by Luft Hansa inspectors in the Dornier shipyard Manzell, and approved for commercial operation.

Luft Hansa sends pilot Urban to Lake Constance to join Merz in the cockpit. Except for the four engine mechanics Schmidt, Jäger, Baur and Dorsch, all Dornier veterans, and engineer Siller, flight engineer on the Germany flight, a new Luft Hansa crew comes aboard. This includes radio operator Friedl, ship's purser Prömel, boatswain Ploog, the new engine mechanics Straub, Goos and Groeber as well as steward Knackfuß and on-board photograhper Bundermann. The difficult task of advertising for the European tour lies in the hands of Luft Hansa advertising manager Angermund as "Super cargo of the Do X."

Surprise Visit on Lake Starnberg

On Saturday morning, April 29, 1933 Horst Merz takes his old pilot chair and steers the flying boat, now as the new commander, from Lake Constance to Lake Starnberg. He remembers a special experience on this day: "... Sightseeing flights are scheduled for the afternoon. During a short break, which we take after a mooring maneuver near Undosa, I notice a commotion on land. Shouts of 'Heil!' and raised arms. The Führer Adolf Hitler is here! After a brief personal announcement and greeting – he thanks me with a heartfelt handshake and the words, "Hey, we know each other already!" – and introduction of my crew, we summon our old Do X battle cry, a triple hip hip hooray! for the Führer.

Then he enters the ship as the first passenger of the year and writes in our guest book. After takeoff, I ask him if he wants to come into the cockpit where I have made the co-pilot chair available for him. He comes and sits at the dual controls on my right for forty minutes. This is a great opportunity for me to see him and find out about his goodwill and understanding for aviation. He observes all the instruments attentively, feels the ribs, remarks on how great the

Greeting on the dock of the Undosa baths on Lake Starnberg. Reich Chancellor Adolf Hitler, in office for three months, and Do X commander Horst Merz before their sightseeing flight on April 29, 1933. (Estate of H. Merz)

Lake Starnberg, the Do X's first stop on its European tour, after taking off from Lake Constance. The flying boat docked at the Undosa bathhouse on April 29, 1933.

vibrations caused by the engines are, and even once takes the wheel himself for a few minutes. A lap of honor over Munich and Feldherrnhalle occupies his full attention. After a real 'Hitler landing' on Lake Starnberg, whose smoothness amazes him, I still have the chance to show him the details of our ship."

The stopover on Lake Starnberg has yet another highlight in store: even Claude Dornier has arrived. Oskar von Miller, founder of the German Museum in Munich, checks in with the entire museum board of directors for a sightseeing flight on the Do X. On May 7th, a Sunday, he goes with his wife and son Rudolf and a prominent group of guests on board the flying boat, which takes off into the sunset. Rudolf von Miller recounts: "I sit on a window seat across from Mrs. Berta Krupp who, like my parents, is very excited. I feel absolutely safe on this flight and got a small taste of the great transatlantic and round-the-world flights of the giant flying machine. The flight takes off late in the afternoon and the sun has already set. I'll never forget how we quickly we gained altitude after the successful takeoff from the lake and how the sun suddenly rose again over the western hills of Lake Starnberg. I perceived it as a symbol of global aviation rising out of the darkness and into a bright future."

From the photo album of the aircraft's radio operator Friedl (fourth from the left). The Do X crew at a brewery tour in Munich during their stopover on Lake Starnberg. Those identified in the picture are (from the left): on-board engineer Siller, mechanics Schmidt and Baur, radio operator Friedl as well as Curtiss engineer Harvey Brewton and commander Horst Merz with glasses. Fourth from the right is engine mechanic Karl Dorsch. Sixth from the left is Walter Angermund, Lufthansa press officer and in front of him, flight captain Urban raises a glass to his comrades.

During tours of the aircraft's interior on the dock of the Undosa bathhouse from May 1st to 4th, around 10,000 people shuffle through the flying boat in the first two days alone. The crewmembers are rewarded with a tour of the Franziskaner Brewery in Munich. In the meantime, dignitaries from Prien am Chiemsee make arrangements for a layover on the Chiemsee on the flying boat's next flight to Passau, which is not scheduled on the Do X's original route plan. Luft Hansa director and advertising manager Angermund as well as commander Merz agree and the landing on Chiemsee is planned for Monday, May 8th, around 4:00pm. But bad weather prevents the take-off from Lake Starnberg from taking place on this day. On Chiemsee, in the rain and cold, a massive crowd of people wait for the flying boat. Curious onlookers travel from as far as Lower Bavaria, but it is put off until May 9th.

On Tuesday, May 9th, a sad day for the Do X, the flying boat is to splash down at 9:30am on the Chiemsee near Prien. Due to the notorious Lake Starnberg fog, which is typical regional weather in the spring and fall, the planned start of 8:30 must be delayed again. It is set for 10:00am, in the hopes that the fog will have dissipated by then. The flying boat casts off from Undosa and a barge tows it to its starting position on the west shore. Around twenty passengers come aboard there by motorboat. The passengers are made up primarily of reporters, but Colonel Franz Ritter von Epp (1868-1946), Reich Governor in Bavaria since April 10th, is also on board. Accompanying him are Luft Hansa district manager Franz Hailer (1886-1969) and aviation enthusiast and cavalry captain Carl Braun (1885-1945) from Prien, who initiated the flight of the Do X to Chiemsee. At 10:24am take-off is successful.

Coming over Rosenheim, the Do X approaches the Chiemsee. The giant bird lands quite well near the stonewall of Herrenchiemsee, observed from the hill between Breitbrunn and Plötzing. After the landing at 11:15, the motorboat Rudolf of Chiemsee-Schiff-fahrt Feßler tows the Do X to Stocker Bay where she is moored. Because they must continue on at 5:00pm, she is available for tours for only a very short time. After takeoff toward the south, over the forest of the Herreninsel with a contrail over Prien, the flying boat disappears near Traunstein with a northeasterly course toward Passau. Well over 10,000 excited people watch the spectacle.

Before takeoff of the Do X from Lake Starnberg to Chiemsee. On the morning of May 9, 1933, a motorboat brings the important passengers on board. (From left to right) Do X on-board photographer Bundermann, the boat driver and an accompanying police officer, Luft Hansa district manager Franz Hailer, Reich Governor Franz Ritter von Epp and cavalry captain Carl Braun from Prien in an old army uniform from the imperial era. (from the collection of Lino von Gartzen, Starnberg)

Splashdown of the Luft Hansa Do X on the Chiemsee on May 9, 1933.

An Incorrect Approach With Fatal Consequences

In the meantime, hundreds of impatient and curious onlookers wait for the flying boat on the shores of the Danube near Schalding above Passau. By around 6:15pm, the spectators are shifting from one foot to the other. Black storm clouds and thunder and lightning from the west promise to bring rain showers at any minute. On the water, out in the open, during a storm is not the most pleasant place to be. And suddenly there it is! A giant white thunderbird rolls past from the west over the heads of the spectators in order assess the length of the splashdown line. A wide curve and then the Do X hovers, now approaching the Danube from the east against the direction of the storm. On this spot, at the beginning of the Kachlet reservoir, the river flows less than one meter per second, almost as smooth as glass under the aggressively sinking flying boat. There is no breeze in the looming atmosphere just before the storm breaks loose.

The flying boat touches the surface of the water almost horizontally and then makes a short bound about one meter high before it sets down a second time. This time jerked strongly with a "tail landing," as pilots call it. The water of the Danube splashes about behind the stern of the ship and the onlookers don't believe their eyes when the spray disappears. The Do X's tail unit is gone, actually it snaps off and is hanging, only held to the stern by the steering cables. Walter Urban, nicknamed "gaffer" and future flight captain at Syndicato Condor in Brazil, comments on the incident as the second pilot from the right pilot chair: "Mr. Merz, we lost our tail!" Horst Merz sits there petrified. "How? Was I too fast? I had to land quickly because of the weather situation." His thoughts are racing. Before a Luft Hansa tribunal, Merz will later state that the setting sun blinded him and, before setting down, he could not accurately estimate altitude due to the intense reflection of the smooth water surface.

The Interavia correspondence from May 22nd reads: "On the planned European tour of the Do X, the flying boat suffered damages after a hard landing in Passau. Although this is not described as se-

The beginning of the end of the Do X on May 9, 1933 on the Danube near Passau. The short jump of the flying boat after the initial contact with the water.

Dragged in the water. A so-called tail landing, for which the Do X tail unit is not designed.

The impact on the water breaks off the entire stern after rib #6 and the tail unit.

With a broken off stern end and loosely hanging tail unit, the Do X continues on after the failed water landing.

That looks awful. With the outer four engines holding against the current of the Danube, the damage can be seen.

With the parish church St. Salvador of Schalding in the background, the tail unit of the Do X only hangs by steering rods. The end of the stern is immersed in the Danube.

rious, the repair will take two months due to a lack of facilities for docking the flying boat in Passau. Therefore, sightseeing flights will only be conducted to Vienna, Budapest and Switzerland." The media response to the accident on the Danube remains low, as little as possible should reach the outside and understandably no one has an interest in spreading the event journalistically.

For the Reich Aviation Ministry, the affair surrounding the state-owned flying boat is irritating because the planned propaganda effect of the 1933 European tour fails. Luft Hansa withdraws its commitment immediately and has the LUFT HANSA lettering on the bow painted over with the base color. Photos from the months thereafter show the Do X with the brighter rectangle on the spot where was bow was painted. The Reichspost had announced major airmail transport with the Do X on its European tour. Transport from Passau is planned, but after the accident the mailbags pile up in the main post

office of the Danube city and nobody knows what to do with it now. In the weeks that follow, the spectrum of postal markings range from postponement via transport restrictions to return to sender. Much to the delight of Do X philatelists today, incidentally, since this enhances their collections.

And how does Dornier react? The Do X 1a has already drawn many a worry line on the foreheads of those responsible, so the latest bad news does not really make much of a difference. The main thing is that doesn't cost them any money. The de facto owner of the flying boat is the German Reich and Dornier withdrew from its operation. So the buck was passed on to Luft Hansa, who also have the entire crew under their wings.

Could Claude Dornier and his men remain calm? Hardly since so much heart and soul went into their visionary aircraft. Any damage hurts in a figurative sense and Dornier wants to know exactly what has happened.

The official epilogue to the events on the Danube near Schalding follows on June 17, 1933. On this Saturday, the "accident tribunal" of Deutsche Luft Hansa is held in the lecture hall of the airline in Berlin Tempelhof. In addition to head of ruling council Schwartz, four experienced professional are a part of the tribunal as assessors. District manager Schiller leads the sea flight department of the airline company. Flight captain Kaspar is one of the very experienced Dornier Wal pilots of DLH and flight captain Wagner flew the Do X during its testing until fall 1930.

Assessor and Dornier director Heinrich Schulte-Frohlinde has been petitioned more as a test manager of the Do X than a partner of Deutsche Flugschiff Gesellschaft. Apparently, Claude Dornier and Walter Diele, co-pilot of the flight from New York to Berlin during the Do X's second Atlantic crossing, are also supposed to be present. But they are tied up or don't want to come. The following experts sit at the table: Undersecretary Friedrich Christiansen, who is advancing at the Aviation Ministry as well as former Do X commander and engineer Dr. Harmsen, Dipl. Ing Uding and Dipl. Ing Achterberg. The accident tribunal receives additional explosiveness through the presence of Luft Hansa board member Freiherr von Gablenz and other company specialists. According to the list in the protocol: in "also present were," the last on the list is "as well as the person involved, Mr.

Merz." This is quite interesting since all the other men are noted with titles. In this situation, Horst Merz is no longer Dipl. Ing., commander, flight captain or first pilot, but simply just: "Mr. Merz." The disrespect is relativized by the authors of the initial proceedings report for the Dornier company in Friedrichshafen. As director of Dornier Metallbauten and as the organizer of the Do X's Germany flight, Heinrich Schulte-Frohlinde is very familiar with the overall problem of the first pilot of the Do X and has quite a different opinion of Mr. Merz.

Standing Before Lufthansa's "Accident Tribunal"

Before the three-hour round of deliberation occurs, there is a film screening. A cameraman had caught the failed Danube landing on celluloid. The film repeats several times so that those present can get an exact picture of the incident. After the extensive description of the accident from Horst Merz's point of view, a round of questions from the expert panel begins. It is determined that a similar landing with a powerful rearing up of the flying boat and dragging down of the tail has already been documented in photos from Frankfurt. During the Germany flight, Horst Merz landed on the Main. Then, the question directed to the Dornier representatives is whether the company's flight division knew that a suction effect was taking place in certain take-off and landing situations. It was known, but with such a minimal impact that it hadn't caused any damages until Passau and therefore didn't have to be addressed constructively. "In truth, the avoidance of the suction effect on the flying boat in smooth water is generally only considered a question of piloting." Over the course of the debate, the analytical observations by pilots and engineers increasingly narrows down the cause of the accident.

Upon glancing at the threatening storm, Horst Merz, not wanting to hover for too long and approaching at a speed of 25km/h that was too fast, probably sets down on the water too hard. He puts forth his the argument from his side that he was blinded by the setting sun and it's reflection on the water's surface, and thus had falsely estimated the height. Then come the merciful words by Freiherr von Gablenz that probably in this case too, various circumstances had caused the accident. The tribunal withdraws for deliberations and after thorough discussion comes to the following assessment: "The accident of the Dornier Do X flying boat #1 on May 9, 1933 in Passau stems from fact that the land speed was too high, that very unfavorable water and landing conditions existed, and that a suction effect took place on the flying boat to a degree that was previously unknown. It has been determined that the influence of the high land speed contributed 20%, the influence of the unfavorable landing conditions caused by the muggy weather, smooth water and the surrounding mountains contributed 60%, and the influence of the suction effect 20%." Since majority blame by the pilot, according to the principal view of the commission, can only be considered if more than half of the causes are attributed to him, the pilot is not at fault for the damages incurred. Horst Merz gets off with a slap on the wrist.

For the Dornier people, the clearance and allocation of blame for the accident is secondary, as long as it remains a matter of Luft Hansa or the state authorities. Within Dornier, the trust in Horst Merz's aeronautical ability emerges with plenty of scratches. Too many preventable incidents have occurred in the last two years, and those involved with his accident with the flying boat in the Bay of Gando on February 3, 1931, with serious consequences for the Do X ferry flight to the USA and for Dornier Metallbauten, are still dealing with the aftermath. Heinrich Schulte-Frohlinde makes no secret of his opinion. For him, the "Passau splashdown" was a pilot error. But what really irks him and the Dornier leadership is the alleged twenty percent accident influence by the suction effect on the stern during the splashdown on smooth water, which implies a shortcoming of testing or even a construction fault of the Do X 1.

Claude Dornier and his design engineers have become very sensitive to such silent accusations. One of the reasons for that is the crash of Luft Hansa's Merkur D-585 "Puma," which makes more headlines than usual for Dornier Metallbauten GmbH in September 1927. Among the six victims, is German ambassador to the USA Baron von Maltzan. Until clarification of the cause of the crash, a dismantled half of the wing unit, Luft Hansa's entire Merkur fleet, around thirty machines, is decommissioned for several weeks by the Reich Ministry of Transportation. The German Research Institute for Aviation (DVL) in Berlin Adlershof determines to be the cause of the accident to be a fatigue fracture of a bolt on a wing part, caused by previously unknown vibrations. As a result, all Dornier Merkur airplanes receive reinforced wing parts at the factory – named "Maltzan struts" by pilots. A costly affair for Dornier Metallbauten and anything but beneficial to their image.

A Difficult Repair Under Open Skies

The initial inspection of the damage to the Do X 1 on May 9, 1933 reveals that a quick repair will be impossible. The four meter-long piece of the airframe lies torn up on the floor of the Danube. The snapped-off tail unit hangs over the breaking point of the stern. How did this kind of damage occur? The official accident investigation report from June 30, 1933 describes the sequence of events: "The pilot brings the flying boat, with a weight of 42t, in horizontally just over the water and then sets it down flatly on the water without throttle. The flying boat is traveling at a speed of about 135-140 km/h. The flying boat jumps out of the water about 1 meter high and then sets down on the water again at 135km/h. At this, the pilot pulls slightly on the elevator and performs a water landing while employing the flying boat's pitch elevator. Shortly after touchdown, during the run out, the flying boat rears up, continues its movement forward, and is eventually sucked into the water by the tail of the fuselage. When the base of the tail, which is not designed to resist water forces, but rather only stresses originating from aerodynamic forces, immerses in the water, it gets hammered in directly behind rib #6. After the base of the tail rips open, water flows with elementary force into the interior of the ship. This and the water pressure from below, rips the tail end up from behind and breaks the rear spar of the vertical stabilizer off. During this process, the rudder control is rammed upward and

broken off backwards underneath the central housing; it remains hanging by the steering rods. The 900kg tail unit of the ship, robbed of its rear supports, now tilts backward and down under the influences of weight and aerodynamic forces and rips rib #6 out of the flying boat's skin. The ship runs out without taking any further damages."

The following has to be explained about the ribs. These cross reinforcements in the flying boat's hull are numbered consecutively from the rear to the front. Rib #1 is located about 60cm away, measured from the end of the stern to the front. Rib #6 is a bulkhead rib. In front of rib #6, about 3.5 meters from the end of the stern, the waters of the Danube drive into the bottom of the boat, force the stern segment upward and rips it off. In the process, the entire stern bond is stripped down, as the later re-

Temporarily securing the rest of the tail unit on the stern of the flying boat in rainy weather.

Towed by a motorboat down river to Heinig.

The destroyed tail unit of the Do X and a crane hook in Heining.

Danube to accommodate the giant aircraft for this. Without repair and restoration of its flight capability, the Do X would never leave.

After the initial shock, those responsible reflect on why they flew to Passau in the first place. Visitor bridges are constructed, and for a few weeks the flying boat can be toured. In Altenrhein, the new construction of the stern segment from rib #1 to rib #8 and a new tail unit with all elevators and rudders begins. At Dornier, the water impact during the tail landing is accepted as the cause of the damage and reinforcing the stern seems inevitable. Five additional ribs, between ribs #3 and #8, are built into the new stern. The rib spacing is thus shortened from its original 70cm to 35cm and the reinforcement doubles the stability on the critical point. After the

With a provisional hoist. Positioning the stern end of the Do X for the new tail unit to be attached.

trieved parts show. Only the tail unit remains hanging on the stern stub. After tethering the broken off remains of the tail on the flying boat, a motorboat tows the damaged Do X two kilometers downriver to the small port of Passau-Heining on the evening of May 9 in pouring rain. There the advance party has chosen the flying boat's original mooring for the stopover in Passau. Today it is the homeport of the Passau Motor-Yacht-Club.

In May 1933, on the basin of the left bank, there is a river construction site with a pontoon, and on it a backhoe with a boom with which the several hundred kilogram tail unit can be salvaged. The small river port on the west shore of the Danube, on the former river kilometer marker 356.5, today 2232.5, only consists of a dammed square basin with a 1.4 meter water depth. In the 20x75 meter basin, the Do X just fits with a 10.6 meter width over the sponsons and a 40.90 meter length over everything. Apparently, Heinrich Schulte-Frohlinde is among the observers of the accident. The test manager of the Do X 1 is on the spot immediately and appears horrified about the possibilities, or better yet, impossibilities of repairing the flying boat here out in the open, without cranes, without paved ground surfaces, etc.

In any event, the repair must take place there. There is no better place downriver or upriver on the

Out in the open and with a great deal of improvisation. The difficult repair of the Do X's stern end in Heining in July 1933.

Ready for takeoff on the Danube. On September 5 the Do X flies back to Lake Constance and splashes down at Altenrhein.

A look into the newly constructed stern of the Do X with additional ribs built in. In the background is the bulkhead rib #6 with manhole.

re-manufacture and delivery of the necessary components from Altenrhein, the difficult repair out in the open in Heining follows. The technicians have to make do with provisional platforms, cranes and scaffolding to align the new tail unit onto the flying boat. At the end of August 1933, the repair work has ended and with head test pilot Richard Wagner at the wheel, some test flights take place. On September 5, Wagner flies the Do X back to Lake Constance with Dornier technicians and mechanics on board as the crew. Only radioman Friedl is borrowed from

Luft Hansa for the flight. The only payload on board: several mailbags.

The flight from Passau to Altenrhein on September 5, 1933 is the last official postal flight of the Do X. The Do X disappears from the public's interest. But not for Dornier. Since the beginning of September, the Do X again belongs to the German Research Institute for Aviation, as the propriety rights in the German aircraft registry documents.

Suction Effect On the Stern – Yes or No?

Shortly before the meeting of the accident tribunal, the Italian Do X 2 has an accident in Augusta on June 9, 1933, with similar damages to the stern of the Do X 1a in Passau. Until a meeting date, there is still no official information about the exact course of events surrounding the Do X 2's accident. In September 1933, details of the Italian accident are made available to Dornier and the Aviation Ministry, and now everyone can get to the bottom of the "disastrous suction effect on the stern of the flying boat." The RLM issues a testing order to Dornier Metallbauten GmbH, in which the DVL is to participate.

The measuring device assembly in the stern of the Do X during testing by DVL on Lake Constance in October 1933.

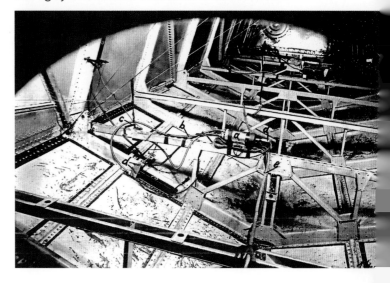

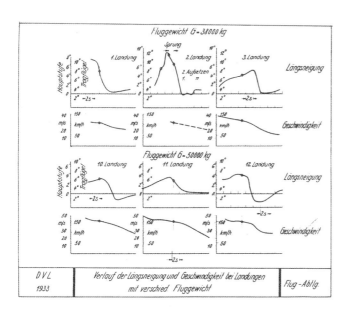

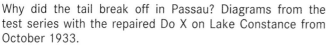

Why did the tail break off in Passau? Diagrams from the test series with the repaired Do X on Lake Constance from October 1933.

After the repair in Heining and the return flight to Lake Constance, the Do X tail unit gets a new coat of paint in Altenrhein. A swastika on the tail fin for the first time.

Yet to be clarified is: "… whether, and under what circumstances, a suction effect on the stern can be determined by further observations with landings on smooth water." These tests take place from September 15th to 21st, 1933 on Lake Constance.

A total of fifteen takeoffs and landings with take-off weights of thirty-eight to fifty tonnes in various water depths from two to eighteen meters were not able to prove a suction effect, much less clear up the matter. Even the extensive installation of "DVL crack expansion plotters" in the stern of the Do X and elaborate measuring lines with takeoff and slow-motion cameras do not provide any results. Flight captain Wagner, who performs the first twelve test landings, succeeds on only the second of three splashdowns on September 15th to force the Do X into a similar tail landing situation like the one observed in Passau. The new stern remains undamaged. A logical conclusion actually, since the double-strength construction counters the water impact with more resistance than the original stern of the Do X 1.

On September 21, RLM Undersecretary Friedrich Christiansen shows up in Altenrhein with two confessed seaplane pilots in tow. They are there to show the Dornier people how it's done. Flight captain Fritz Kiessner from Lufthansa trains airline pilots in Travemünde for transatlantic service and flight captain

Jobst from Studnitz has just come from aircraft catapult testing in the South Atlantic. In June, he had completed several flights with the eight tonne Dornier Wal Monsun between the catapult ship Westfalen and Bathurst and Natal. The result of their efforts with the Do X is meager. The summary reads: "DVL research report FB 26 – testing the Dornier Do X 1 flying boat in Altenrhein after the ferry flight from Passau … During testing, no special occurrences, which could offer a complete explanation of the incident in Passau, appeared, and it is also hardly believable that this will be possible with large-scale testing. In addition, systematic model experiments would have to be performed in a towing tank … According to observations made, the accident in Passau was caused by a concurrence of an excessively high land speed and the position of the aircraft."

The end of the Do X as a commercial aircraft has begun. A commercial operation with a fourteen-man crew, twelve fuel-guzzling engines for only sixty-six passengers and little additional payload, does not pay off. In the next months, a swastika is painted on the port side of the tail fin, in accordance with the former "aviation flag regulation" from June 6, 1933. The Do X then bobs up and down for a year in Altenrhein and Manzell on Lake Constance.

The Do X Artifact From Passau

In March 1980, a few newspapers report that dredging work in the Danube near the A3 autobahn bridge in Scalding have found fragments of the Do X tail unit from a depth ten meters. Numbers and markings clearly prove that they belonged to the Do X. The imposing autobahn bridge near Schalding, about thirty-five meters high and over 1,000 meters long, is the approximate location of the Do X's failed splashdown on May 9, 1933 at 6:15pm, where the tail impacts, breaks off and sinks in pieces to the floor of the Danube. The Motor-Yacht-Club Passau e.V., which operates its boat harbor in Heining, displays the Do X artifact in its clubhouse that probably came from this excavation.

The Do X artifact from Passau is a rusted torpedo cleat made of aluminum cast with pitted efflorescence on a ripped out section of the stern's planking. Each of these cleats, for belaying the rigging, are spaced a half a meter from the end of the stern, at the height of cross rib #1 of the hull, and screwed down tightly on each side of the flying boat. The retrieved specimen was located on the port side just over the weld of the underside planking with the side planking. At least eight steel countersunk bolts with slits and nuts on the inside hold the cleats to the duralumin sheet metal of the side planking. Noteworthy, and typical for the Do X, are the model and kind of riveting of the duralumin corner profiles and adjacent cover plates with aluminum rivets. The setting heads of the round-head rivets can be seen on the outside. The inside of the artifact with fragments of rib #1 show the closing heads of the rivets. The sheet metal, the profile and the aluminum rivets are only oxidized with few pits, the steel bolts of the screw joint, though, are corroded. In the meantime, the Do X artifact from Passau has found its rightful place in the Dornier Museum in Friedrichshafen.

Virgin tail unit of the Do X before its first flight on July 12, 1929, still with green protective coating. The cleats for belaying the rigging on each side of the end of the stern are clearly visible.

Destructive forces. A piece ripped out of the stern's planking during the flying boat's accident on the Danube. Discovered after nearly fifty years in the mud of the Danube. (Photo: Ch. Maier, Passau)

Terribly mangled by pitting corrosion. Aluminum cast cleats for belaying of rigging. Originally bolted on the port side of the Do X's stern. (Photo: Ch. Maier, Passau)

A particularly difficult task. Transport through the eye of a needle – under a railway underpass toward the Lehrter train station. (Dornier GmbH, EADS)

A Home in the Museum

The RLM in Berlin had planned to build a German aviation museum ever since mid-1934. And again it is the ex-commander Friedrich Christiansen who intervenes with the course of the flying boat's fate. On his way up in the aviation hierarchy of the National Socialists, he makes asserts his influence in the Aviation Ministry. He wants to ship the Do X to the new Berlin Aviation Museum. We can assume that Claude Dornier is not asked whether he likes this plan, which means the absolute end of his Do X in the future of commercial aviation.

In issue number twenty-two of the magazine Flugsport from October 31, 1934, interested observers read: "The Do X flying boat, which everyone knows has been sitting at the shipyard of the Dornier factory in Friedrichshafen for a long time, took off from Friedrichshafen on October 14th at 8:52am for a flight to the North Sea and Baltic Sea and splashed down in Norderney on October 19th at 3:10pm. The command has flight commodore Christiansen from the Aviation Ministry, the well-known pilot of the Do X on the America flight. The pilot is flight captain Kiessner. Navigation officer Niemann and four other old members of the Do X America flight are also part of the crew."

Nineteen men are on board the Do X for its last journey. After splashdown and fueling in Norderney, they continue on to Wyk on Föhr on October 20th. The Sylter Zeitung from 10/23/1934 reports: "... led by flight commodore Friedrich Christiansen, the Do X flying boat arrived unexpectedly on Saturday morning at 11:00 in front of the Wyker Reede and landed smoothly on the water. The flying boat is known to be on the flight from Norderney to the Baltic Sea. On the way there, "Fiede" Christiansen made a detour to his hometown Wyk auf Föhr. The news of the Do X's arrival at Wyk's harbor, spread like wildfire and soon everyone on the island knows about it. The ship is made available for tours. Like its first visit to Wyk, the Do X is again seen by countless people." On Sunday, October 21, at 12:30pm the Do X takes off from Wyker Reede on its last flight to Travemünde. It arrives there after one hour and five minutes and splashes down on the Pötenitzer Wiek. The flying boat is moored in Travemünde-Priwall, and at the turn of the year 1934/35, the deletion of the legendary tail number D-1929 (nineteen twenty-nine) of the Do X from the Germany aircraft registry.

Now deleted from the aircraft registry, the Do X can of course no longer fly to Berlin. Due to its dimensions, the flying boat would become a monstrosity when transporting it over land. The transport on inland waterways, in contrast, seems to be no problem. Using the Flender aircraft dock at the testing site in Travemünde, the tail unit, engine system and the wings as well as the sponsons and command deck are dismantled from the fuselage and loaded onto a barge. The self-floating fuselage of the Do X is towed by a riverboat and the larger parts travel on a cargo barge. They go over the Elbe-Trave canal, the Elbe and the Havel to Berlin's West Harbor.

Arrival of the self-floating Do X fuselage in Berlin's West Harbor. (Dornier GmbH, EADS)

After an exciting transport on special low-loaders of the German National Railway through the dark Berlin streets, the Do X finds a new home in the new museum's "German Aviation Collection." After World War I, the Research Institute for Aviation begins with the collection of noteworthy aircraft. Back then, of course, no museum ideas are behind it, but rather practice-oriented, technical interest. The DVL's purpose is to test airframes, engines and other equipment and the technical approval of aircraft devices. Over the years, it adds a model collection of airplanes, which later forms the foundation for the great aviation museum in Berlin. With increasing interest at all levels for aviation and flying in the early-1930s, the founding of a museum in Berlin is among the forced museum activities in Germany. The exhibition palace, Alt Moabit 4 to 10 near the Lehrter train station, which has gone unused for some time, is chosen as the exhibition site. After extensive reconstruction, the largest aviation museum in the world at the time is created from various German aviation collections. Upon its inception, the collection is comprised of eighty airplanes, most of which are contributed by DVL.

The transport of the Do X to the museum turned out to be quite adventurous. Arriving in Berlin's West Harbor, the precious load, weighing up to ten tonnes and measuring forty meters long, is raised onto a specially built transport trailer. On May 27, 1935, at 11:00pm, the unusual convoy, hauled by tractors, makes its way to the museum. The Berlin public utility company even has to temporarily remove the catenary above that railway. A later report describes the scene: "The route leads over the Putlitz bridge, whose crossing takes about three hours. The following junction into Stephanstraße requires another two hours and a very complicated and time-consuming undertaking that only specialists can handle. Further routing of the Do X transport leads from Stephanstraße over Perleberger Straße and Lehrter Straße to Invalidenstraße. This section of roughly three kilometers takes another three and a half hours. On the morning of the following day, there is one more hurdle to overcome, which presents the biggest problem for the team transporting the fuselage. Now the

The pride of the exhibition until hit by an aerial mine. (Dornier GmbH, EADS)

Museum visitors in front of the Do X's bow stem.

crew shoves the precious cargo, the proverbial "camel through the eye of a needle," under the railway viaduct through to the Lehrter train station. Arriving there without damages, the giant is reassembled under not-so-favorable conditions and presented to the public as a masterpiece of aircraft construction."

On June 20, 1936, the German Aviation Collection opens its doors for visitors and the Do X shines in freshly painted splendor. When the visitor comes into the entrance hall, he walks on a carpet, flanked by smaller airplanes, that leads directly to the "Giant of the Skies." The construction of a footbridge here, similar in design to the one used on the Germany flight, also proves successful. The museum visitor climbs up on the sponson, sideways on to the foredeck, and down again on the other side. Among all the aircraft in the museum, the Do X is the main attraction until the beginning of World War II. A plan to set up an airplane cafe on the passenger deck of the Do X in order to also celebrate airplane weddings never comes to fruition.

Nazi propaganda view of the Do X in the entrance hall of the museum.

Title page of the museum guide of the German Aviation Collection in Berlin.

The tortured spirit of the well-traveled Do X is finally at peace under a protective roof. But it doesn't last long. Seven years later, the war will demand its sacrifice. In anticipation of damage, smaller exhibits from the collection are brought to safety in Pomerania. The flying boat remains behind, alone in the giant hall. It can't be transported away with the facilities of wartime in 1943. The first bombing damage to the museum comes during a massive attack by English bombers on the nights of November 23rd and 24th, 1943. The Do X barely survives unscathed. But during one of the many night attacks on Berlin in the spring of 1944, an English aerial mine penetrates the hall's roof above the Do X and detonates inside the flying boat. Its explosion shreds not only broad segments of the exhibition hall but also ends the existence of the Do X. Only a pile of twisted metal debris

Only duralumin scrap metal remains. (Dornier GmbH, EADS)

remains. Until the disposal of the building ruins in the early-1950s, only scrap metal collectors and souvenir hunters visit the wreckage. During the first cold winter of the post-war period, the remains of the wooden propeller, among other things, probably made its way into someone's stove or oven to warm up soup or hands. Smart metal recyclers make diverse objects of use from the duralumin scrap, such as kitchen trays, fence posts, and the like. Nothing remains of the proud German aircraft engineering. Today, only the memories of the first wide-bodied aircraft in aviation history live on.

The same, whether big or small. Even then, Do X fever gripped collectors and model builders.

Who, What, Where and Why?

Answers To the Most Frequently Asked Questions About the Do X

Trapped in Bubaque. In the hot and humid rainy season on the equator, the Do X cannot take off after twenty-one attempts and a take-off weight of around fifty tonnes. (Photo: Dornier GmbH, EADS)

What was the bitterest day for Dornier Flugzeuge AG in Altenrhein?

On the morning of November 5, 1930, it had finally come. The crew of the Do X flying boat prepares itself for the trip around the world. On this day, the first stage follows the Rhine from Lake Constance to Amsterdam. With seventeen men on board, the Do X takes off at 11:30am. The excitement and expectations of all those involved is great. But the mood in Berlin is quite different. As the Do X is taking off, the end of the incorporated company Dornier-Flugzeuge has been decided in Altenrhein. Probably the bitterest day for the business director of DoFlug, Alfons Keppeler (1895-1947). He has to go to the Ministry of Transportation in Berlin to speak and answer questions in the emergency meeting: "Determining the Overall Costs of the Do X and Closing the Altenrhein Factory." The result: shutdown of the Altenrhein factory and voluntary liquidation of DoFlug AG. A bitter day for those who played a significant role in building up the factory.

Born on January 6, 1895 in Friedrichshafen, Alfons Keppeler finds a business apprenticeship at the Luftschiffbau factory in Friedrichshafen after graduating from high school in Ravensburg. His youthful drive leads him to Italy in 1921 where he is promoted from authorized representative to executive director in Claude Dornier's aircraft factory in Marina di Pisa in 1922. By 1926, his life's work is forever connected to DoFlug AG in Altenrhein. The most modern aircraft factory in Europe at that time is built and organized under his leadership. It is intended to be the aircraft hangar for the series production of the Do X flying boat. Until his death on November 12, 1947 in Rheineck, Switzerland, he leads the factory's commercial operations in which three Do X flying boats are developed. After the liquidation of the incorporated company, the factory operates under the name "Dornier-Werke, Altenrhein."

What happened on Tuesday, July 26, 1932?

On Tuesday, July 26, 1932, around 1:40pm, the twelve-engine Do X flying boat flies the first stage of its legendary Germany flight, at a few hundred meters altitude, from Travemünde to Kiel. Navigation officer Wilhelm Niemann and passengers in the luxuriously furnished cabin of the middle deck look skeptically out of the port side portholes at the threatening mountain of black-gray storm clouds over the green island Fehmarn. On the starboard side, the sun shines on the unaffected Fehmarn Belt and a three-masted barque under full sail. The crew is whistled on deck to greet the Do X as it flies by. "That's the Niobe, the training sailboat of the Imperial Navy," remarks one of the passengers, as it slowly disappears from their field of view. No one on the flying boat can anticipate the tragedy that would unfold over the next half an hour on the waters of the Belt. A sudden thundersquall capsizes and sinks the boat in only three minutes and sixty-nine crewmembers are killed. The death of the forty-seven young sailors, career candidates of the Imperial Navy, who were having class below deck, is especially tragic. A national disaster that overshadows the everyday politics of that month. After landing in Kiel, Wilhelm Niemann learns of the incident and immediately volunteers to help the Navy search and rescue units. But help comes too late.

How long was the Do X 1a in the air on its round-the-world flight?

As we know, the Do X 1a spends most of its time during the two-year journey from November 5, 1930 to November 14, 1932 taxiing on the water or lying on land. For the entire flight distance of 43,482km, the Do X needs around 258 hours, just about eleven days of pure flying time.

What did the passenger cabin of the Do X 1a look like?

There are no color photographs of the interior design of the passenger cabin. Color photography is not yet the standard in 1930 and our view into the cabins today is black and white. Interior designer Emil Rau delivers a progress report for the implementation of his design and a room description to Altenrhein. After the completion of the upgrade of the Do X, he reports in the November 1930 issue of Fachblatt für den Holzarbeiter (Eng: 'Woodworker's Joural'): "If the construction of this air giant in Altenrhein has already evoked admiration from all sides by its technical originality and its large proportions, then one would hope that its interior design will be noticed with interest in our industry circles. It is no ordinary task to manage a minimum of weight with an artistic effect and still provide the best in solidity. Beforehand, let it be said that the company responsible, J. Keller Co. in Zurich, has still substantially fallen short of the already extremely closely calculated weight, to which the pleasant cooperation with the leading figures of the hangar contributed a lot. The ground plan shows the distribution of individual rooms, which together claim a length of around 23m (half of the fuselage length). From the entrance arranged on both sides in the front third, there is room toward the front for sixteen passengers, half of which can be transformed into a sleeping compartment. Yellowish-brown, striped taffeta is used as the wall material, the furniture is upholstered with colorful horsehair fabric, the small curtains of green rep. The beige-colored, thick carpet increases comfort and, along with other objectively used insulating materials, takes away a large part of the engine sound. An 80cm high parapet panel, polished here in walnut, is led through all rooms and hides technical installations. Small folding tables, each with two benches, are also arranged everywhere. Further ahead lies a very cozy smoking cabin outfitted with zebrano panels, eight leather chairs and bouclé rug together with adjacent bar niche, in which a steward caters to the refreshment needs of the passengers. Moving backward from the entrance, one enters the large lounge through a cloakroom alcove situated on both sides. Almost 7m long and 3.5m wide and separated by only two ribs, this room calculated for twenty-six passengers represents superbly in its beautiful golden ambiance. The walls are covered by polished cherry tree panels with yellow-ground chintzed craquelé with Chinese patterns; the front and rear seating groups are covered with plain green velour, the center seats with plain red velour. Green curtains enliven the walls with portholes. Here too, like in all rooms, the floor is covered with a soft, plain carpet. The rearmost section is arranged the same way as the front passenger room, but the benches here have striped velour covers and the woodwork is finished with polished mahogany. The kitchen and two restrooms complete the passenger cabin … The quickly advancing technology of our time will still prompt some new construction, even in the interior design, as it has done in this case. Maybe aircraft and airship construction will assume the role to convince the traditional carpenter how wasteful he is throughout his life with 'wood.'"

What were ozite underlays used for in the Do X?

A contemporary description of the Do X's passenger deck furnishings reads: "… with ozite underlay." The ozite carpet underlay: "A practical luxury for the practical housewife" as the contemporary advertisement announces, is indeed practical but also a luxury. The ad from 1929 continues: "Ozite is a new elastic, felt underlay that gives your carpet luxurious softness and depth. Every step is dampened to silence. Your carpet's life expectancy doubles at the same time because friction with the floor is eliminated." Furthermore, the buyer had to look out for the orange-colored edging of the felt underlay since this was the mark of the original product. The designers of the Do X used ozite underlays between the metal floor and the carpet to dampen walking and vibrations.

How much did the Italian Do X 2 and Do X 3 flying boats cost?

Claude Dornier's cost estimate for the construction of a Do X flying boat totaled 1,470,000 Reichsmarks in 1925. The order and purchase price of 2,370,900RM is agreed upon in June 1928 with the German Reich as the buyer and DoFlug the supplier.

Around the same time, Claude Dornier finalizes a construction contract with the Italians for two more Do X flying boats. The Do X 2 and Do X 3 flying boats are delivered at a fixed price of 2,000,00RM each (today 10,000,000 Euros). The political outrage in Italy creates a stir. The response: this is way to expensive. Why don't we build this ourselves? Where are our jobs going? Because Italy is just waiting for a mistake from Altenrhein so that they can pull out of the controversial contract, Dornier and the Reich ministries agree to liquidate DoFlug starting in June 1932, once the Do X 2 and 3 are completed.

Why was the Deutsche Flugschiff Gesellschaft (DFG) founded?

In 1932, extensive support measures by the German Reich are necessary for the financial difficulties of the company Dornier Metallbauten GmbH (DMB). One demand by the Ministry of Transportation, and especially by the Ministry of Finance, during the restructuring process is the dissolution of the Do X operation from DMB. Under this pressure, the Deutsche Flugschiff Gesellschaft was founded in Friedrichshafen, at the instigation of DMB, on March 24, 1932. Acting partners are Otto Milatz and Heinrich Schulte-Frohlinde, both Berlin directors of DMB. The sole purpose of the new company is the operation of the Do X 1 flying boat. Capital is set at 20,000RM; the founders each assumed half of the capital with 25% to be paid in. The funds were made available to those named due to special contracts on the part of DMB. According to the contracts, the founders, as partners, were only trustees for DMB. The funds advanced (loans) were granted interest-free, with the obligation and the right to return the shares to DMB against the offset of loans. The company, whose headquarters are in Berlin, is only granted one economically active fiscal year. After 1933, DFG only exists as a shell company.

Why do crewmembers have a seaman's record book?

The Do X 1a is declared a seagoing vessel for international air service, and not as an airplane. Thus simplifying approaches and calls at ports since the established maritime laws apply (air transport laws are complicated at that time). All important data about the flying boat and its crewmembers is therefore listed in a ship's articles, like with seagoing vessels, and is part of the ship's papers. Every crewmember also gets a seaman's record book. The port authority notes all personal and travel information in it. The seaman's record book is maintained by flight mechanic Ernst Brombeis for the second Atlantic crossing from New York to Berlin. As a representative of Captain Christiansen, Wilhelm Niemann certifies the signing off of Brombeis on November 21, 1932 and the period of service during the Atlantic flight and the German tour from April 19, 1932 to November 14, 1932, lasting six months and twenty-five days. The port authority confirms the pension insurance verification for Ernst Brombeis. Normally, the monthly pay is also stated in the seaman's record book, but this information is missing here. In addition to a rather low base pay, the crewmembers get daily allowance and mileage allowance, which are scaled according to position and function. Some of the officers of the ship's command receive their salaries from their parent companies, like Newmann from the Hamburg-America Line, radio officer Kiel from DEBEG and pilot Merz from Luft Hansa.

What was the command hierarchy on board?

On the Do X, Friedrich Christiansen organized the hierarchy and duties like on a ship. Constant watch with an officer and two men are also a part of this, as is the appointment of Wilhelm Niemann as his proxy and first officer on board. Three officers on the Do X are allowed to carry the title "captain" and all three are a "skipper for international voyages" as the license was known then, which justifies the appointment captain. Christiansen valued his title, and the blurred boundaries from commander and captain irritate not only the contemporary newspaper reader. He carries the professional title of captain and his official position is commander on board the Do X. Wilhelm Niemann, also a skipper for international voyages, attached little importance to his title. His official position as navigation officer on the Do X (for him, shortened to: N-O "Do X") was enough. The third skipper for international voyages was Horst Merz. Like all ap-

pointed flight captains for transoceanic operation, he also attended the Lübeck School of Navigation for his license. Flight captain Merz's official position on the Do X was first pilot. After commander and first officer, the next level of officers is equal, which applies to pilots, radio operators and mechanical engineers. Even if Horst Merz likes to portray it differently in later years, Commander and Captain Friedrich Christiansen has the say on board. Merz only flies under directive and not on all parts of the route.

Why DORNIER or LUFT HANSA on the bow?

Company names and logos on vehicles are the code of either the owner, manufacturer or the operator. This also applies to the Do X in chronological order. After the engine conversion and the planned flight to the USA in sights, the Do X receives a new light silver/gray coat of paint in July 1930. For the rollout from the factory hangar in Altenrhein, with new Curtiss engines, DORNIER gleams in large capital letters on both sides of the bow. The ownership situation of the Do X 1 flying boat can be explained today with few words. The aircraft hangar of Dornier Flugzeuge AG (DoFlug) belongs to the German Reich as majority shareholder. Operators of the factory are Claude Dornier as executive director and chairman, Johannes Keppeler as business director and Paul Berner as technical director. With almost its own company in Switzerland, the German Reich orders the Do X for the estimated purchase price of 2,370,900 Reichsmarks in June 1928. According to the Reich Finance Ministry in July 1932, the total cost for constructing the Do X 1 comes to 3,966,594.49 Reichsmarks. Calculated for inflation, this totals about 19,832,972 Euros. By April 1933 the state-owned Do X is bought and paid for. Dornier functions as manufacturer and later is appointed operator of the flying boat by the Transportation Ministry. All planning and subsequent organization of the flight operation takes place at Dornier Metallbauten GmbH (DMB) in Manzell. Production, assembly and testing takes place at DoFlug in Altenrhein. DoFlug is allowed to present its logo on the stem of the Do X and the "great" name of spiritual power is shown off for everyone to see on the sides of the bow. DORNIER as image advertising for the manufacturer and operator. Superficially, Luft Hansa was not involved with the events of 1933. They know about the numbers game of manufacturing and operating costs of the Do X and management does not scramble to change it. They have made their without the new Aviation Commissioner's pen stroke. Hermann Göring orders the transfer of the Do X to Luft Hansa, which is listed as the owner in the German aircraft registry from May 1933. LUFT HANSA was the owner of the Do X, even though only for five months, and presented their name on the bow.

Why an "X" in the type designation?

Starting around 1922, new Dornier airplanes received a so-called type name, for example: Delphin, Falke, Libelle, Wal and others, which were communicated inside and out. After the restructuring and renaming of Zeppelin Werk Lindau GmbH to Dornier Metallbauten GmbH (DMB), a new system of type designation is created beginning in October 1924. Following the company's abbreviation "DO," new airplanes receive letters in alphabetical sequence as the type designation. There is no chronologically logical system here, except that the alphabet is limited by the number of letters. With the start of design work on the Do X, the construction department in Manzell still used project numbers. It was called "Dornier Metall-Giant Flying Boat for Air Transport Purposes" and in December 1926 "Type Do X 12x500hp." In early 1927, DMB came up with the type letter "X."

Claude Dornier once said that he was asked if the "X" referred to the unknown quantity in a mathematical sense. This doesn't seem logical since there was no unknown factor for Claude Dornier's Do X, when the technical decision making was taken care of. More likely is a banality with the naming. Claude Dornier allegedly said: "Just take any random name!"

Why flying boat and not seaplane?

In his 1931 speech About Flying Boats, Claude Dornier defines the term: "I understand a 'flying boat' to be an aircraft that is also at home in the water and serves to transport large payloads across the sea. It is equipped with a central hull, similar to a ship's, which has several 'decks.' Apart from its size, the flying boat differs from the normal airplane in that the basis of its service on board largely depends on a division of work and conforms as nearly as possible to the operation of seafaring ships. According to the general definition, the vessel has a closed hull with several decks. Listed from top to bottom these are the command deck, passenger deck and service deck. A boat, in contrast, is open on top or at least comes with a closing deck. The Dornier Wal, for example, is a seaplane and the Do X is a flying boat. This, by the way, should not to be confused with an airship, like the Zeppelin, which floats in the sky rather than flies like the flying boat.

Why is the Do X sometimes referred to as a he instead of a she?

"Thousands of Cologne Residents Visit the Do X" is the headline of the Stadtanzeiger für Köln und Umgebung in its morning edition #183 on Thursday, September 22, 1932. The flying boat landed on the Rhine during its Germany flight and moors in Riehler Floßhafen. The article continues, "With kit and caboodle, on water and on land, they are on their way – a carnival atmosphere surrounds the flying boat" and ends with the question: "He or she? How can we even talk about the Do X, when we don't know what gender this thing has? Now don't just say it's neuter because despite most diligent searching, no representative of this gender is to be found in Cologne. The argument takes place exclusively between men and women. The city Cologne, several Cologne tour companies and shipping lines say "he." Or is it only the opinion of the Cologne poster artists, who hang sign boards 'to the (male article) Do X' on Niehler Straße, on the Hohenzollern bridge and several other streets. Maybe our Cologne painters also thought the people were walking to the zoo. And the people walk, bike, swim in droves. The riverbanks are all full of people. Jupp and Stina steer their two-seater toward the Do X from the Rhine side. Flags flying on its topmast, the steamship brings the Schmitz family to the flying boat. Do X emblems and Do X postcards swarm on the beach. The male Do X and the female Do X sound joyfully confused here! … Every question is answered by the attentive command: the Do X cost 2.5 million, but now Dr. Dornie could manufacture the machine in series production for 1.5 million

... now comes the important question: what does the crew of the flying ship say? Is the Do X a he or a she? The disappointment is great. 'The crew is not in agreement about this either!' ... and the long walk, on which one can reach the engines, feels like a romantic embodiment of technology itself, in all its practicality. In a word: the Do X is so beautiful that one should quietly concede the honorable female article."

This is the train of thought and the observations of the time. Even this representative of the journalistic fraternity noticed that everyone who has something to do with water or shipping is talking about the Do X. Even with the airships of Graf Zeppelin, people referred to the Graf Zeppelin in professional exchanges as the LZ 127, or later to the Hindenburg when LZ 129 was meant. Does the masculine title have something to do with the impressive size of the airship or the flying boat? Subliminally yes. For centuries now, every ship has had to have a name with which the launch was made public and the newly built construction of wood and steel made capable of being registered. Ship names serve as identification. Measurement certificates, testing certificates and other documents are issued in the name of the ship. Franz Patocka from the Institute for German Studies cites the female article before ship names, as an example of "prototype semantics." "The association of ships with containers that protect and accommodate, have always led to the typical notion of something female." For many experts, this archetypical concept of the femininity of ships – no matter whether in English or in German – is the reason for the use of the feminine article for ship names.

The seafaring nations Holland and England, as models for German ambitions on the world's oceans, do not have as many problems with a gender defining article before a ship's name as we Germans do. Our grammar rules state: "Ship names are feminine, with exceptions." And these have been unique in the first half of the last century. The naval power of the German Empire produced these exceptions beginning in 1880.

For example, "His Majesty's Ship" (S.M.S – Seiner Majestät Schiff) of the Imperial German Navy, the armored cruiser Fürst Bismark, put into service on April 1, 1900, cannot possibly be female as a warship. It is called the (male article) Fürst or the (male article) Fürst Bismark. Female ship names are left out of the merchant marines. War ships, the bigger the clearer, are designated male in general usage and zeitgeist of the next decades. The last German battleships of the Second World War are called the (male article) Bismark and the (male article) Tirpitz.

Carried over to the linguistic usage of the 1920s from the Imperial era, Dornier Metallbauten in Manzell refers to the Do X flying boat as simply the (male article) Do X.

Can Do X also be written as DO-X?

Karl Kössler, former director of the Federal Aviation Authority in Braunschweig, commented on the spelling of DO-X or Do X: "The Americans and the Russians have a hyphen between the company abbreviation and the type designation, but not us. The company letters on very first airplanes at Dornier, with a large 'D' and the logically small 'o,' formed the slowly introduced standard for the uniform denomination of airplane models from 1929 on, which was insisted upon by the German Army Ordnance. From then on there were Ar(ado), He(inkel), Ju(nkers) or Kl(emm) airplanes. But all had the pattern of a capitalized first letter and a small second letter, regardless of its origin. Focke-Wulf airplanes were designated by 'Fw' and the airplanes built by Messerschmitt at the Bayerische Flugzeugwerk by 'Bf.' The Do X was no exception." This is correct, according to the technically oriented usage beginning in the 1930s.

But where does the notation DO-X, with capital letters and hyphen, come from? Apart from being listed on some design drawings, this notation was present on the flying boat beginning in October 1930. The ferry flight to the USA has been planned out and its clearance as a seagoing vessel in European and international harbors has been organized with the help of HAPAG shipping line in Hamburg. But a visible ship's name, whose importance is mentioned above, is missing. Just before departure on November 5, 1930, craftsmen from the painter's workshop in Altenrhein paint it on the flanks of the command deck underneath the windows. In large, black uppercase letters, which is common with ship names, and with a hyphen. "DOX" without a hyphen would have taken some getting used to and since they were on the way to the USA, where hyphen are customary, it came before the "X." One name designation of the legendary flying boat is therefore also DO-X. Whoever wants to use the exact type designation from October 1930, has to write "Do X1a."

The three Do X flying boats at a glance				
1	Factory #	Type Designation	Name	Tail Number
1	Do X1 / Do X1a	None / Das	None / Do-X	D-1929
2	Do X 2	Vas	R.I. Umberto Maddalena	I-REDI
3	Do X 3	Vas	Alessandro Guidoni	I-ABBN

What do the type designations of the Do X flying boats mean?

Beginning in 1926, Dornier Metallbauten GmbH expands their type designations for new airplane constructions with a three-letter code. In this additional code, the first letter designates the installed engine with the first letter of the manufacturing company. Apparently, though, consistency is not always possible, as the type designation of the Do X with water-cooled Curtiss Conquerer engines shows. For Curtiss, there is a "D" and DMB codes the Fiat engines of the Italian Do X 2 and 3 with a "V." Other examples: "B" for BMW, "G" for Gnôme-Rhône, "J" for Junkers, "S" for Siemens, etc. The first letter of the code is always capitalized, the following two letters are written in lower case letters. The second letter, always a vowel, hints at the purpose: "a" for transport, "e" for testing, "i" for military, and "o" for transoceanic mail service. The third letter characterizes the design of the machine: "l" for land plane and "s" for seaplane.

The Do X with the works number DoFlug 1 and Siemens engines carries the type designation "Do X1 Sas." After conversion to the Curtiss engines, the type designation becomes "Do X 1a Das."

Where does the tail number D-1929 on the tail and the wings come from?

Since August 1, 1922, an aviation law is in effect in Germany that governs the regulations and installations as well as the tail numbers of airplanes. Every approved aircraft should be clear and visibly recognizable to everyone and reveal its identity. With the assignment of nationality indicators as part of the Paris aviation agreement of October 13, 1919, no one considered Germany. Convinced of the future relevance of German air transport, the "A" for Allemande is suggested by a French-speaking national, but this is out of the question. The Germans give themselves the nationality indicator "D." And so the first German aircraft numbers begin with the familiar "D" as does

the current tail number from the German aircraft registry. The Reichsamt for Aviation and Automotive Vehicles implements this into the Transportation Ministry. Dornier's formal application for approval of the Do X is handed over to the German Research Institute for Aviation (DVL) by the Reichsamt for technical testing of the machine in early-1930. With a take-off weight of forty tonnes, several acceptance flights are performed by Joachim von Köppen, the head of the flight department at DVL, starting on February 14, 1930. Without objections, the Do X receives a model approval on February 20 and in October 1930 it is assigned the tail number D-1929. The months-long period in between result from the conversion from air-cooled to water-cooled engines. The maiden flight year 1929 has nothing to do with the tail number. It is a pleasant coincidence for Dornier. The last tail number assigned in 1929 is D-1770 and not until October 1930 does the Reichsamt allocate the tail number D-1929.

This numbering system has its limits and proves to be a failure for practical applications. In 1934, the Reichsamt comes to D-3466. But who is really interested in how many airplanes are circling the German skies? Hints to the kind of machine – from passenger aircraft to airship, sport plane or hot air balloon, or the weight of the aircraft, etc. – are much more interesting. Such classification characteristics can only be organized with letter groups, as has been practiced abroad since 1919. On March 20, 1934, the conversion of aircraft numbers on civilian machines takes place. Now, instead of a "D" with a hyphen, comes a four-digit lettering group with informational value. Incidentally, the Do X tail number is only written in black lettering. Red tail numbers are an invention of the Japanese aircraft manufacturer Otaki from 1968, which some illustrators still paint on unchecked.

Sources and Additional Reading

Primary Sources

Bundesarchiv (Federal Archives), Berlin
Reichspostministerium
– "Einrichtung und Aufhebung von Posthilfsstellen 1929-1939"
(R 4701/18533);

Reichsfinanzministerium
– "Reichsbeteiligung an der Dornier AG für Flugzeuge, Finanzierung der Entwicklung und des Baues des Flugbootes Do X 1, Sanierung der Gesellschaft" (R 2/5596);
– "Dornier-Metallbauten GmbH, Stützung durch das Reich, Kosten der Indiensthaltung des Flugbootes Do X 1931" (R2/5597)

Deutsche Lufthansa AG, Company Archives, Frankfurt
"Do X Flug," correspondence and materials for the dispute between Horst Merz and Rudolf Cramer von Clausbruch. Compiled and annotated until 1979 by Franz Preuschoff, DLH South Atlantic pioneer and the first DLH chief engineer as well as company archivist after World War II. Collection of materials in three parts with forty-five positions altogether.

Deutsches Museum, Archives, Munich
Correspondence between Claus Bergen and the Deutsches Museum from 1925 to 1934 (Administrative Acts: VA 0375).

Dornier Stiftung für Luft und Raumfahrt (Dornier Foundation for Aeronautics), Friedrichshafen
Archives and collection of the Dornier Museum
Photos, correspondence and reports about the history of the Do X

EADS, Dornier GmbH, company archives, Friedrichshafen
Photos, correspondence and reports about the history of the Do X
– "Zusammenstellung der Starts und Flüge der DO X für die Zeit 12. Juli 1929-14. November 1932," list according to the personal records of DO X flight mechanic Ernst Brombeis.
– "DO-X Erprobung am 12. Juli 1929" Altenrhein, July 15, 1929 Schulte-Frohlinde, 4 pages.
– "Schema einer Rentabilitätsberechnung für den Luftverkehr zwischen Lissabon und New York" created by Deutsche Luft Hansa AG and by director Erhard Milch, transmitted on 4/4/1927, 8 pages.
– "Sensationeller Bericht der einzigen Frau, die im 'DO X' mitflog" Berliner illustrierte Nachtausgabe # 120 from Wednesday, May 25, 1932, continued in the following editions.
– "Homing DO-X flies to Newfoundland" report in: New York Times from May 19, 1932.
– "DO-X Awaiting Sunny Atlantic, Woman in Crew" report in:

New York Herald Tribune from May 20, 1932, page 2.
– "Mrs. Putnam at Harbor Grace (...) DO-X at Holyrood" report in: The New York Sun from May 20, 1932.
– "Bericht und Anhang der Deutschen Revisions- und Treuhand-Aktiengesellschaft Berlin über die bei der Deutschen Flugschiff Gesellschaft m.b.H., Berlin vorgenommene Prüfung des Jahresabschlusses zum 1. März 1933 und des Zwischenabschlusses zum 31. Mai 1933" 12 pages and 3 attachments.
– "Bericht und Anlage der Deutschen Revisions- und Treuhand-Aktiengesellschaft Berlin über die bei der Dornier Metallbauten G.m.b.H. Friedrichshafen ausgeführte Prüfung der Kosten des Fluges des Do X von Rio de Janeiro nach New York." from April 9, 1932, 5 pages and 6 pages attachment.
– "Dornier-Geschichte" by Heinrich Schulte-Frohlinde, unpublished manuscript from 1959, 120 pages.

Lenggries Gemeindearchiv (Lenggries Municipal Archives)
List for the estate of Claus Bergen, created on July 28, 1988
(559 reference numbers – oil, tempera and watercolor paintings, drawings, studies and sketches with handwritten location information).

Estate of Flight Captain Horst Merz
Pilot of the Do X and rapporteur of the Reich Transportation Ministry, photos and memorabilia for the history of the Do X.

Estate of Captain Wilhelm Niemann
Navigation Officer of the Do X crew from October 1930 to November 1932
– "Wilhelm Niemann und das Flugschiff Do X. Zum 60. Todestag von Kapitän Wilhelm Niemann am 21. März 1995," photocopied material collection from the Dornier Archives, Friedrichshafen.
– Photos, newspaper clippings and postcards, personal information and correspondence with Lena Niemann (daughter)
– "Langstrecken-Navigation in Luftfahrzeugen über Land und See im Inund Ausland" speech by W. Niemann before the 28th general assembly of the Society for Aeronautics in Berlin on January 22, 1935, published in Hansa, the German Maritime Journal, Hamburg 1935 # 26, 27 and 28.
– "Willhelm Niemann, Leben und Werdegang" in Hansa, the German Maritime Journal, Hamburg 1935, # 13, page 541.

Estate of Radio Operator Friedl
Radio officer of the Do X Luft Hansa crew, March to September 1933, Hormann collection, Rastede, photos from Friedl's album "Fliegerei 1928-1935."

Estate of Engineer Heinrich Schulte-Frohlinde
- "Das Flugschiff Do X, gesehen vom Standpunkt des Fliegers" speech by H. Schulte-Frohlinde held on March 11, 1930 in the Ring der Flieger, Berlin 1930, unpublished speech manuscript, 29 pages.
- Article: "Das Dornier Riesenflugschiff, Do X'" in Wiener Bilder, 1929, number 29, page 6 (with photo of Schulte-Frohlinde and Wagner).

Saxon State and University Library Dresden
Center for scientific reporting about aviation research,
Deutsche Versuchsanstalt für Luftfahrt e.V. (ZO 7400)
"Forschungsbericht FB 26 vom 15. Dezember 1933, Erprobung des Flugschiffes
Dornier Do X1 in Altenrhein nach dem Überführungsflug von Passau" (1997.4.000783.001 / SL)
State Archives of the Canton of St.Gallen (Switzerland)
Photos, correspondence and reports about the history of the Do X
Collections: W 241 Dornier-Werke Altenrhein AG and W 241/3 Bildarchiv

Secondary Sources

Braunburg, Rudolf. Kranich in der Sonne: Die Geschichte der Lufthansa. Munich, 1980.

Brembach, Hellmuth (Ed.). Adler über See: Fünfzig Jahre deutsche Marineflieger. Oldenburg/Hamburg, 1962.

Busjan, Béatrice/Schubert Corinna. Flugzeugbau in Wismar: Erinnerungen an die Norddeutschen Dornier-Werke. Wismarer Studien Band 9, Wismar, 2005.

Christiansen, Friedrich. "Die Fernflüge des Flugschiffes Do X 1930/32." Zeitschrift des Vereines deutscher Ingenieure, May 27, 1933: 77, 21.

Christiansen, Harro. "Der Weg des Flugschiffes DO-X nach Berlin."
Deutsche Gesellschaft für Schiffahrts- und Marinegeschichte e.V. Lectures for the XVIII conference. Berlin, Herford on Sept 23, 1989.

Dischl, Stahel, et al. Schweizerischer Luftpost-Katalog, Handbuch. 2nd ed., Zürich, 1949.

Dornier, Claude. Aus meiner Ingenieurlaufbahn. Zug/Schweiz 1966

Dornier, Claude. "Das Flugschiff Do X." Speech at the annual assembly of the Wissenschaftliche Gesellschaft für Luftfahrt (WGL). November 6, 1929 in: Yearbook 1929 of WGL, Berlin: 1929, S. 45-65.

Dornier, Claude. "Über Flugschiffe, Erfahrungen, Vergleiche, Folgerungen und Ausblick." Speech held at the 1931 University conference of Technical University Munich, special edition from "Wissenschaftliche Vorträge" Munich: 1931, 19 pages.

Dornier, Marcel. Palette meiner Jugend: Erinnerungen eines Malers. Starnberg: 1993.

Dornier, Tilgenkamp. Do X: Das größte Flugschiff der Welt. Zürich: 1931.

Dornier GmbH. "DO X 1929." Anniversary reprint of the Swiss AERO REVUE from 1931 and 1932. Friedrichshafen: 1979.

Dornier GmbH (Ed.). "Do-X Verkehrs-Flugschiff." Dornier Typenblatt. Munich: around 1975. 4 pages, 21 b/w photos, 2 drawings.

Dornier GmbH. Dornier, eine Dokumentation zur Geschichte des Hauses Dornier. Friedrichshafen:1983.

Dornier-Post (company newspaper) Supplement: "Durch dick und dünn mit dem Führer." 3, May/June 1939.

"DO-X Weltreise-Bilder." 72 picture cards with album of Peter Kölln Mühlenwerke (Haferflocken), Elmshorn: 1933.

"E-Stelle See: Die Geschichte der Flugerprobungsstellen Travemünde und Tarnewitz." Steinebach-Wörthsee o.J. (3 volumes).

Field, John C.W. Unlucky Giant: Mail-carrying German Dornier Do-X, 1929-33. (Paperback, Publisher: FJ Field, ISBN: 0852370180).

Fölz, Gerhard. "Besuch des Flugzeugriesen Do X in Schleswig Holstein." Luftfahrt zwischen Nord-und Ostsee: Von den Anfängen bis zur Gegenwart. Neumünster: 1975.

Grieder, Karl. "Dornier Do-X: Geschichte eines Riesen-Flugschiffes." Der Lehrling. Schweizerischer Metall- und Uhrenarbeitnehmer-Verband 1974.

Grieder, Karl. 50 Jahre Dornier Do-X. Geschichte eines Riesenflugschiffes. Schaffhausen: 1979.

Gronau, Wolfgang von. Im Flugboot nach Amerika. Berlin: 1936.

Gröber, Roland (Leverkusen). "Do X am Starnberger See." Vom Einbaum zum Dampfschiff: Jahrbuch 2 des Förderverein Südbayerisches Schiffahrtsmuseum Starnberg. Starnberg: 1982.

Gröber, Roland. "Immer wieder neues von der Do X." Vom Einbaum zum Dampfschiff: Jahrbuch 3 des Förderverein Südbayerisches Schifffahrtsmuseum Starnberg. Starnberg: 1983.

Gütschow, Fred. Die deutschen Flugboote: Flugboote, Amphibien-Flugboote und Projekte von 1900 bis zur Gegenwart. Stuttgart: 1978.

Gustosa, Corrado. "Da Amsterdam a Lisbona a Bordo del DO-X." Rivista Aeronautica, Rom Jahrg. 7, 4, April 1931, 66 pages.

Haberer, Erich. "Katalog der Deutschen Luftpost" Teil 3 ...DO-X Luftpost..., Weil der Stadt 1999.

Harms, Günter. Katalog der DO X Post 1981. Stuttgart: 1981.

Hindelang, Eduard (Ed.) Marcel Dornier: Gemälde- Zeichnungen-Graphik. Published by the Langenargen Museum, Sigmaringen: 1983.

Heinkel, Ernst. Stürmisches Leben. (Ed. Jürgen Thorwald, pseudonym for Heinz Bongartz), Stuttgart: 1953.

Höker, Paul Oskar. "Im Dornier-Flugschiff Do X." Velhagen & Klasings Monatshefte. 4, pp. 539-546, Berlin: 1930.

Hofbauer, Leder, Schmelzle. Die Welt der Überflieger: 75 Jahre Nordatlantikflug Ost-West. Bonn: 2003 (History, Biography, Philately).

Hormann, Jörg-M. Elite im Dritten Reich: Die Geschichte der Deutschen Akademie der Luftfahrtforschung 1936-1945. Garbsen: 1988.

Hormann, Jörg-M. "Zeppeline, Marineluftschiffe und Marineflieger." Museum guide of the German Airship and Marine Aviation Museum AERONAUTICUM, Nordholz, Hamburg 2001.

Hormann, Jörg-M. Ein Schiff fliegt in die Welt: 75 Jahre Dornier-Flugschiff Do X D-1929. Bonn: 2004.

Hormann, Jörg-M. Flugschiff DO-X, die Chronik. Bielefeld: 2006.

Hormann, Jörg-M., Zegenhagen Evelyn. Deutsche Luftfahrtpioniere 1900-1950. Bielefeld: 2008.

Hormann,Jörg-M., Kliem, Eberhard. Claus Bergen: Marinemaler über vier Epochen. Hamburg: 2002.

"Hundert Jahre Deutsche Luftfahrt." Ed. Museum für Verkehr und Technik, Berlin, Gütersloh 1991.

Italiaander, Rolf. Wegbereiter Deutscher Luftgeltung: Neun Lebensbilder. Berlin: 1941.

Jung, Dieter, Wenzel, Berndt , Abendroth, Arno. Die Schiffe und Boote der deutschen Seeflieger 1912-1976. Stuttgart: 1977.

Kresting, W., Scheuvens, C. (Ed.). "Zweimal mit Do X über den Ozean" Mein Führer durch das Jahr 1933, Das Jahrbuch für die gewerbliche und kaufmännisch tätige Jugend Deutschlands. Edition D for young people interested in metal machining, Wuppertal-Barmen: 1932.

Langsdorf, Werner v. Flieger und was sie erlebten: Siebenundsiebzig deutsche Luftfahrer erzählen. Gütersloh: 1935.

Luftfahrt International, Nr.8."DO X das erste Flugschiff der Welt" as focal point, Nürnberg: 1975.

Mantey, Eberhard von (Ed.). Die Kapitäne Christiansen: Nach Logbüchern erzählt. Berlin: 1933.

Matthias, Joachim. "Mit Do X fliegen fünfzehn Personen über den Ozean" (4 pp.) in: Adler Bücherei "Die große Brücke" Im Flugzeug über Meere und Kontinente, Ed. Wehrbetreuung der Luftwaffe. Berlin: 1943.

Matthias, Joachim and Heinz. Tod und Sieg über den Weltmeeren: Das Buch der Ozeanflieger. Berlin: 1939.

Nagel, Alfred. "Die beiden Luftriesen Do X und D 2000: Zwei Wunderwerke deutscher Flugtechnik." Monatshefte für Literatur Kunst und Wissenschaft. # 3, September 1930.

Nowarra, Heinz J. Dornier DO X, das erste Großraum-Flugschiff der Welt, Sonderheft der Waffen-Arsenal-Reihe, Friedberg 1990.

Pletschacher, Peter. Großflugschiff Dornier DO X: Eine Bilddokumentation über das erste Großraumflugzeug der Welt, 1929, 1. Auflage, Stuttgart 1979.

Pletschacher, Peter. Großflugschiff Dornier DO X, Authentische Bilddokumentation des ersten Großraumflugzeugs der Welt (1929). Überarbeitete und erweiterte 3. Auflage, Oberhaching 1997.

Pfister, Gertrud. Ein Leben zwischen den Welten: Antonie Strassmann – Ein biographischer Versuch, aus: "Olympisch bewegt" Festschrift zum 60. Geburtstag von Prof. Dr. Manfred Lämmer, Köln 2003

Regnat, K.H. Vom Original zum Modell: Dornier Do X, Bonn 1998

Ries, Karl. Recherchen zur Deutschen Luftfahrzeugrolle, Teil I = 1919 bis 1934, Mainz 1977.

Saris, Wilhelm P.B.R. Deutsche Lufthansa 1926-1945 Geschichte, Bekleidung, Abzeichen, Norderstedt 1999.

Seeger, Hartmut und Spicker, Ralf. Dornier-Flugzeuge, (22 S.) in: "Pioniere des industriellen Designs am Bodensee", Friedrichshafen 2003.

Seifert, Karl-Dieter. Die deutsche Luftfahrt Der deutsche Luftverkehr 1926-1945 – auf dem Weg zum Weltverkehr, Bonn 1999.

Schneider, Rolf. Die Do X Story, Essen 1969.

Schmidt, Fred (Hrg.). Kapitäne berichten – Ein Buch von Männern und Schiffen, Berlin 1936.

Straßmann, Antonie. Atlantikflug der Do-X, in: Malina, J.B. (Hrg.) "Luftfahrt voran! Das deutsche Fliegerbuch," Berlin 1932.

Szigeti, Martin. Hinter den Kulissen der Do X, in: "Flug Revue," Stuttgart Juni 1999, S. 24-25.

Tilgenkamp, Erich Dr. Das Dornier-Flugschiff DO-X Sonderdruck der Schweizer, "AERO REVUE," Zürich 1931.

Tilgenkamp, Erich Dr. und Dornier, Maurice. Dornier Do-X D-1929, Mit dem ersten Flugschiff der Welt über drei Kontinente Sonderdruck der Schweizer, "AERO REVUE" Zürich, 1932.

Tittel, Lutz "100 Jahre Claude Dornier, Metallflugzeugbau 1914-1969", Friedrichshafen 1984

Träger, Susanne. In 80 Tassen um die Welt Gastlichkeit und Porzellan – Ausstellungskatalog, Band 46 des Deutschen Porzellanmuseums, Hohenberg/Eger, 1996.

Wachtel, Joachim. Claude Dornier: Ein Leben für die Luftfahrt, Planegg 1989.

Wachtel, Joachim. Claude Dornier: Ein Leben für die Luftfahrt. 2. von Jörg-M. Hormann überarbeitete und erweiterte Auflage, Bielefeld 2009.

Wittemann, A. Die Amerikafahrt des Z.R.III" Mit dem Luftschiff über den Atlantischen Ozean, Wiesbaden, 1925.

Wuest, Walter. Sie zähmten den Sturm: 75 Jahre Aerodynamische Versuchsanstalt Göttingen, Göttingen, 1982.

Zegenhagen, Evelyn. Von Aufwind in den Sturzflug. Rollenbild, Chancen und Beschränkungen deutscher Sportfliegerinnen der Zwischenkriegszeit, in: Ausstellungskatalog "Frau und Flug. Die Schwestern des Ikarus," Zeppelin-Museum, Friedrichshafen, 2004.

Zegenhagen, Evelyn. Himmelstürmerinnen. Deutsche Sportfliegerinnen 1928 bis 1945, in: Montagskolloquium des Deutschen Museums, München, 29. November 2004.

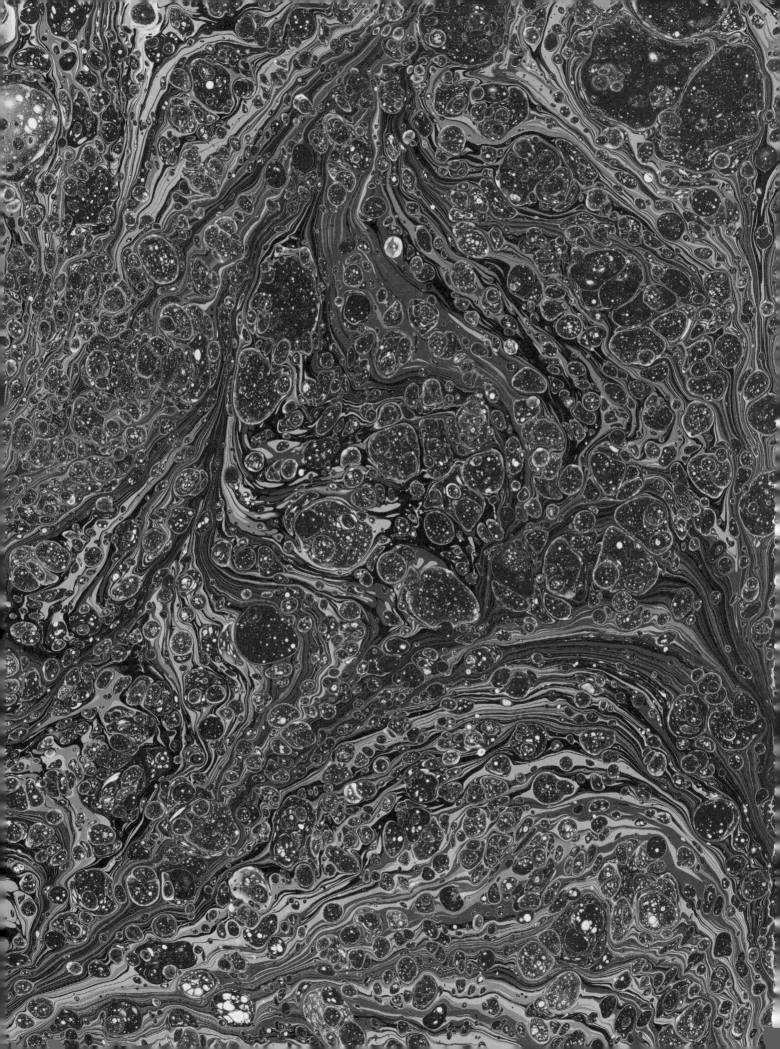